The Travels of Frederick Bruce Thomas
1872–1928

MAR 2013

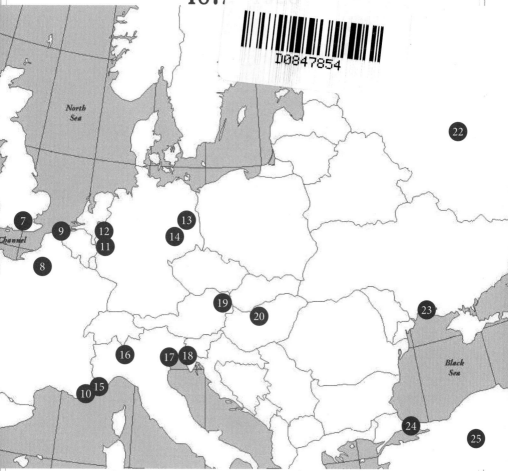

7 - London
8 - Paris
9 - Ostend
10 - Cannes
11 - Cologne
12 - Düsseldorf

13 - Berlin
14 - Leipzig
15 - Monte Carlo
16 - Milan
17 - Venice
18 - Trieste

19 - Vienna
20 - Budapest
21 - St. Petersburg
22 - Moscow
23 - Odessa
24 - Constantinople
25 - Ankara

THE BLACK
RUSSIAN

Also by Vladimir Alexandrov

Andrei Bely: The Major Symbolist Fiction
Nabokov's Otherworld
Limits to Interpretation: The Meanings of Anna Karenina

THE BLACK RUSSIAN

Vladimir Alexandrov

Atlantic Monthly Press
New York

B
Thomas, F
Alexandrov

The quotations from Prince Andrey Lobanov-Rostovsky on pp. xvii–xviii are reprinted with the permission of Scribner, a Division of Simon & Schuster, Inc., from *The Grinding Mill: Reminiscences of War and Revolution in Russia, 1913–1920* by Prince A. Lobanov-Rostovsky. Copyright © 1935 by The Macmillan Company. All rights reserved.

The quoted passage on pp. 178–179 from Morris Gilbert, "Alors, Pourquoi?" *The Smart Set*. Vol. LXXII, No. 3 (November 1923), 47–48, is reprinted with the permission of Hearst Corporation.

Published simultaneously in Canada
Printed in the United States of America

FIRST EDITION

ISBN-13: 978-0-8021-2069-4

Atlantic Monthly Press
an imprint of Grove/Atlantic, Inc.
841 Broadway
New York, NY 10003

Distributed by Publishers Group West

www.groveatlantic.com

13 14 15 16   10 9 8 7 6 5 4 3 2 1

For Sybil, who heard it all first

CONTENTS

CONVENTIONS

All dates for events in Russia prior to 1918 are given in the "Old Style" (O.S.) calendar: the Julian calendar that was in use until that year and that was thirteen days behind the Gregorian, "New Style" (N.S.) calendar used in the West during the twentieth century (during the nineteenth, it was twelve days behind). Occasionally a double date is given for clarity in connection with events that were also important in the West: e.g., August 2/15, which means August 2 according to the O.S. calendar and August 15 according to the N.S. calendar.

Russian personal names and place-names are given in their most accessible forms. For Turkish personal names, I use the spelling in my sources. For Turkish place-names, I give the forms used in Western sources during the time I describe, rather than present-day names: thus, "Constantinople" not "Istanbul"; "Pera" not "Beyoğlu"; "Galata" not "Karaköy"; "Scutari" not "Üsküdar"; "Grande rue de Pera" not "İstiklal Caddessi."

Estimates of what different currencies and sums from the past would be worth in today's dollars are determined by calculators at http://www.measuringworth.com/uscompare/.

PROLOGUE

Life or Death

The catastrophe should never have happened. On the morning of April 1, 1919, William Jenkins, the American consul in Odessa, a major Russian port on the Black Sea, walked from his office to the London Hotel, where the French army of occupation had set up its headquarters. He was alarmed by the previous day's setback on the front—Red Guards had driven Greek and French troops from yet another town to the east—and by the hysterical rumors that were sweeping through the scores of thousands of refugees who had fled to Odessa from Soviet territory. He wanted to meet with the French commander himself, General Philippe d'Anselme, and to ask him point-blank what he was going to do in the face of the deteriorating situation. Shortages of food and fuel in the city had become critical. A typhus epidemic was breaking out. Radicalized workers were mutinying and stockpiling guns. And Odessa's notorious criminal gangs vied with the Bolshevik underground in robbing homes and businesses, and murdering anyone who got in their way. Jenkins had compiled a list of twenty-nine Americans in the city, including, against all odds, a black man from Mississippi accompanied by a white wife and four mixed-race children. As consul, Jenkins was responsible for the entire group's safety and was beginning to doubt the resolve and reliability of the French.

Although he would not know it for another thirty-six hours, Jenkins's fears were well founded. The French high command in

Paris had concluded several days earlier that their military intervention in the Russian civil war had been a mistake. However, General
d'Anselme skillfully concealed this behind his blunt military manner
and proceeded to lie to Jenkins's face.

He began by pretending that he was sharing a confidence
with Jenkins, who was, after all, the official representative of an
important ally, and admitted that it might perhaps be necessary
to evacuate some of the old men, women, and children in Odessa
because of food shortages. But when Jenkins pressed the crucial
point of a general evacuation of the city, d'Anselme assured him
that there was absolutely "no question" of the French army abandoning Odessa.

Jenkins left French headquarters reassured. The following
day, Wednesday, April 2, he received written confirmation of what
d'Anselme had told him. The French commander also broadcast his
message to the city at large by publishing announcements in the local
newspapers to the effect that although some civilians would have to
be evacuated—he used the strangely callous expression "all useless
mouths"—the military situation was secure.

In truth, however, the French had already decided to withdraw
all forces from Odessa. But rather than organize an orderly evacuation
that might take two weeks—which would have been the only way to
accommodate 70,000 troops, their equipment, and anywhere between
50,000 and 100,000 civilians—d'Anselme and his staff decided to keep
their decision secret as long as possible. The city was dangerously
overcrowded and they hoped to prevent panic. What they achieved
instead was the exact opposite and would become known around the
world as the French "debacle" in Odessa.

Wednesday passed relatively calmly. All the government offices
were open and working. After the sun set, the only disturbances were
the occasional, familiar crackle of gunfire and detonations of hand
grenades as the city's criminals and Bolsheviks began their nightly
depredations. In the inner and outer harbors, the French and other

Allied warships rested reassuringly at anchor. The bivouacs of the Greek, Senegalese, and Algerian Zouave regiments were quiet.

Then, almost by chance, Jenkins learned the incredible news. Around 10 p.m., Picton Bagge, the British commercial attaché in the city, came to him with urgent and confidential information. He had heard from the captain of HMS *Skirmisher*, a British torpedo boat in the harbor—the captain in turn having gotten it from a French admiral in Odessa—that the French had decided to give up the city.

Jenkins was stunned: not only had d'Anselme lied to him, but the French withdrawal meant that the Bolsheviks would be in Odessa in a matter of days. Jenkins also realized that as soon as word got out, the hordes of White Russian refugees from Moscow, Petrograd, and other places in the north would stampede out of terror that the Bolsheviks would massacre them. With escape by land cut off, the only way out was across the Black Sea, and there were not nearly enough ships for everyone. He would have to rush to get his flock aboard a ship while there was still time.

Most of the Americans trapped in Odessa were in Russia because of business and charitable ventures with which Jenkins was familiar. But the black man who had recently come to see him was unlike anyone he had ever met in Russia before. The man gave his name as Frederick Bruce Thomas and claimed he was an American citizen who owned valuable property in Moscow. He explained that his passport had been stolen from him several months earlier during his harrowing escape by train from Moscow and that he had no other documents to prove his identity; neither did his wife, who he said was Swedish, nor his four children. He was presenting himself at the consulate to claim the protection for himself and his family to which his American origin entitled him.

As Frederick anticipated, his black skin and southern drawl identified him as convincingly as any official piece of paper could have done.

But as he also surely knew, any assistance that Jenkins would give was risky: it could be a return ticket to the world of American racism. During the past twenty years, every time Frederick had filled out an application to renew his passport in Western Europe or Russia, American consular officials had noted his skin color on it; the Europeans and Russians, by contrast, seemed never to care about such matters.

However, this time Frederick was facing an even bigger risk. He had concealed something very important about himself when he met Jenkins and could not be sure he would not be found out. Four years earlier, soon after the Great War began, in a move that may have been without precedent for a black American, Frederick became a citizen of the Russian Empire. He had thus automatically forfeited his right to American citizenship, and this meant that he no longer had any moral or legal claim on American protection. But Frederick never told the United States consulate in Moscow what he had done; and, as far as he knew, the Imperial Russian Ministry of Internal Affairs, which presented his petition to Tsar Nicholas II for approval, had also not informed the United States embassy in Petrograd. As a result, neither Jenkins nor any other American official, in Russia or in Washington, was likely to have known the truth.

It was Frederick's good fortune that Jenkins had no reason to doubt his story. During the past year, many people escaping from Bolshevik Moscow had experienced far worse than stolen documents. Trains lumbering across the lawless and war-torn expanses of Russia constantly risked attacks by armed bands, both political and criminal, who robbed and murdered civilians at will. And because black Americans were hardly known in Russia, Jenkins could never have imagined that Frederick was anything other than what he claimed to be, even if Jenkins had never heard of Frederick's fabulous career as a rich theater owner in Moscow. The consul therefore accepted that the smooth-talking, sophisticated, middle-aged black man with the big smile was an American, although he would qualify this in his official report to the State Department by noting that "Mr. Frederick

Thomas" was "colored." Jenkins also dutifully added him, his wife, and their four children to the list of people he would try to get on board a ship.

The choice for Frederick had been stark: to lie to Jenkins and escape or to stay in Odessa and risk death. When, in the first months of 1919, it became increasingly obvious that the French were not going to succeed in nurturing a White Russian crusade against the Bolsheviks—a prospect that had originally made refugees in the city delirious with joy—the hopes of people like Frederick that they would be able to return home and reclaim their former lives and property began to sink. In a paradoxical reversal, the Russian citizenship that had provided Frederick with valuable protection in Moscow during the outburst of patriotism at the beginning of the Great War had now become a liability. The Bolshevik Revolution had destroyed the society that had embraced him and allowed him to prosper. His theaters and other property had been nationalized and his wealth stolen. In the poisonous atmosphere of class warfare that the Bolsheviks created, he risked arrest and execution simply for having been rich. By contrast, nationals of the United States and the other Allied powers who had succeeded in getting to the French-controlled enclave in Odessa could turn to their countries' diplomatic representatives for help. And because after the war the Allies had sent a large fleet to Constantinople, the capital of the defeated Ottoman Empire, and transformed the Black Sea into their dominion, the diplomats were backed up by military strength.

The hour was late, but the news Jenkins had gotten was so shocking that he decided he could not wait until morning. He immediately began to contact all the Americans in the city, instructing them to gather their belongings as quickly as possible and get to the harbor while they could still find cabs. He also started burning all the coded telegrams in the consulate and packing the secret codebooks. By working through the night, Jenkins was able to round up the entire group. And by early in the morning on Thursday, April 3, he had gotten them onto two ships: HMS *Skirmisher*, which had agreed to take most of the American consular and other officials; and *Imperator Nikolay*, a Russian ship that the French had placed at the disposal of the consuls from several Allied countries—France, Great Britain, Greece, and the United States. The American contingent on *Imperator Nikolay* was one of the smallest: in addition to sixteen other civilians, it included Frederick; his wife, Elvira; and his three sons, who ranged in age from four to twelve—Bruce, Frederick Jr., and Mikhail. There was supposed to be a fourth child, his seventeen-year-old daughter Olga, but she had unexpectedly disappeared at the last minute and no one knew where she was.

Olga was not staying with the rest of the family and had been put up in a hotel. Perhaps this was because of the severe overcrowding and shortage of rooms in a city filled with refugees, or perhaps her relations with Elvira, her stepmother, were strained, as they would be later for her brother Mikhail. Whatever the reason, the sudden call from Jenkins late at night had caught Frederick by surprise. As he rushed to gather his wife, sons, and what little luggage they could take with them, he turned to the British acting consul general Henry Cooke, who was working with Jenkins, for help in getting word to Olga to come to the ship without delay. Cooke agreed to send someone to Olga's hotel. But when the messenger returned, he brought the distressing news that she had already left and that her new address was unknown. It was possible, Cooke suggested, that Olga had decided to try to get on board one of the other ships in the harbor.

There was no way to verify this during the Thomases' flight through the sleeping city. And once he was on board, Frederick could not risk going back on shore. At any moment, word of the evacuation could leak out, and then Odessa would erupt, and the streets would become impassable. Despite the relief he felt because his wife and sons were almost out of danger, it must have been excruciating to wait within easy reach of the shore, helpless to do anything.

The hurry to get on board also cost Frederick what remained of his fortune. At its peak on the eve of the February Revolution in 1917, it had amounted to about $10 million in today's currency. All he had left now was what he happened to have on hand—"less than $25," as he later described the sum, which is equivalent to perhaps a few hundred now. Thursday, April 3, also proved to be the last day that any of Odessa's banks were open and clients could make withdrawals, but Frederick had boarded *Imperator Nikolay* before they opened.

As the sun climbed higher over the city, the anxiety of rushing to the ship was gradually eclipsed by the tedium of waiting. *Imperator Nikolay* continued to sit at anchor as one delay followed another. First, there were problems with the engines, which needed twenty-four hours to get up steam in any case. Then the crew suddenly deserted in support of pro-Bolshevik workers in the city and replacements had to be found. More and more refugees kept boarding, including many Russians. The French had still not announced the evacuation officially, although rumors were spreading and agitation in the city was growing.

Finally, on the following morning, Friday, April 4, d'Anselme published in the Odessa newspapers the announcement of an immediate evacuation. A Russian naval officer, Prince Andrey Lobanov-Rostovsky, saw what happened in the London Hotel when people heard the news and when they suddenly realized that they would need exit visas from the French to get on board a ship:

> In an instant bedlam reigned. . . . The lobby was filled with wildly gesticulating people. The elevators were jammed. Two streams of humanity, going up and down the stairs, met on the landings between floors, where free-for-all fights took place. Women caught in the crush were shrieking, and from these landings valises came tumbling down on the heads of those who were below in the lobby.

Adding to the chaos was a violent mob that had gathered in the street and was trying to force its way into the hotel. A unit of French soldiers, rifles at the ready, took up positions in the lobby behind the bolted doors. With great difficulty, and "risking being crushed," Lobanov-Rostovsky pushed his way to the upper floor, where he "succeeded in getting past some hundred people who were hammering at the doors of the rooms occupied by headquarters, claiming visas." Once inside, he got a written order allowing him to board a ship leaving that morning; he then escaped by a back door and hastened to the port. The steamer on which Lobanov-Rostovsky got passage turned out to be the same one that had been designated for foreigners, *Imperator Nikolay*, so his memoirs provide a glimpse of the fate he shared with Frederick.

The panic was even worse in the harbor because the ships that were supposed to carry the refugees to safety were within sight and almost within reach. In Jenkins's words, the "confusion was indescribable." A crush of tens of thousands of panicked civilians poured down the streets from the upper city and flooded onto the docks, trying to get past armed Allied sentries, struggling with their luggage and waving their documents in the air.

Discipline among the French colonial troops and other Allied troops had been weak to begin with. The sudden evacuation eroded it further. Greek soldiers on the docks hacked at the engines of brand-new automobiles with axes, then pushed them into the water, so that the Bolsheviks would not get them. Cooke saw drunken soldiers looting supplies they were supposed to be evacuating while their officers stood by and watched. Just before setting sail, a British captain noticed several drunken French soldiers from Senegal grab two young Russian women who were on the dock and push them screaming into a shed. He intervened and was able to get the women on board his ship. As he went up the gangplank behind them, one of the soldiers ran alongside with his rifle and took a shot at him, but missed.

At last, before dawn on Sunday, April 6, 1919, *Imperator Nikolay* weighed anchor and set its course for Constantinople, four hundred miles across the Black Sea. Bolshevik troops were already entering Odessa. They were a rough and unimposing-looking band of only three thousand men. Even though numerous armed workers in the city supported them, the French evacuation of tens of thousands of troops in the face of such a weak force seemed especially cowardly.

For the Russians on board it was a deeply poignant moment. As *Imperator Nikolay* churned into the darkness, the last vestige of their homeland was disappearing off the stern. The electrical station in Odessa was not working, and there were no lights visible in the city except for a red glare from the fires that were breaking out in various quarters. The occasional cries and gunfire that had been audible near the shore no longer reached the ship, and the only sounds were the thrum of the engines and the murmur and shuffling of passengers on deck. The sea was calm.

For Frederick, the moment would have been no less moving. This was the second time in his life that he tasted the bitterness of exile. The first happened thirty years ago, when he escaped to Memphis with his parents after a white planter tried to steal their farm in Mississippi. Then, racial hatred had determined his fate. Now, it was class hatred, which for the Bolsheviks was as ingrained in the nature of existence as race was for most Americans. This was also the second time that a sea voyage marked a major change in his life. Twenty-five years ago, when he crossed the Atlantic from New York to London, he was young, had aspirations, and was eager to see something of the world. Now, he was forty-seven, had lost more in Russia than most men ever dream of having, and was unlikely to be surprised by anything else that life could still throw his way. He was also leaving Odessa almost twenty years to the month after he had arrived in Russia, a country that had been as unknown to him then as Turkey was now.

Overnight, most of the refugees aboard *Imperator Nikolay* had become homeless paupers heading into an unknown future, and for many the conditions on board deepened their emotional suffering. The ship had been built just before the war and was designed to carry 374 passengers in comfort; now, it was crammed to overflowing with 868 refugees. With the exception of some rich people who managed to get a few private cabins, the conditions for almost everyone else were very hard. Picton Bagge, the British attaché who had brought Jenkins word of the evacuation, was also on the ship and was shocked by how cruel the French were, especially to the defenseless Russians, who had no diplomats to protect them.

> The filth on board was almost indescribable and nothing could be obtained except by payment. A glass of water, for instance, cost 5 rubles. The men had to wash by drawing up buckets from the sea, whilst the women had to pay 25 rubles each to go into a cabin where they could wash. . . . The French went out of their way to ill-treat and insult them, and the ill-feeling which had been growing during the French occupation of Odessa had now become one of intense hatred.

Even though Jenkins was aboard another ship, Frederick and his family were still under official American protection and were thus probably spared some of the overt brutality that the French inflicted on others. Nonetheless, the passage could not have been easy, especially for Elvira and the boys.

After a voyage of some forty hours, on the evening of April 7, *Imperator Nikolay* entered the Bosporus, the narrow strait separating Europe from Asia, and anchored a few miles south of the Black Sea, near Kavaka, a small town on the Asian shore now called Anadolu Kavağı. The site was then, and still is, dominated by the ruins of an ancient castle, with its twin, also ruined, on the European side. These enigmatic monuments from the Byzantine and Genoese past were among the first sights that *Imperator Nikolay*'s passengers saw that showed them how far they had traveled from home. Other steamers from Odessa arrived that night, and by morning there were half a dozen, all overflowing with evacuees.

The refugees had reached what they thought would be safety only to discover that their ordeal was not over. French officers came on board *Imperator Nikolay* and posted Senegalese sentries everywhere. The passengers were treated like prisoners and ordered to disembark so that they could undergo medical examinations and quarantine on shore. Because there was an epidemic of typhus in Odessa and lice spread the disease, the Allies had made "severe delousing" mandatory for anyone arriving from Russia.

The French procedures were driven by legitimate public health concerns, but they were also humiliating and the guards treated the passengers harshly. Lobanov-Rostovsky described what Frederick and his family must have endured: "It was a pathetic sight to see the barges, overloaded with men, women, and children, leaving for the Kavaka quarantine station. Old men and women of good families and wealth, accustomed to luxury and courteous treatment, were stumbling down the gangway under the oaths and coarse shouts of French sergeants who were treating them like cattle."

The disinfection itself was painfully slow and primitive. Once the barges docked, men and women were separated and made to enter a barrack-like building through different doors. Inside, they were ordered to undress, to put all their clothes in mesh bags, and then to proceed into what proved to be a large communal shower room. There they had to wash as best they could, after which they moved into a third hall, where, eventually, their bags were tossed back to them. One young man recalled how shocked he was when he saw what had happened to his clothing. The delousing process consisted of putting the bags through a chamber filled with high-temperature steam that was supposed to kill any vermin. But the heat and moisture also warped and scorched leather shoes, shrank fabrics, and baked wrinkles into garments that could not be smoothed out. Women in particular were distressed to see their dresses ruined, which stripped them of the last vestiges of their dignity.

The Americans had not been at war with Turkey. However, they were allies of the occupying powers in Constantinople, and had important diplomatic and commercial interests in the country, which they supported with a squadron of warships. Jenkins and his group might have expected to benefit from their special status, but this did not happen. As much as a week after *Imperator Nikolay* arrived at Kavaka, the commander in chief of the Allied army in the East, the French general Franchet d'Espèrey, was still declining all requests from senior representatives of the other Allies for authorization to allow their nationals into the city, before they went through delousing and passport controls. Some of the refugees bribed guards and managed to slip away, to the great annoyance of the French. In light of Thomas's experience greasing palms in Moscow and the discomfort suffered by his family, he must have been tempted, even though he had very little money.

Despite such hardships, whatever doubts any of the refugees had about evacuating with the French were quickly dispelled. Within days of the Bolshevik occupation of Odessa, reports began to arrive about the reign of terror that they initiated against the city's remaining "bourgeoisie." They levied a tribute of 500 million rubles in cash on residents whose names were published in local newspapers. Those who did not pay were thrown into prison or forced to do manual labor, such as cleaning the city's streets. The Cheka, Lenin's dreaded secret police, began a campaign of bloody revenge against the Soviet state's political and class enemies. Hundreds were tortured and executed, including women and children. The nine-year-old heir of an old Polish noble family, the Radziwills, was purportedly killed to stop the family's succession. People became so desperate that they tried to escape from Odessa at night in small boats, hoping to reach Greek and French ships at sea. After he got to Constantinople, Frederick would attempt to find out what happened to Olga, but he would not learn anything about her fate for several years.

In the meantime, even after delousing, the Allied groups faced still more hurdles. The ship that would take them the dozen miles south to Constantinople had to be disinfected. Nationals were also kept together for the first dozen days and put under medical surveillance to see if they developed any signs of typhus. Judging by the time they spent in transit, Frederick and his family were forced to go through all the steps of this rigorous plan. Communiqués exchanged by the French authorities indicate that no Allied passengers from *Imperator Nikolay* were released into the city prior to April 17, and the Thomases arrived on April 20, a full two weeks after leaving Odessa. The experience of the evacuation had been so traumatic that Jenkins felt he was on the verge of a "nervous collapse" and soon applied to his superiors for transfer "immediately to a quiet post in a civilized country." The refugees did not have this luxury.

Kavaka is little more than an hour from Constantinople by boat, but the approach down the narrow, sinuous channel of the Bosporus provides no foretaste of the grand panorama that lies ahead. The country on either side is rustic and quietly picturesque, with an occasional village, hotel, or mansion on the shore and an old ruin on a hilltop. Only when the boat navigates a final, right turn and the steep banks part does the entire magnificent city unexpectedly swing into view.

The first sight of Constantinople is breathtaking. Straight ahead, shimmering in the distance and dominating the promontory known as Seraglio Point, stands the old Topkapi Palace and beside it, rising into the sky, are the delicate minarets and giant domes of the mosques in Stambul, the ancient Byzantine and Muslim heart of the city. By the water's edge on the right, the boat soon passes the sultan's Dolmabahçe Palace—a vast, low building of gleaming white marble, its straight lines softened by elaborate carvings that look like frozen sea foam. Minutes later, the small houses by the shore begin to multiply and swarm up the steep slopes of Galata and Pera, the European sections of the city, over which stands the stubby cylinder of the Galata Tower. To the left, across a mile-wide expanse of choppy water, is Scutari, Constantinople's foothold in Asia. As the boat approaches the dock near the Custom House on the Galata shore, yet another body of water comes into view on the right—the Golden Horn, a long natural harbor separating Stambul from Galata and spanned by a low-lying bridge. The entire vast waterway is filled with vessels: dozens of gray European and American warships, ferries churning back and forth, rusty freighters, and countless small boats under sail or with oars bobbing in every direction.

Frederick had suffered the kinds of losses in Russia that many weaker and less savvy men would have been unable or unwilling even to try to recoup. When he landed in Constantinople, he had hardly any money and no way to support his wife and sons. Because he had no documents, it was unclear how the diplomats in the American consulate general would treat him. He was, for the first time, in a non-Western country, one that was in turmoil as its centuries-old traditions crumbled and rapacious European politicians plotted its dismemberment.

But he still had his wits, drive, and experience. And it was not in his nature to yield to despair, or to settle for a modest compromise. He resolved instead to reinvent himself once again, to match wits with the historical forces that had brought him to Constantinople, and to gamble big in an effort to rebuild all that he had lost.

1

THE MOST SOUTHERN
PLACE ON EARTH

Despite their remarkable success, Hannah and Lewis Thomas could never have imagined what the future had in store for their newborn son, who lay swaddled in their log cabin on November 4, 1872, and whom they decided to name, very grandly, Frederick Bruce. They had been slaves until the Civil War, but in 1869, four years after it ended, a sudden reversal of fortune gave them their own two-hundred-acre farm in Coahoma County, Mississippi, in the northwestern corner of the state known as the Delta.

As black landowners, the Thomases were in the smallest of minorities. Out of some 230 farms in Coahoma County in 1870, blacks owned only half a dozen, and the Thomases' was the second largest of these. Their achievement was all the rarer because in the years after the war, blacks in the Delta still outnumbered whites nearly four to one. Most of the land was owned by a handful of white families; many other whites, like most blacks, owned nothing.

Early in 1869, before the spring planting season had started, at a public auction in front of the courthouse door in Friars Point, a town on the Mississippi River that was then the Coahoma County seat, Lewis bid on a sizable piece of land consisting of fields, forests,

swamps, and streams (called "bayous" in the Delta). It had belonged
to a white farmer who had lived in another county and died without a
will; as a result, the probate court had instructed the man's lawyer to
sell the property for whatever he could get. Lewis probably knew the
farm well. It was near the land in the Hopson Bayou neighborhood,
about twenty-five miles southeast of Friars Point, that still belonged
to his former masters, the Cheairs brothers. When the auction was
over, Lewis had won with a top bid of ten cents an acre. He had three
years to pay the total of $20 in annual installments of $6.66²/₃ each,
with interest at 6 percent. Even with the severe economic depression
in the Delta after the Civil War, this was an extremely low price.

The Thomases did not wait long and set to working their farm
that same spring. Their first season was a stunning success. The value
of all their crops was estimated at $5,100, equivalent to approximately
$80,000 today. In less than a year, they had recouped their first in-
stallment many hundreds of times over and had become one of the
most successful black families in the region.

Nature created the conditions in the Delta that allowed human ingenuity and effort to succeed. Despite its name, the Delta is the Mississippi River's inland flood plain, and is located some three hundred
miles upstream from the Gulf. Coahoma County was still a semi-
wilderness in the decades after the Civil War, and its character and
appearance were largely products of the Mississippi's annual spring
floods. The dark alluvial soil these deposited, combined with the
long and hot summers, made the region extraordinarily fertile. Well
into the beginning of the twentieth century, Coahoma County was a
dense forest of giant cypress, tupelo, and sweet gum trees, as well as
sycamore, poplar, pecan, maple, and numerous other species. Many
of the trees were as thick as a man is tall and soared a hundred feet or
more. Amid the trees were jungle-like growths of underbrush, vines,
and cane, in many places fifteen to twenty feet high, which made pas-

sage extremely difficult. The interlacing network of swamps, lakes, and bayous created by the spring floods further impeded travel by land. Roads were hard to build and water was the primary means of transportation throughout the nineteenth century.

After the county was formed in 1836 from what had been Indian lands, word spread quickly that cotton grew there to an amazing six feet in height, nearly twice as tall as anywhere else in the South. Slave-owning whites were the dominant settlers from the start because intensive labor was necessary to clear the forests and drain the land for planting. They usually came by water, often on Mississippi riverboats, which were the simplest means of transporting large and heavy loads. After reaching the Delta, they transferred their families, cattle, slaves, and other possessions onto shallow-draft flatboats that they poled via sinuous paths, turning whichever way the interconnected bodies of water allowed, until they reached a likely bank on which to land.

At first, cultivated fields were narrow strips along rivers and bayous. It took years of arduous work for the slaves to expand them inland by felling the trees, uprooting the stumps, and clearing the brush and cane. Despite a rapid increase in settlers in Coahoma County, which encompasses nearly six hundred square miles, the population by 1860 was only 6,606, of whom 5,085 were slaves. And throughout the Delta as a whole at this time just 10 percent of the land was under cultivation.

Nevertheless, Coahoma and several other nearby river counties quickly became among the wealthiest in the entire country. When the Civil War began, cotton constituted 57 percent of total American exports, and the state of Mississippi alone grew one-quarter of it. This made the biggest slave owners rich and allowed them to live luxuriously. Over time, they built large mansions, filled them with expensive furniture, collected art, and traveled to Europe. During the fall and winter social seasons, they indulged in dinners, parties, and lavish balls.

By contrast, the lives of slaves were more brutal in the Delta than in most other places in the South because of the difficult terrain and the prolonged annual agricultural cycle that the warm climate made possible. The large financial investment that many planters made in what was then a remote location, and their hunger for profits from spectacular crops, caused them to drive their slaves especially hard. Working conditions were aggravated by the clouds of mosquitoes that bred in the standing water every spring. From April to September, these insects made life so unbearable that whites who could afford it would leave for resorts in the North or escape to higher and cooler ground. The Delta was also a singularly unhealthy place to work. Epidemics, including yellow fever and malaria, as well as various waterborne diseases, killed thousands. Blacks suffered more than whites, and black children were the most vulnerable population of all.

Little is known about Lewis and Hannah before they bought their farm. Slaves wrote very few memoirs because owners tried to keep them illiterate. Planters rarely kept detailed records about their slaves that went beyond the kinds of inventories used for cattle.

However, it is possible to surmise that like almost all other freedmen in the Delta, Lewis and Hannah worked the land between the end of the Civil War in April 1865 and early 1869, when he bid on their farm. This is how they could have earned the money necessary for the first annual installment. That they immediately became very successful when they struck out on their own implies that they were not novices.

When the Civil War ended, many freedmen believed that the federal government would institute land reforms by confiscating large plantations, dividing them into parcels, and giving the parcels to individual black farmers. This did not happen. The compromise solution that developed throughout the South was various forms of tenancy, especially sharecropping. Under this system, which was already established in parts of the Delta by 1868 and would persist well into the twentieth century, a black family would lease a piece of land from a white owner in exchange for a percentage of the crops the family raised. The cost of whatever supplies and services the family received from the landowner, such as food, clothing, medical care, farming implements, and building materials, would be deducted from the family's share of the crop. However, because the tenant often had to pay the landowner as much as 50 percent of the crop, many freedmen remained impoverished. Those who did succeed in accumulating enough capital to be free of debt at the end of a harvest, and who thereby felt empowered to bargain with the landowners for better conditions during the next season, often tried to rent land. But landowners, as well as the Ku Klux Klan, tried to thwart black land rental, which they feared would deprive them of control over black labor and could lead to the widespread transfer of Delta lands from white hands to black. This may have been what Lewis faced prior to 1869. Nonetheless, his bid of $20, with one-third down (equivalent to perhaps $100 today), could have been within the financial reach of a family that worked either as hired hands or as sharecroppers.

Hannah and Lewis experienced the other hardships of black life in the Delta as well, including the region's notoriously high mortality rate. Frederick had three older brothers and one sister—Yancy, who was born a slave in 1861; William, who was born free in 1867; Kate, born around 1868; and John, born in 1870. Two died young—Kate around 1870, and William a few years later. Frederick left no recollections of any of these siblings, and nothing further is known about them.

Frederick's mother, Hannah, died when she was around thirty-five; she may have died giving birth to him in 1872. Lewis then married another woman, India, who was a few years younger than Hannah. She was born in Alabama in 1843, and was probably brought to the Delta before the Civil War by a white planter. Frederick would later identify India as his mother, and this confirms that she entered his life when he was very young and raised him.

It is possible that Lewis and India were drawn to each other in part because they both stood out in the local black community. He was by all accounts a friendly, hardworking, intelligent, and socially conscious man. By the time of Frederick's birth in 1872, he had also been well off for several years, and not only by black standards. Various evidence has survived indicating that India was a good match for him. Most notable is that she would join her husband in pursuing a number of legal actions in the Coahoma County courthouse; this was rare for black people in general, and even more so for a black woman. That she persisted with lawsuits on her own after being widowed made her rarer still. India was also literate, which was exceptional for a former slave (and suggests that she may have been a domestic before the Civil War). Her first name was unusual, too, for a black woman, and even the way she signed documents distinguished her from most freedwomen: she used a middle initial, "P." Although Lewis could neither read nor write, on occasion he also used a middle initial, "T," perhaps imitating India. These are small gestures, but under the circumstances, they imply a certain defiant pride in one's own identity, and a resistance, however subtle, to the kind of self-effacement that whites expected from blacks. The resemblance between Lewis's and India's strong character and Frederick's behavior in later years suggests that they had a very decisive influence on him.

The names that appeared in the Thomas family also fit this pattern of exceptionalism. Although she was in her forties, which was an advanced age to bear children in the nineteenth century, India had a daughter at some point in the 1880s and named her Ophelia. Like Bruce, Frederick's middle name, Ophelia was an uncommon name among black Americans in the postbellum South.

Frederick was most likely named after Frederick Douglass, the former slave who became a celebrated abolitionist, author, and statesman. Douglass was widely known throughout the United States starting in the 1850s, and his name would have appealed to black people like the Thomases. A possible source of Frederick's middle name, one that was quite near at hand, was Blanche K. Bruce. He was a former slave who became a rich landowner in Bolivar County, Mississippi, during the late 1860s, and a politician both there and in Tallahatchie County, before being elected in 1874 to the United States Senate, where he was the first black man to serve a full term. Because Coahoma County shares borders with both Bolivar and Tallahatchie counties—and the latter was very near the Thomas farm—it is possible that the Thomases knew Bruce personally. In later years, Frederick continued to pay considerable attention to the implications of personal names. He always used his middle initial when he signed his name, and often wrote out "Bruce" fully. In Moscow, when he was starting to put down roots, he adopted a typically Russian name and patronymic—Fyodor Fyodorovich. He also kept his first and middle names alive in his family by naming his youngest sons, who were born in Moscow, Frederick Jr. and Bruce.

"Ophelia" suggests evidence of her parents' unusually broad cultural awareness, or at least that of India, since she was the literate member of the couple. The nearest plausible source for the name was Harriet Beecher Stowe's famous antislavery novel *Uncle Tom's Cabin*, which was published in 1852 and became the second biggest best seller in the United States in the nineteenth century, after the Bible. In the novel, Miss Ophelia St. Clare is an admirable secondary character who manages to overcome her northern prejudice against blacks. India might have known of the novel even without having read it because of its fame and notoriety in the South, where slave owners angrily attacked it.

Farming was a family affair out of necessity, and the work it entailed sheds light on how the Thomases lived after they bought their farm and on what Frederick's childhood was like. During the final third of the nineteenth century, the major cash crop in Coahoma County remained cotton, followed by corn. Clearing the land, plowing and seeding it, weeding the fields until the plants were tall enough to shade the ground, and then picking the cotton and ears of corn when they had ripened and dried sufficiently were chores not only for men and women but also for children, as soon as they were six or seven and big enough to manage a hoe or drag a sack. Everyone had to pitch in with the other tasks as well. Farm families grew their own vegetables, raised chickens and hogs, and kept a milk cow or two if they could afford it. They needed mules, horses, or oxen to pull the plows, to haul the crops, and for other heavy work like ginning the raw cotton and baling it; all the animals had to be fed and watered regularly.

Hunting and fishing were also a part of a farmer's life in the Delta, for whites and blacks alike, because these were the simplest and cheapest ways to provide meat for the table. At the end of the nineteenth century the woods were full of deer, bears, panthers, wolves, opossums, and many other small animals; there were turkeys, ducks, and other fowl. Catfish, buffalo fish, trout, bowfin, crayfish, alligators, water moccasins, and snapping turtles as big as washtubs filled the waterways. Even after the Civil War, alligators preyed on domestic pigs so regularly that children had to be warned constantly to be on guard lest they be seized too.

The daily, weekly, and seasonal rhythms of agricultural labor and life on the edge of a wilderness would have largely determined the world that Frederick knew from earliest childhood. Church and school would have been the most important exceptions, but these probably started later. Most of the year, chores filled the daylight hours, playmates were scarce in the sparsely populated countryside, and amusements would have been whatever one could devise.

A child growing up in the Delta would probably never forget its smells and sounds, because of the way these imprint themselves on one's consciousness. Smells such as the sweetness of sun-warmed tangles of honeysuckle; the heavy brown aroma of newly turned loam behind a plow in the fields; or the delectable, banana-like scent of the pawpaw tree that sometimes grows on riverbanks. A farm in the Delta was like an island in a vast green sea, and the sounds one heard came mostly from nature. At dawn, the dew-laden air was filled with the cries of mourning doves, the staccato rattle of yellow-headed woodpeckers, and the grating calls of crows that flapped by on heavy wings. During still, hot summer days, the fields would resound with the oscillating buzz of grasshoppers. At dusk, the big-bellied bullfrogs would mark the end of day with a bass chorus that would alternately swell, then fade, while the last mule team trudged back from the fields, and the final, flat, ringing blow of a hammer on a distant anvil dissolved in the growing darkness.

After 1869, the Thomases emerged from the anonymity that typified the lives of most black people in the Delta. As landowners they had to interact with the white power structure of Coahoma County and began to leave traces in governmental records. The consequences of this would be far-reaching for them as well as for several prominent local planters.

During the 1870 United States census, Lewis and Hannah were canvassed for detailed information about their farm production. From this it is known that their exceptionally successful first year's crop included 48 bales of cotton, each weighing 450 pounds; 250 bushels of sweet potatoes; and 300 pounds of butter. Most of the $5,100 they earned that year came from cotton. In a way that the majority of black people could scarcely imagine, the Thomases had become independent and self-reliant landowners, with their own home, fields, animals, and freedom to set priorities.

They had also started farming on a fairly large scale. The 48 bales they produced indicate that a sizable portion of their land was planted with cotton, perhaps 70 out of 200 acres. Sweet potatoes would have required additional acreage, as would fodder for their animals. The 1870 census recorded that the Thomases owned seven mules or asses, seven working oxen, four milk cows, and six other unspecified "cattle." Fourteen draft animals were too many for Lewis and Hannah to use by themselves in tilling the land or in ginning and baling the cotton. Moreover, Hannah would have been busy with many other responsibilities, including her children, housekeeping, the milk cows, the vegetable garden, chickens, and the like. From the very beginning of their land ownership, the Thomases could not have managed without either hired hands or sharecroppers to help with the work. For a black family to employ other freedmen was a remarkable change in the normal labor relations in the Delta. And it also made the Thomases stand out in the eyes of their white neighbors.

During the next decade and a half, the Thomases engaged in many land transactions as their fortunes, and the Delta's economy, waxed and waned. In 1876 they actually lost ownership of their farm for a year because of debts, but they repurchased most of it in 1877. They then gradually built it up to 400 acres in 1880, 504 in 1884, and 625 in 1886. The core of the Thomas property straddled what is now Highway 49, two miles south of Dublin and twelve miles southeast of Clarksdale, where Hopson Bayou comes closest to the road.

As records in the Coahoma Chancery Court show, the Thomases regularly used their land as collateral for loans and as capital to repay debts. Banks were scarce in Coahoma during the 1870s and 1880s, and a farmer who needed cash or supplies before he could sell his current harvest would often mortgage all or part of his land, frequently together with all his farm animals, tools, equipment, and buildings, to a bigger and richer local landowner. Once the farmer sold his crops, he could pay off his mortgage, which, in addition to principal, would include annual interest, usually between 6 and 10 percent a year, and usually for a period from one to three years. Between 1870 and 1886, Lewis signed financial agreements of this kind eight times with five rich, influential white men for sums ranging from $2,600 to $9,600 (the latter would be around $200,000 today), and he often had notes coming due once or even several times a year. In this way, the Thomases' total acreage varied over the years: they would sell or buy pieces of property as obligations demanded or opportunities allowed.

A constant feature of Lewis's efforts, and India's as well, judging by her active role when things began to go badly for them, was trying to increase the size and profitability of the farm. Lewis even tried to branch out beyond farming by setting up a steam-powered sawmill on his land with a white English emigrant as a partner in 1873. This initiative is notable because it foreshadows what Frederick would discover years later in London—the English did not impose a color line on black Americans.

As Frederick was growing up, he could not have missed hearing about his parents' business dealings. These transactions were frequent; people on a farm lived in tight quarters; and children are always curious. Even a vague awareness of his parents' financial plans and deals would have given him a sense of life broader than an endless cycle of labor, food, and sleep—a sense that very few other blacks in the Delta would ever get. Frederick never returned to rural life or farming after he left Mississippi. However, he also never gave up the idea that true success was defined by growth. This may have been a commonplace of American enterprise and capitalism in general, but it is also something that he witnessed at home as a child.

However, material gain was not the only thing that moved Lewis and India. In 1879, they made a dramatic change in their own lives and in the life of the black community in the Hopson Bayou neighborhood by donating land to establish a new church. In light of how few blacks owned any land in Coahoma County, the Thomases' donation demonstrated their unusual generosity. This initiative would also have done much to expand Frederick's worldview and sense of life's possibilities.

Before and during the Civil War, it was common for slaves to attend their masters' churches. Afterward, the sweeping changes in the social order led whites to refuse to let the newly emancipated blacks participate in the life of their churches, and freedmen either left their old congregations or were expelled. On June 14, 1879, the Thomases sold three-quarters of an acre of their land on the west side of Hopson Bayou to the African Methodist Episcopal Church for the token sum of one dollar. It may have been India's initiative even more than Lewis's because, typically, the mother in a black family took a special interest in spiritual matters, and India's signature accompanies Lewis's "X" on the deed. When it was built, the Thomas Chapel, as it became known, was probably a small log cabin, like virtually all new buildings in Coahoma County in those days, including the residences of planters. It was also one of the earliest A.M.E. churches established in the county after the "mother," Bethel A.M.E. Church in Friars Point.

It was not the first church in the Hopson Bayou neighborhood, however, and the initiative that the Thomases made toward their fellow freedmen may well have struck whites in the area as presumptuous because, once again, the Thomases were standing out. The Cherry Hill Methodist Church, around which the town of Dublin eventually grew, and which was two miles northwest of the Thomas Chapel, had been there since the 1850s. Lewis would have known it because its congregation included his former owners, the three Cheairs brothers, and their extended family. In fact, it is quite possible that Lewis and Hannah had attended the Cherry Hill Church with their masters, but that they had been excluded from it after the Civil War.

The churches in rural Mississippi typically extended their role far beyond worship and served local residents as gathering places for various purposes, including entertainment, politics, and especially education. The 1880 United States census indicates that Frederick and his brothers Yancy and John attended school during the previous year. It is likely that the boys' school shared space with the church their parents helped found; it is possible that India taught there. The boys' school "year" would typically not have lasted more than four months, thus leaving them free to help on their parents' farm the rest of the time. In a small one-room country school such as this, children would have been grouped in different corners by approximate age and ability (in 1879, Yancy was around seventeen, John was ten, and Frederick was seven). All would have been taught by one teacher, and education would not have gone beyond the third or fourth grade.

If the Thomas Chapel was also used as a school, it was probably the first one in the area for black children. The Bureau of Refugees, Freedmen, and Abandoned Lands, a federal agency established in 1865 for the purpose of aiding newly freed blacks, had originally been charged with organizing schools in the South, in addition to providing various other forms of assistance. When southern state legislatures took over their black school systems, funding was cut and some schools were closed. As a result, in 1880 only one in four black boys aged ten and over was literate, in comparison with four out of five for southern whites. Frederick and his brothers were in very select black company in the Delta by virtue of their schooling as well as their parents' land ownership and social leadership.

The Thomas family's prominence, however, would also be the cause of its ruin. The second major turning point in their lives again involved their farm but it was, unfortunately, for the worse.

Early in 1886, at a time when the annual cycle of cotton farming had come to a close, William H. Dickerson, a rich and well-known white landowner in Coahoma County, showed up at the Thomases' farm. Seeing him arrive would not have surprised Lewis and India, because they had had regular business dealings with him during the past eight years. They had borrowed money from him twice (and once from his father) by mortgaging their property in the usual fashion. As they saw it, their relationship with Dickerson was based on friendship and honesty. They had paid off all their notes on time, a fact that Dickerson had officially acknowledged. They also trusted Dickerson to such an extent that over the years they had relied on him to keep accurate accounts for them of the numbers of bales of cotton they delivered to him for sale and of the various goods and supplies they received from him.

This time, Dickerson's visit was not a friendly one. He showed Lewis and India a wad of papers he claimed were letters from other white landowners in the area who had written to him, and then began to read extracts aloud. The Thomases' neighbors complained that Lewis "had become very obnoxious" to them "because of his owner-ship of property to a considerable amount." They did not want Lewis "to reside among them" any longer and, knowing Dickerson's long-standing relations with Lewis, warned Dickerson "to close out" his business dealings with Lewis.

Dickerson then revealed his second reason for the visit and began to play the double role he had apparently intended all along. First, he underscored the implied threat in the letters by stressing that it was "dangerous" for the Thomases to remain on their farm. Lewis and India would have understood very well what this meant. Then Dickerson delivered his second blow. He announced that Lewis and India owed him nearly $13,000. This was a very large sum for the time, the equivalent of roughly $300,000 in today's money. Dickerson told them they had accumulated this debt over a number of years and he was ready to seize their personal property and to have it sold to satisfy the debt. Then he got to what was pre-sumably his motive all along. Playing on their supposed friendship, Dickerson suggested "an amicable settlement." If Lewis signed a deed transferring the entire 625-acre farm and all the Thomases' personal property to him, Dickerson would give Lewis $2,000 plus "two good mules and a wagon." In other words, Dickerson would provide the Thomases the means to escape with their lives and a stake to start over somewhere else in exchange for everything they owned. He thus cunningly tried to present himself as their "savior." To cinch the argument, Dickerson then reminded Lewis that if his property was sold for his debts, the sum realized might be less than the amount due and Lewis not only would be penniless but would have a "large debt hanging over him."

Initially at least, Dickerson's multilayered trap worked. Lewis and India thought they knew him well. So, they must have reasoned, if Dickerson was good enough to warn them of the dangers they faced from the whites around them, and if he said that they had to sign their farm over to him to make things right between them, he must be telling the truth, and they had to do what he said. Accordingly, on February 10, 1886, they signed the deed, although for a reduced and recalculated debt of $9,600.

Lewis and India had lost everything that they, and Hannah, had worked for during the past seventeen years. But at least they could get away from Coahoma County with their lives and children. Or so they thought. They waited one week, then another. The promised wagon and two mules never arrived, and neither did the $2,000. When Lewis sought out Dickerson and confronted him about the delay, the white man flatly denied ever having made the promise.

Given Dickerson's wealth and prominence, it is hard to understand what would have motivated him to try to take the Thomases' land in the first place. He owned around eight thousand acres between Clarksdale and Friars Point, of which four thousand were under cultivation, as well as a store with goods worth $8,000 and various buildings and land in Friars Point worth more than $50,000; and he had interests in several Friars Point factories. The Thomases' 625 acres and other possessions were minuscule in comparison. Could Dickerson have been seeking to take what he believed was legally his? Or could it be that the rich white man thought he could simply brush the black couple aside because their success was "obnoxious" to his racist sensibilities? Subsequent events would suggest that the

Thomases had become victims of an ignominious episode in the Dickerson family's past.

For the Thomases, Dickerson's reneging on his promise meant they were now destitute. But rather than meekly accept this new blow, Lewis and India found the strength to rally. They began to doubt what Dickerson had told them. Although they did not keep many paper records on their farm, they did have good memories, especially when it came to cotton harvests. Furthermore, Lewis and India had tenants or sharecroppers who had worked their land and who also remembered what years had been good, middling, or bad. When they all put their recollections together and tallied the bales of cotton they produced each year and what the bales were worth, and when they recalculated all the other business transactions that they had naively entrusted to Dickerson's reckoning, Lewis and India could not understand how they could owe him the enormous sum he claimed. Had Dickerson in fact credited them for all the cotton that they had delivered to him? Was not the interest he had charged them "excessive and usurious"? Had he not "wrongly charged them" for "illegal and unwarranted items"?

Also very troubling was Lewis and India's discovery that none of their white neighbors had actually written the threatening letters to Dickerson that he had pretended to read to them. They concluded that Dickerson had invented these in order to frighten them, to make them anxious to get out of the county, and to accept his low offer of a buyout. Fighting him would be difficult because of his and his family's wealth and prominence. But the Thomases felt so wronged by what he had done that, in an extraordinary display of courage, they resolved to seek justice anyway.

Swindles such as this were not rare in the South and often had a crippling effect not only on the victims but also on their children. A young black man in a different state whose father had been cheated out of his property by whites concluded: "it weren't no use in climbin too fast . . . weren't no use in climbin slow, neither, if they was goin to take everything you worked for when you got too high."

However, Frederick learned a very different lesson, judging by his behavior in subsequent years. He was thirteen in the spring of 1886 and old enough to understand the kind of elaborate deception that his parents were facing. Growing up in Coahoma, he would have known from earliest childhood the belittlement, hostility, and violence to which blacks were routinely subjected. But his parents' reaction was hardly the usual response to such treatment, and it showed him the possibility of fighting for what was his no matter who the opponent or how slim the chance of victory. Even though the circumstances would differ markedly in Moscow and Constantinople, Frederick would show the same kind of tenacity there when he faced attempts by merchants, moneylenders, and lawyers to cheat him.

The Thomases must have been greatly encouraged by the willingness of a small team of prominent lawyers (all white, of course) to take on their case—George F. Maynard and the brothers Will D. and John W. Cutrer. John, or "Jack," Cutrer was also a politician with good connections who would marry well and become a rich, notorious, and flamboyant figure in Coahoma County. (In 1890, in the midst of the protracted Thomas lawsuit, he would shoot dead in broad daylight a white newspaperman who had questioned the purity of his white ancestry; and he would get away with it.) By contrast, Dickerson had only one lawyer, Daniel Scott. This imbalance suggests that there may have been some degree of antipathy among leading whites toward Dickerson—and the suggestion is borne out by later events.

On May 6, 1886, Lewis filed a lawsuit in the Coahoma County Courthouse in Friars Point against Dickerson. He sought to cancel the deed transferring the farm to Dickerson; to have the accounts between them reexamined, recalculated, and purged of usurious interest and illegal charges; and to receive credit for all the sums to which he was entitled and which Dickerson had denied him. Dickerson must have been taken aback by the audacity of Lewis's lawsuit. Not only was this black man trying to wrest a fine piece of property from his hands just when he had seized it; he was also impugning a white man's honor in full public view and with the assistance of other leading whites.

But there was even more reason for Dickerson to be outraged. The lawsuit would also resurrect memories of a series of scandals in his family's past involving an especially sordid intersection of race and money.

The Dickerson family's roots in the area went back to the early days of white settlement in Coahoma County. Around 1847, three brothers from Maryland—Peter, Levin, and George Dickerson— bought land and established what became several of the largest and richest plantations in the county's northwest quadrant. Peter was William Dickerson's father.

The first scandal in the family involved Levin, William's uncle. He never married but chose instead to live more or less openly with a black woman named Ann from 1855 until his death in 1871. Although before and during the Civil War many white men in the South kept slave women as concubines and sexually assaulted slaves at will, interracial marriage had been illegal under slavery. An open liaison was still a rare occurrence even after the Civil War and was seen as deeply shocking by white planters. Moreover, Ann and Levin had two children, Susan and Oliver, and Levin acknowledged them despite their "illegitimacy." These two embarrassing offspring were William's first cousins. When Levin died, leaving "a large real and personal estate" worth $115,000, his two children assumed they would inherit it all. However, Peter Dickerson and his family had other plans. Peter himself, his daughter Mary, and her husband, W. N. Brown, sued in the Coahoma County Chancery Court to get possession of Levin's land and property by claiming that they alone were his legal heirs. They won, and Mary and her husband took over the plantation from Susan and Oliver to work as their own.

Despite the racial barriers they faced, Susan and Oliver decided to fight back and appealed the lower court's decision to the Mississippi supreme court. It is testimony to this body's honesty and diligence, and to the unusually liberal moment in Mississippi during Reconstruction in October 1873, that the state supreme court overturned the lower court's decision. It ruled that Ann and Levin Dickerson had lived in a state of de facto marriage after the Civil War, and therefore their mixed-race children were Levin's legal heirs. As a result, Susan and Oliver received their inheritance, and Peter Dickerson, his daughter, and his son-in-law had to give up the plantation.

There is thus a resemblance between William Dickerson's attempt to take Lewis and India's property and the attempt that his father, Peter, and members of his family made to take Susan and Oliver's. Moreover, because William was eighteen years old in 1873, he must have known every last detail of the shameful story, even if there is no evidence that he had been directly involved himself.

Everyone else in Coahoma County would have known about it as well, because the state supreme court's decision legitimizing a white-black marriage and recognizing mixed-race children as legal heirs was so shocking that it reverberated throughout Mississippi. One newspaper in Jackson, the state capital, angrily condemned the decision because it equated "the sanctity of the marriage tie" to "the beastly degradation of concubinage" and because it let "copulation thrive."

There can be no doubt that everyone in the large Dickerson clan who was still alive in 1886, when William made his move against the Thomases, remembered the 1873 decision. Indeed, it is possible that when William first rode out with the threatening "letters" intending to scare off the successful black man, he had the earlier reversal in mind and was hoping for a form of revenge. What he could not have anticipated, however, is the way his plan would backfire and how this would lead to uncanny reminders of the family fiasco in 1873.

The case Lewis brought against William Dickerson was complex and dragged on in the Coahoma County Chancery Court for nearly three years (before undergoing a spectacular twist that would give it new life for another five). It is unclear how the Thomases lived in the interim, without the farm that had been their livelihood. Perhaps this is the time when they ran a boardinghouse in Clarksdale, as Frederick recalled later. Both sides in the suit asked for and received extensions to gather additional evidence and testimony; there were additional delays.

When the court finally handed down the decision on April 19, 1889, it could not have been a bigger shock, especially for William Dickerson. Lewis and India Thomas won on all counts. Not only did the court order Dickerson to return the property to them, but a recalculation of the accounts between them showed that he owed the Thomases a sum nearly identical to what he had claimed they owed him in 1886. The court also summarized Dickerson's behavior in a way that was even more insulting than the verdict itself. He had made "misrepresentations" to the Thomases, had betrayed their naive trust in him, and had cheated them when he did not deliver the promised wagon, mules, and money. Incensed, Dickerson swore that he would appeal to the Mississippi supreme court.

Although the Coahoma court's decision was a resounding confirmation of the Thomases' claims, other powerful forces were at play around their case as well. One would not necessarily have expected truth and justice alone to triumph in a case in the Delta that pitted a black couple against a rich and well-established white planter. It is possible that personal relations between Lewis and influential whites in Coahoma County could have played a role in how the court viewed him and even in the trial's outcome, especially if William Dickerson had enemies. And he did.

Coahoma County was a contentious place in the 1880s and there were many causes that divided whites. One of the major issues for some was the location of the county courthouse. It had been in Friars Point since the 1860s, but in the 1880s a faction formed that wanted it moved to the growing town of Clarksdale. A leader of this group, and a son-in-law of Clarksdale's founder, was none other than Jack Cutrer, one of the Thomases' lawyers. By contrast, Daniel Scott, William Dickerson's lawyer, was a well-known proponent of keeping the courthouse in Friars Point. The two factions went so far as to disrupt each other's meetings, to arm themselves with clubs and guns, and to threaten each other with bodily harm. Their conflict became so notorious that news of it was reported as far away as Boston in 1887. At stake were not only the seat of local power and the trickle-down effect this would have on local business and development. Even more important was where railroads would be built through the Delta to link Memphis and points north with Vicksburg and ultimately New Orleans. Peter Dickerson owned a plantation ten miles north of Clarksdale but only three from Friars Point. He succeeded in having a train station built on his property in 1889 and named it after his son William. Perhaps this kind of bold and lucrative initiative put the Dickersons at odds with Cutrer and his Clarksdale allies and influenced the Cutrer brothers' decision to take on the Thomases' case. Local political and electoral rivalries may have played a similar role as well.

A year after the Coahoma court had delivered its verdict, the supreme court of Mississippi considered William Dickerson's appeal during its April 1890 term. In their official "Opinion," the justices complained that they found the hundreds of pages of testimony and documents they had to review overwhelming and unclear. As a result, the ruling they handed down was mixed and confusing.

On the one hand, the justices affirmed the lower court's decision to cancel Lewis's transfer of his land to Dickerson in 1886. This would seem to have been a confirmation of Lewis's victory. But on the other hand, the justices undermined the entire evidentiary basis of the lower court's decision and thus of Lewis's victory by ordering that his accounts with Dickerson be recalculated. They also ridiculed the Thomases' other claims against Dickerson, the lower court's procedures, and the portrait that his lawyers had painted of

Lewis as a simple and uneducated black man. The only real criticism of Dickerson was that on occasion he charged the Thomases too much interest. Nevertheless, it is clear that the justices did not find the Thomases' case against Dickerson to be entirely without merit (or, perhaps, the influence of local Coahoma politics a matter of complete indifference).

The two sides in the lawsuit must have found the supreme court's decision confusing as well. Lewis and his lawyers naturally focused on the part that appeared to favor them. Thus, on June 7, 1890, Lewis asked the local court to issue him a "writ of assistance" so he could get his property back, a request to which the court agreed. At the same time, the court ordered that all accounts between him and Dickerson be reexamined to determine once and for all who owed what to whom.

Dickerson's plans had been thwarted for the second time by the unlikely coalition of a black couple and the local white judicial system. He immediately decided to reappeal to the Mississippi supreme court. The stakes had now risen for the Thomases, and fighting Dickerson had become more difficult, but they were not about to give up. During most of this time, they did not have possession of their farm or receive income from it, and they could not have had much cash on hand. Consequently, two days after Dickerson announced his intention to reappeal, the Thomases deeded one-half of their farm to their lead lawyer, Jack Cutrer, as a retainer and gave him a lien on the remainder in case he incurred any other expenses. Because they badly needed some money just to get by, the deed also stipulated that Cutrer would give them ten dollars in cash when they signed.

William Dickerson and his family were unlikely to have been the only whites in the county who saw the Thomases as troublemakers needing to be taught a lesson. By the late 1880s, Mississippi was becoming the "lynchingest" state in the entire country. This would have been a prudent time for the Thomases to leave. In fact, they appear to have abandoned Coahoma County and moved to Memphis during the summer of 1890, after they deeded their farm to Cutrer. This was the nearest city to Friars Point and was located only some seventy miles away, which meant that it was far enough to establish a safe distance from possible threats but close enough to allow them to keep an eye on the lawsuit's progress.

By 1890, Memphis had a population of some sixty thousand, with 56 percent white and 44 percent black, and was a major business hub. It was the largest inland cotton market in the United States and shipped 770,000 bales a year to fabric mills at home and abroad, especially to England. River transport on the Mississippi and railroads linking the rest of the country with the South further enhanced the city's economic importance and made it an attractive place to seek work.

Although Memphis became a temporary haven for the Thomases, it was hardly a model of racial tolerance. In 1866, the city had seen one of the worst race riots in the South following the Civil War; and in the 1880s lynchings began to increase. But Memphis was also big enough to allow a new black family to blend in without trouble.

Lewis and India rented a house at 112 Kansas Avenue, at the corner of Carolina Avenue, in the Fort Pickering section on the city's southern edge. In those days, this was a suburban and mostly black part of town. The house was a roomy, long and narrow, two-story frame structure with a yard on two sides and a stable in the back, in the middle of what might be called today a mixed residential and industrial zone. It was a busy, noisy, smelly, and gritty place. A wood yard was directly across the street, and the Milburn Gin and Machine Company, which occupied an entire city block and included various manufacturing shops and storage areas, was diagonally across. The depot for the Kansas City, Memphis and Birmingham Railroad lay one block to the west. Tracks from one of its branches passed right in front of the Thomases' house and forked several doors away; another set of three tracks ran directly behind the stable in their backyard. The screech of steel wheels and the howls of steam whistles as trains went back and forth on all sides, the billows of acrid black coal smoke, and the dust that settled everywhere must have been a shock at first for country youngsters like Frederick and Ophelia, who were used to the lush green vistas, placid bayous, and sweet-smelling breezes of Coahoma County.

But the city offered tantalizing opportunities that were not available back home. Lewis needed to find work and was able to get a job as a flagman with the KCM&B Railroad. Because the house that he and India rented was too big for just their family, they decided to use part of it as a boardinghouse for India to run. She not only was a good cook but may already have had experience with lodgers in a boardinghouse in Clarksdale.

Frederick got a job as a delivery boy for Joseph A. Weir, a white merchant who owned a well-known market on Beale Street that advertised "Fine Meats, Oysters, Fish, and Game." This is the first urban job that Frederick had about which there is any information, and it is intriguing to note how it foreshadows his occupations in future years and in distant locations, which always involved some form of service and sophisticated cuisine.

Frederick also tried to continue his formal education in Memphis. He enrolled "for a short time" in Howe Institute, a school for black youth. Established in 1888 as the Baptist Bible and Normal Institute, it was renamed the following year in honor of Peter Howe, its white founder and chief benefactor. When Frederick was a student at Howe, the principal was most likely Joseph Eastbrook, a Congregational minister and lifelong educator originally from Michigan, and one of the teachers was Eastbrook's wife, Ida Ann, who had been born in New York. Contacts with tolerant and enlightened white people like these from the North were probably Frederick's first, and would have given him an entirely new sense of how whites could treat blacks. Howe Institute tried to meet a patchwork quilt of different educational needs. It provided everything from religious instruction to academic subjects to vocational training in such skills as sewing and nursing for girls and carpentry for boys. A local newspaper pointed out that a "specialty" of the Howe Institute was "furnishing trained houseboys for the people of Memphis—sending into this service as many as 100 a year." Because Frederick would work for many years as a servant, although at a considerably more sophisticated level than a newspaper reporter in Memphis could have imagined, it is possible that he received some training in the relevant skills and deportment while at Howe. His careful, calligraphic handwriting later in life suggests the influence of formal schooling as well.

Frederick's stay at Howe and in Memphis would prove short, unfortunately. Two new tragedies were waiting that would strike his family unexpectedly and would finally destroy everything his parents had achieved.

Among the boarders at Lewis and India's house was a black married couple, Frank Shelton and his wife. According to Memphis newspapers from October 1890, which strove to outdo themselves in describing Shelton in the most lurid terms, he was a "trifling" and "worthless negro" with an "evil disposition," "a reputation for brutality," and "brutal instincts." Even his wife was quoted as describing him as "very cruel, stubborn and desperate." Shelton was about thirty years old; had a smooth, dark brown complexion, a big nose, and a thick chest; was five feet ten inches tall; and carried a scar on the back of his head, which his wife said he had gotten in a fight with his employer at a sawmill in Alabama. He was a brakeman on a railroad and had come to Memphis about five months earlier.

By contrast, all the newspapers described Lewis in very positive terms. He was a "very reputable colored citizen," an "industrious," "intelligent," and "conscientious" man who was never known to participate in the fights and barroom brawls that often spilled out onto the streets of Fort Pickering. He and his wife were able to rent their house through their "industry and economy" and lived "comfortably" on their earnings. In 1890, Lewis was in his mid-fifties and India in her late forties. Expressing the norms of the time, the newspapers described her as "aged" and him as an "inoffensive old negro."

On Friday, October 24, for some unknown reason Frank Shelton refused to pay his rent and had an argument with Lewis, who told the Sheltons that they would have to leave their room. They were gone only overnight, however, and after they made amends Lewis allowed them to return. The calm did not last. The following evening, Shelton got into an argument with his wife and assaulted her brutally. He knocked her down, dragged her out of the house, and stamped her face with his feet. According to one account, Shelton also beat her with a spade so badly that her face and head were "horribly disfigured and bruised." Lewis saw the attack from a distance and hurried over, pleading with Shelton to stop. When he realized that this was not doing any good, he went to call a policeman. Shelton saw what Lewis was doing and, fearing arrest, stopped his assault. But before running away, he yelled a chilling threat to Lewis: "I will get even with you for this, if it takes me ten years! You are my meat!"

The next morning, Sunday, October 26, at about nine o'clock, Shelton's wife went to the police herself and asked them to arrest her husband for the beating he had given her. An Officer Richardson was dispatched to deal with the matter. He approached the Thomases' boardinghouse, planning to watch it from a distance in the hope of catching Shelton if he should return. Eventually, Richardson caught sight of him and rushed forward, shouting to him that he was under arrest. When Shelton started to run, Richardson drew his revolver and fired, but the shot went wide. Shelton turned a corner and disappeared.

The following night, Monday, October 27, Lewis went to bed as usual. Around 3 a.m., Shelton got into the Thomases' house, crept up the stairs to Lewis and India's room on the second floor, and entered it quietly. He was carrying a sharp-bladed ax and must have paused by the side of the double bed until he could make out his target in the dim light. Lewis was asleep, faceup, lying next to India. Shelton raised the ax, took aim, and brought it down hard on Lewis's face. The sound of the heavy blow roused India. She propped herself up on her elbows and glimpsed her husband struggling to rise with his arm outstretched; then the steel flashed and another heavy blow descended upon Lewis. India screamed in terror. Shelton dropped the ax, dashed out of the room, and ran down the stairs.

India's screams roused the household. Frederick, Ophelia, Shelton's wife, and the other tenants rushed into the room. After several moments of panic, someone got a light, which illuminated a horrific scene. Lewis was writhing in agony on the bed, blood pouring in streams from a gaping wound that extended from his left temple to his mouth. The first blow had cut through his cheekbone and fractured his skull. The second blow had caught his arm above the elbow when he raised it in a futile attempt to protect himself and had cut through the muscle and bone, almost severing it. Lewis struggled to rise several times as blood poured onto the bed and pooled on the floor near the ax that Shelton had dropped. It took several more frantic moments before someone had gathered sufficient wits to telephone for a doctor and the police. The blow to Lewis's face had nearly killed him. The doctor who arrived could do nothing to help because of the depth of the wound and the amount of blood that Lewis had lost. Somehow, Lewis lingered for six more hours, unconscious, until he finally died at 9 a.m.

Two justices arrived to carry out an autopsy and conduct an investigation. Testimony by all the witnesses pointed conclusively to Shelton. The Memphis police department quickly spread the news that he was the prime suspect. A day later, he was spotted sneaking onto a train heading for Holly Springs, a town in Mississippi some thirty miles southeast of Memphis. When he tried to escape the guards who were waiting for him, they killed him in a fusillade of shots. On the following day, in a display of professional zeal that was also strikingly insensitive to India's trauma, the Memphis police sent her down on the afternoon train to identify her husband's murderer. There was no doubt, and the case was closed.

Back in Coahoma County, the news of what had happened to Lewis could hardly have displeased William Dickerson. This black man had caused him a lot of trouble over the years and his death must have seemed like a just reward or even a wish fulfilled. There is no suggestion, however, that Dickerson was somehow behind Lewis's murder. It was merely bad luck, and the price that Lewis paid for his decency when he decided to help a woman with an abusive husband.

Shortly thereafter, Dickerson got more news that must have cheered him. In October 1890 the Mississippi supreme court issued an explanation of its previous decision. It now stated that the chancery court should never have returned the disputed land to Lewis before recalculation of the debt between him and Dickerson was completed.

But any illusions Dickerson might have had about Lewis's death putting an end to the lawsuit were quickly dispelled. On December 24, 1890, barely two months after the murder, India petitioned the chancery court to be recognized as the executor of her deceased husband's estate. As part of the process, she had to take an oath at the courthouse in Friars Point. Her willingness to come back to a town where she would face serious hostility from some quarters proves she was a remarkably determined woman and could not be cowed easily. On January 10, 1891, she revived the lawsuit against Dickerson in her own name and in the name of her two children, Frederick and Ophelia.

The case would continue with long interruptions and various convolutions for nearly four more years. It outlived both of the original litigants: William Dickerson died on February 18, 1894, at the relatively young age of thirty-nine; his widow, Lula, stepped into the breach to continue the fight, just as India had done. In the end, the decision the Coahoma County Chancery Court handed down on November 28,

1894, stated that India owed Lula a much-reduced amount of money. India had to auction off land to raise it, and a year later she was still remortgaging the property to raise money quickly for other reasons, possibly for Frederick.

Through all this time, India continued the case in her and the children's names, despite the fact that her family had effectively fallen apart and its living connection with the farm in Coahoma was severed. She stayed on in Memphis for a year after the murder, although in a different house from the one she had shared with Lewis, and in 1892 she moved to Louisville, Kentucky, presumably with Ophelia, where she got a job as a cook for a prosperous white jeweler. She worked for him for several years and appears to have died in Louisville sometime in the mid-1890s. The fate of Ophelia is unknown.

Frederick had turned eighteen on November 4, 1890, a week after his father was murdered, and left Memphis shortly thereafter; his subsequent recollection of the exact year was hazy. Decades later, when he had occasion to tell his life story to various Americans he encountered abroad, he did not always hide that his parents had been slaves, as some other black Americans did, but he never mentioned his father's murder to anyone. Perhaps the memory was too traumatic for him. The only reason he ever gave for leaving Memphis is that living near the railway junctions in Fort Pickering had "stimulated a desire" in him "to travel."

There is no reason to doubt that this part of what he chose to reveal was true. Indeed, it is easy to imagine a young man on the verge of adulthood being drawn by the lure of the railroad—by the sight of trains arriving from famous cities across the South while others depart for the even more alluring North, their plangent whistles receding in the distance, promising change. Eighteen was the right age to become your own man, to escape the white southerner's heavy gaze, to see something of the world, and to find a home elsewhere.

2

TRAVEL AND TRANSFORMATION

During the next decade Frederick traveled widely, and for a young black man of his era every step he took was a highly unusual rejection of his past. He left the South and lived only in cities. He mastered urban skills and moved in worlds that became progressively more white. And he would eventually leave the United States.

From Memphis, Frederick traveled a short distance west and crossed the Mississippi into Arkansas. Because Arkansas had been a slave state, and its eastern portion was much like the Delta bottomlands in appearance, history, and reliance on cotton and corn, Frederick did not find it appealing and spent only two months there. He then turned north and "drifted" to St. Louis, as he put it. This was a longer trip of some three hundred miles and represented a more resolute change.

In 1890, St. Louis was the fourth-largest city in the country, with a population approaching five hundred thousand, and had begun the quintessential American form of urban growth—upward, via steel-framed, multistory buildings. Its industrial and commercial bustle, its surprisingly white crowds in which not even one person in ten was black, and its air filled with snatches of spoken German, Czech, and Italian must have appealed to Frederick. After spending just a few months there he headed even farther north to a city that epitomized the young, powerful, polyglot, brash United States.

By 1890, Chicago had captured the world's imagination as the embodiment of the "American miracle." In just two generations, a frontier settlement established in 1833 had grown into the second-largest city in the country, with a population of 1.1 million; it was overshadowed only by New York's 1.5 million, and was the fifth-largest city in the world. Rather than being stunted by a devastating fire in 1871, Chicago's growth accelerated in the last decades of the nineteenth century as the city rebuilt itself into a modern metropolis and became a center of industry, commerce, and transportation. Chicago, with the world's first skyscrapers, became an icon not only of American technological prowess and economic might, but of modern industrialized civilization in general.

Emigrants from the Old World eager to reinvent themselves flooded into Chicago. They included Germans, Irish, Scandinavians, Poles, Lithuanians, Czechs, Italians, and Jews from several Eastern European countries. In 1890, an astounding 78 percent of the population had been born abroad or had foreign parents. An observer remarked that there were regions in the city where you could pass an entire day without hearing a word of English. It is bitterly ironic that American blacks, who were still concentrated largely in the South and who lived under conditions that were no better, and often worse, than those suffered by landless peasants in Ireland or impoverished laborers in Germany, did not have the same opportunities for change that many white foreigners were given. In fact, there were very few blacks in Chicago at this time; of the total population, they made up only 1.3 percent—about 15,000 people—with men somewhat outnumbering women. Even if many of the foreign emigrants in Chicago barely scraped out a livelihood and lived in filthy slums, they were at least given a chance to come to a place where they might be able to improve their lot. By contrast, Frederick's arrival was part of a feeble trickle of native-born southern blacks who had started coming to Chicago in the years after the Civil War. The "Great Migration," when hundreds of thousands would start streaming north in search of economic opportunity and to escape the intolerable conditions at home, would not occur until decades later, during and after World War I.

At first, Frederick got a job similar to the one he had in Memphis —except that this time he worked as a "boy" for a flower and fruit seller rather than for a butcher. Michael F. Gallagher was the owner of what was probably the most successful floral business in Chicago during the late 1880s and early 1890s, with a main store in the fashionable city center. On the eve of the Columbian Exposition of 1893, Gallagher opened a second store in an even more visible location on the city's main lakefront thoroughfare and announced his newly achieved prominence by advertising his business as "Florists to the World's Fair."

Everything about Frederick's first job in Chicago prefigures his future life and career. By working for Gallagher, he had entered what can be called an elegant service industry, one that existed for the benefit of people with money and social standing. No matter how lowly or demanding Frederick's own labors might have been, he was nevertheless involved in providing adornments to those who could afford to pay for such luxuries. The kinds of customers he most likely saw and interacted with at Gallagher's would also have presented him with models of gentility, and forms of posturing, that he would need to learn to understand and to satisfy.

Although Frederick had moved five hundred miles north of Memphis and a world away from the South, at the end of the nineteenth century blacks in Chicago were still hardly free to do or to become anything they wanted. After working for Gallagher for "8 or 9 months," as he recalled, Frederick launched into a profession that would be his mainstay for the next twenty years as well as his springboard to wealth: he became a waiter. By setting out on this career path, Frederick also assumed one of the few roles that was available to him because of the racist labor patterns in the city.

One-third of the entire black population were employed in domestic and personal service, a category that included workers in Chicago's myriad restaurants and hotels, in private homes, and on trains as Pullman porters. When Frederick entered the profession around 1892 there were some 1,500 black men working as waiters everywhere in the city, from chains of inexpensive restaurants to elegant hotels.

Especially in the upscale dining rooms, the black waiter's job in those days was complex, demanding, and competitive—more so than is usual today, and differently. By reacting immediately and cheerfully to the client's wishes—and all the clients in the expensive restaurants were white—the black waiter could be seen as simulating the enforced obsequiousness and racial subordination that had been, and still was, the norm for all blacks in the South. Even if the diner was a lifelong northerner for whom slavery had been an abomination, he would still be likely to enjoy the sense of privilege and worth that an exaggeratedly deferential black waiter would confer on him for the duration of the meal. An efficient waiter who strived to be likable also got bigger tips.

However, black waiters in Gilded Age America were not just gifted or cynical actors. They also took pride in their profession, which required tact, charm, dignified deportment, and mental and physical agility. Waiters who served the financial and political elite in the grand hotels and restaurants of the nation's second-largest city acquired an enhanced sense of personal worth as well as a heightened social status in their own communities.

If the first job one has in a given profession acts as a tuning fork for the career that follows, Frederick started at a pitch of the highest quality. The Auditorium Hotel, where he began as a waiter, was the most important new building in Chicago and had one of its most elegant and modern dining rooms. Built between 1887 and 1889 on what is now South Michigan Avenue, it was hailed at the time of its completion as the "chief architectural spectacle of Chicago," a symbol of the city's civic progress, and even hyperbolically as the "eighth wonder of the world." Frederick had found his niche in urban life: after the Auditorium Hotel he spent the next "one and a half years as waiter" in other restaurants in the city.

Frederick left Chicago around the summer of 1893, a momentous period in the city's history. The World's Columbian Exposition opened on May 1; on May 9, a banking crisis began, which led to a national economic depression that became known as the Panic of 1893. When the economy collapsed, thousands of workers, including those who had been attracted to the city during the boom period of the world's fair, were left without jobs or prospects of any kind.

Frederick decided that he could do better by heading to New York City. From all accounts, the situation was not as bad there as in Chicago. New York also had more of everything that had originally made Chicago attractive—more people, bustle, excitement, power, towering buildings, and hotels and restaurants where one could find work. New York was the only city in the United States that ambitious Chicagoans envied. And the only siren call that ambitious New Yorkers heard came from the great cities of Europe.

Like Chicago, the New York metropolitan region was still overwhelmingly white in 1893. It was also filled with immigrants from all over Europe and their first-generation children. The wretched poverty of many of them, together with their foreign babble and alien customs, made longtime New Yorkers fear for the future of their city. To acculturate and redeem these motley newcomers, white New Yorkers initiated a variety of reform efforts at the end of the nineteenth century. However, they typically ignored the less numerous native-born blacks who were arriving simultaneously. Blacks were made to feel unwelcome in Manhattan, and many chose to live in the outlying areas. Brooklyn, which would remain an independent municipality until 1898, became especially popular with blacks after the Civil War draft riots of 1863, when white mobs attacked them throughout Manhattan. But even in Brooklyn the black population in 1893 was very small and amounted to only some 13,000 people out of a population of 950,000.

The job that Frederick found after he arrived in Brooklyn was predictable, in both personal and broader social terms. New York was like Chicago, once again, in restricting most blacks to lower-paying, subservient occupations. Within this narrow range of possibilities, however, Frederick was able to carve out a superior position for himself, one that represented an advance over his work as a waiter in Chicago. The Clarendon Hotel in Brooklyn, where he became "head bell boy," was a new, large, prominent, and strategically located establishment in its day. Opened during the summer of 1890 two blocks north of City Hall, it was also just a few steps away from an elevated railroad that ran to the Brooklyn Bridge a dozen blocks away. A cable car service took passengers across the bridge to lower Manhattan and dropped them off within easy reach of New York's City Hall, thus putting the Clarendon at one end of a transportation system that linked the two municipalities' administrative centers.

Frederick was twenty-one at this time, and as the "head" of a crew of bellboys, he had a responsible position that reflected his skill in both serving and managing people. Bellboys would typically be on their feet all day, and because they were always in public view, their physical appearance, from uniform to grooming to deportment, would reflect directly on the establishment where they worked. It would have been his job to give individual bellboys their assignments, to keep track of their hours for payroll, to train beginners, and to resolve complaints made against them. Frederick would have had to balance being a figure of authority toward his coworkers—and since he was black, they could have been nothing else—with being an employee and a servant of whites. It would have been Frederick's prerogative to go out of his way to provide exceptional service to an important client himself.

Frederick's subsequent career shows that he impressed guests at the Clarendon: after working there for some months, he left to become a personal valet to a leading local businessman. Percy G. Williams had taken up temporary residence in the hotel in the early summer of 1894, which is when he probably met Frederick and hired him for the traits that any successful servant would need—resourcefulness and a winning disposition. Williams was in his late thirties and was on the verge of making his mark on the history of American popular entertainment as the biggest owner of vaudeville theaters in the New York area. There is good reason to assume that Frederick learned some valuable lessons from witnessing aspects of Williams's career and character.

This is also the time when Frederick's ambitions began to surpass the lowly roles that American society allowed him to play and at which he had begun to excel. With a good letter of recommendation from a well-known, rich, and respected man like Williams, Frederick could have continued in New York as a personal valet or even a household butler for many years. But in addition to his vocation, Frederick also had a passion for music. And it was strong enough for him to take the extraordinary step of leaving the United States to study.

Years later, Frederick would explain to an American consular official that "he went to Europe on the advice of his German musical professor, Herman," who told him specifically to go to London. Frederick hoped to become a singer. It is possible that his studying voice in New York reflected the famous legacy of black church singing, which he would have known in his parents' chapel in Coahoma County. As far as the German teacher is concerned, nothing is known about the man except that his influence on Frederick was crucial. That he was a foreigner surely explains why he was willing to cross the American color line and take Frederick on as a student; it also explains why he would have looked to Europe as a place to which Frederick could escape to develop his abilities.

*   *   *

In the 1890s, passenger ship traffic between New York City and London was frequent, quick, popular, and affordable. Approximately half a dozen ships left every week during the fall of 1894, transporting thousands of passengers with the most diverse backgrounds and incomes. The vast majority went in "steerage," which was the cheapest way to travel, and which accommodated surprising numbers of laborers, workers, and others on the lower rungs of the economic and social ladders. International travel was also much simpler then than it is today: one bought a ticket and went. Americans did not even need a passport to leave the country.

Frederick left New York in the fall of that year, apparently on October 9, aboard the SS *Lahn* of the North German Lloyd shipping line. Its ultimate destination was Bremen in northern Germany, but on the way it was scheduled to call at Southampton, a major port on the south coast of England that was a popular entry point for Americans. The *Lahn* docked on October 16, after an uneventful seven-day crossing. Direct trains from Southampton to Waterloo Station in central London took two to three hours.

Some of the novelty of arriving in London would have been mitigated for Frederick by the changes he had already experienced in the United States. In fact, the contrast between the Hopson Bayou neighborhood and Chicago was in many ways far greater than that between the two greatest English-speaking cities in the world—New York and London.

But in another and more important way, the change between the United States and England was like climbing out of a ship's dark cargo hold onto a top deck bathed in brilliant sunshine. "Negro," "colored," and "black" did not mean in England what they did in the United States. In London, for the first time in his life, Frederick experienced what most of his brethren back home would never know—being viewed by whites with curiosity, interest, even affection.

It was not that Victorian England was a color-blind sanctuary. For generations, the British Empire had subjugated and exploited entire civilizations in South Asia, Africa, and many other places around the world. In the United Kingdom itself, unabashed racism was directed against the Irish, the Jews, and others. But because there were very few blacks in England at this time, and even fewer American "negroes," the attitude toward people like Frederick was surprisingly accepting—"surprisingly" especially from the point of view of Americans who happened to be visiting the British Isles.

The seeming contradictions of British snobbery dismayed one American visitor, who noted that in the great university towns of England, one could see "negroes" at college balls waltzing with aristocratic young women and ladies of high position, all of whom would have considered it grossly inappropriate even to acknowledge a familiar tradesman in the street. Another American was shocked by the sight of "two coal-black negroes and two white women" in a fashionable London restaurant. "My first impulse was to instantly depart," the American admitted, "for such a sight in the United States would surely not have been possible." But in the end there was little he could do except acknowledge ruefully, "In London a negro can go into the finest restaurants and be served just like a white man."

William Drysdale, a well-known American reporter making a grand tour of Europe—and who would soon have a memorable encounter with Frederick in Monte Carlo—wrote that

> no American negro who reaches London goes away again if he can help it. Here his color does not militate against him in the least, but rather the contrary, because it is something of a novelty. He is received in the best hotels, if his pocket is full enough, in the lodging houses, in the clubs; he can buy the best seats in the theaters, ride in the hansoms—do anything, in short, that

he could do if he had the fair skin and rosy cheeks of a London housemaid. He is more of a man here than he can well be at home, because there is no prejudice against him.

Drysdale approved of the way the English treated American blacks. He had also heard numerous lectures from Londoners about the barbarism of lynchings in the South and the general inhumanity of American whites toward blacks. But he got to know the English well enough not to be taken in entirely by their morally superior attitudes. He pointed out that their criticism of American failings

> would have more force if one did not find out in a short time the particular brand of darky that the Englishman despises most thoroughly and heartily, and that is the East Indian darky. The low-caste Hindu is a beast in his estimation; a creature to lie outside on the mat, and be kicked and cuffed and fed on rice.

"So we all have our little failings," he concluded wryly.

After arriving in London, Frederick applied for admission to a school that he remembered as the "Conservatory of Music." He must have had very little money after paying for the voyage across the Atlantic, because he hoped that he could make arrangements to pay for his tuition and living expenses by working for the school. However, his application was refused. Were it not for the descriptions of how American blacks were treated in London in the 1890s, one might have thought that Frederick was rejected on racial grounds. It was more likely that the school was unwilling to take on a student who wanted to work his way through the program. Or perhaps he was judged to lack sufficient talent, as is suggested by the fact that he did not attempt again to study music in England or in continental Europe. Given the kind of adventurer he had become, he could have tried to enroll elsewhere at a later time if he believed in his own abilities.

He next tried to start his own boardinghouse in Leicester Square. He thus not only shrugged off his failure at the music school but also tried a new way to put down roots in a city that he found attractive. This was, moreover, an endeavor that capitalized on all the experience he had acquired in Chicago and Brooklyn. But whom could Frederick approach in London to borrow the money that he would have needed?

The answer may in fact have been entirely elsewhere. On February 8, 1895, India, who was working as a cook in Louisville, Kentucky, mortgaged the family land in Coahoma County for a two-month loan of $2,000 at an exorbitant interest rate. How she came to be in possession of the land after everything that had happened and why she did this are unknown, but it could have been to get Frederick the money that he needed for his venture in London or to make ends meet as he was trying to set it up. The timing is plausible.

In any event, Frederick overreached himself in London. The plan for the boardinghouse failed, and he had to take a step back into the occupations that he knew best. He first worked in a German restaurant that he remembered as being called "Tube," and then in a "Mrs. James' Boarding House." Shortly thereafter, perhaps in pursuit of a better job, or because of wanderlust, or both, Frederick left England for France.

Frederick's arrival in Paris can be dated closely. He must have gotten there shortly before July 12, 1895, the day he received a letter of introduction from the American ambassador to France, J. B. Eustis, addressed to the Paris prefect, or chief, of police. Writing in French and using the standard phrases for a letter of this type, the ambassador expressed the hope that the prefect would welcome "Mr. Frederick Bruce Thomas," who was residing at 23 rue Brey, when he presented himself to be registered. Among the duties of the office of the prefect was making note of foreigners who planned to live in the city.

The distance across the English Channel between Dover and Calais, which was the port of entry for boat trains to Paris, is only thirty miles, and the thrice-daily ferries in 1895 could cover it in less than two hours. Nevertheless, Frederick's move to France would in some ways be a bigger dislocation than his move to England. However strange the pronunciation and idioms in Great Britain might have sounded to an American at first, the language was still the same, especially for someone whose ears had gotten used to regional variations as different as those of the Deep South, the Midwest, and Brooklyn. But throughout much of the rest of the world in the 1890s, and well into the beginning of the twentieth century, French was the second language of business, government, and culture. A monolingual American arriving in a foreign locale would find few English-speakers outside the major tourist hotels. To live and work in France, or anywhere else on the Continent, Frederick would have to learn French without delay. He had the right temperament to do so: his willingness to leave a familiar world in order to seek new experiences indicates that he was sufficiently confident and extroverted to be a good language student.

Frederick's need to learn French was especially urgent because his job was once again that of butler or valet, which would require him to communicate quickly and easily with his employers, or, if these were English-speaking, with people outside the household, such as shopkeepers and tradesmen. Judging by the addresses he gave in several documents, his employers were well off: all the addresses are elegant buildings that have survived to this day and are located in fashionable districts of Paris near the Arch of Triumph.

France, like England, was accepting of blacks. In fact, the attitude toward blacks in Paris at this time was even more liberal than in London. The reaction of James Weldon Johnson, a black American writer, composer, and intellectual who first arrived in Paris in 1905, conveys what Frederick may have also felt:

From the day I set foot in France, I became aware of the working of a miracle within me. I became aware of a quick readjust-
ment to life and to environment. I recaptured for the first time
since childhood the sense of being just a human being. . . . I
was suddenly free; free from a sense of impending discomfort,
insecurity, danger; free from conflict within the Man-Negro
dualism and the innumerable maneuvers in thought and behavior
that it compels; free from the problem of the many obvious or
subtle adjustments to a multitude of bans and taboos; free from
special scorn, special tolerance, special condescension, special
commiseration; free to be merely a man.

The relative rarity of blacks in Paris made someone like Frederick an appealing object of curiosity and enhanced his chances of
being employed. Because the French were far less conscious of class
differences than their staid English neighbors, it is likely that he
would have found working in Paris more congenial than working in
London. In the streets and in the city's shops, servants were greeted
politely as "Mademoiselle" or "Monsieur" even by strangers who
knew their actual status. A valet's wages and hours would also have
been better than a waiter's.

Because Frederick was also a very handsome young man (as
photographs of him c. 1896 show), Paris would have been a wide-
open field for romantic adventures. A white American who knew the
city well commented, with a hint of envy, that "Frenchmen do not
connect the negro as we do, with plantation days. Fair women look
upon him with love and admiration, as Desdemona looked upon
Othello." Even more relevant to Frederick was the man's remark
that "everywhere you find the same thing. Colored valets traveling
with Americans are raved over by pretty French maids."

Paris in the 1890s was seen worldwide as the capital of modern
urban civilization—a place where everyone with any pretense to
sophistication or social standing longed to be. Frederick's life there

was the last stage of his basic education in the ways of the world. After Paris, with its museums and theaters, monuments and grand boulevards, cafés and fashionable shops, temples to haute cuisine and raucous vaudeville, there was little any other city in Western Europe could offer Frederick that he had not already seen.

During the next three years, Frederick traveled extensively, working in different cities for months at a time, and returned to Paris twice. This involved crossing multiple borders, and even though most European countries did not require passports from visitors, an official government document could still be useful as identification; it would also provide a traveler with protection in case he got into any kind of trouble. Frederick applied for his first passport in Paris on March 17, 1896. Among the questions he had to answer was how soon he would return to the United States, and he responded "two years." However, it is not clear if he meant this or if he simply said whatever he thought would help him keep his options open (American passports had to be renewed every two years). It would not have been in his interest to make the embassy staff suspect that he might have left the United States for good. He also began falsifying his past, something he would continue later as well, by giving Louisville, Kentucky, as his birthplace, and Brooklyn as his permanent place of residence. Perhaps his reasons were that India was still living in Louisville and that not all blacks had been slaves there. Naming Brooklyn might also have forestalled offhand comments from the second secretary at the embassy, with whom Frederick dealt and who, like his father the ambassador, was a southerner.

After Paris, Frederick went first to Brussels and then to Ostend, a popular Belgian resort on the North Sea. There he worked at the Grand Hôtel Fontaine, which, although not particularly expensive, was recommended by Baedeker's, a respected tourist guide at the time. Unlike most of the other hotels in Ostend, which closed for the cold season, the Grand Hôtel Fontaine remained open all year. However, Frederick left and went on to the south of France. The fall of 1896 is probably when he came to the Riviera for the first time, and this is where his expertise and skills were recognized and rewarded in a remarkable way: he became a headwaiter for the season. His employer was a Monsieur G. Morel, the proprietor of the well-known Hôtel des Anglais in Cannes. The hotel, on the northern edge of town, prided itself on having an admirable southern exposure, a beautiful pleasure garden, and a recherché cuisine and cellar, and on providing luxury, comfort, careful service, a lift, hotel baths, telephone, and entertainments such as tennis and billiards. The position of headwaiter in a large establishment like this that catered to a demanding international clientele carried considerable responsibility. It would also have been coveted by experienced, native French waiters. Frederick's command of English—even though his English was heavily accented—would have been an asset for the hotel's restaurant because many tourists from Great Britain came to Cannes. But he could not have gotten the job if he did not have command of idiomatic French, which he would have needed to communicate with the management, the waiters, and the rest of the staff. He would also have needed to develop a good understanding of the psychology and cultures of the different classes and nationalities of Europeans with whom he dealt.

After the Riviera season was over, in the spring of 1897, Frederick returned to Paris, where he worked as a waiter in the Restaurant Cuba on the avenue des Champs-Élysées. He then made an extensive tour of Germany, crossing the country from west to east, and working for short periods in Cologne, Düsseldorf, Berlin, and Leipzig. This zigzagging itinerary shows that he had not yet found a place that suited him entirely and that he was satisfying his curiosity to see other parts of Europe. Like other waiters in Europe, Frederick would have heard much about the strict discipline and perfect service practiced in German restaurants and hotels and might have been interested in sampling this world. But like others before and after him, Frederick probably discovered quickly that German patrons were very difficult to please. From Germany he returned to Paris, and late in 1897 he turned south once more, this time choosing first Nice and then Monte Carlo, the capital of the famous, diminutive principality of Monaco on the Azure Coast, where he would have a memorable encounter with a white American.

Drysdale, the reporter making a tour of Europe, arrived in Monaco with an English friend during the first week of February 1898, from Nice and other points farther west on the French coast. Already much impressed by the beauty of the countryside they had seen from the train, with picturesque hills on the left and the azure Mediterranean on the right, he emerged from the Monte Carlo train station only to be struck anew by the remarkable beauty of the town. At the center was the Casino, a grand, elegant, and lavishly decorated concoction of cream-colored stone. It stood on one end of a large square occupying the hill that towered over the area, and that was surrounded by what Drysdale described as a "fairyland of flowers and tropical plants as you may dream of sometimes but seldom see." The extravagant luxury of Monte Carlo's appearance, and the gorgeously decorated coaches, drivers, and horses that the town's twenty-five hotels sent to the station to meet the train and attract guests, overcame Drysdale's reservations and frugality. He and his friend decided to splurge on the Hôtel de Paris, which belonged to the Casino Company and was, as he admitted, "by many degrees the largest and finest and most expensive in the place." It also faced the Casino, as it does to this day.

After being escorted by a regally garbed bellman to his handsome rooms facing the sea, Drysdale was in the process of unpacking and preparing to ask a maid for some hot water, in French, when he heard a voice behind him say: "Reckon I better look aftah dis 'Merican gemman."

Without looking up, Drysdale guessed who had arrived at his door and felt a wave of relief. After traveling for months through the famous cities of Europe, he was delighted to encounter a friendly black servant from home, someone with whom he could feel "completely at ease," as he put it, and to whom he could confide all the small cares and worries associated with travel. The various Dutch, German, Belgian, and French hotel "boys" had been perfectly obliging and attentive. But this young black man was a "colored friend and brother," someone as familiar as if "you had brought him up from the cradle," someone who, when compared with the Europeans, was "an electric light beside a flickering candle."

Drysdale's affection for Frederick was genuine, even though it was tainted by an unconscious patriarchal racism. Drysdale had been born in Pennsylvania and lived most of his life in New Jersey while he wrote for newspapers in New York City. Nonetheless, his comments about Frederick betray a nostalgia for a romanticized image of the old antebellum South that began to appear among northerners at the end of the nineteenth century, and that centered on the supposedly chivalrous nobility of the planters and their benevolent relations with contented slaves. Drysdale would also have enjoyed being waited on simply because he was a heavy man, and no longer young at forty-six; indeed, he was to die only three years later. Thus, he found it entirely normal to expect that a black man would be an excellent servant; to think of him as a "boy" even though he was in his mid-twenties; to refer to him as "Sambo," as an "ebon" or "sunburnt angel," or as a "dusky brother"; and to record his speech in a way that exaggerated its nonwhite, semiliterate pronunciation (despite the fact that Frederick had probably learned to modulate his native accent when dealing with affluent white clients).

Drysdale also concealed Frederick's real name and referred to him as "George." By doing this, he was consistent with how he concealed the names of others he encountered on his travels, including his English friend, presumably out of consideration for their privacy.

Nonetheless, his choice of "George" may also have been dictated by the custom American whites had of referring to black servants by "generic" names that denied them their individuality. A striking example of this was porters on Pullman trains, all of whom were black and many of whom were former slaves hired after the Civil War. Passengers called every one of them "George" no matter what their names may have been, and did so automatically and "in honor" of the businessman George M. Pullman, who employed them.

Drysdale was of course curious about Frederick's origins and began to quiz him. "I comes from Kaintucky, Sah," was the reply (Frederick continued to misrepresent his origins). "Been on dis side de watah bout fo' yeahs, Sah."

And why had he come to Europe? "To see the worl', Sah."

Part of Drysdale's sense of relief when Frederick appeared came from not having to struggle with French any longer. Instead of "de l'eau chaud," all he had to say now was "bring me a jug of hot water." By contrast, Frederick spoke French fluently and explained that he had learned it while living in Paris for about three years. He had come to the French Riviera several months earlier for additional language study—except that now he wanted to learn Italian. To his disappointment, he found what little was spoken in Nice to be corrupted with French and Provençal, the old language of the region, so that he had moved to Monaco instead. The Italian there proved to be badly flawed as well, prompting him to make plans to leave for Milan in a few weeks.

Drysdale had the opportunity to verify Frederick's ability to speak French on several occasions and was much impressed by how good it actually was. Especially surprising was the cultural transformation that it captured. Although Drysdale said that he found Frederick's "bluegrass dialect" more musical than the band playing in Monte Carlo's public park, he also thought that the "negro dialect" Frederick spoke had such a coercive hold on him that he would never be able to speak "real English." It was therefore a genuine shock for

Drysdale to find that Frederick's black southern accent did not affect his French at all—either when he spoke with Drysdale himself or when he spoke with Frenchmen fresh from Paris.

> Sounds that it seems impossible for him to make clearly in English he makes without difficulty in French. And the effect is very curious in talking with him in both languages. He has had good teachers and speaks excellent Parisian French one minute, and the next minute he says to me in cottonfield English: "Dem boots wet; dey's not done gwinter shine, Sah."

By contrast, Drysdale ruefully acknowledged that his own French was "naturally bad." In keeping with the practices of the time, it is likely that Frederick's language studies in Paris consisted less of classroom instruction than of walking and riding around the city in the company of an experienced teacher and repeatedly imitating both the practical, everyday expressions he used and his accompanying manner and gestures.

The elegance of Frederick's French was echoed by his worldly manner, which Drysdale described as dignified, gentlemanly, and altogether fine. Frederick was also physically striking. He was a bit taller than average at five feet nine, and good-looking, with rich brown skin and generously proportioned features: high cheekbones, large oval eyes, a prominent nose, and a wide mouth that was quick to break into a captivating smile. He also liked to dress stylishly. Everything about Frederick said that he had transformed himself into a genuine cosmopolitan, one who felt free to travel around Europe as his fancy moved him, and without any concerns about being able to find suitable employment whenever he wanted it.

After helping Drysdale settle in, and brushing and cleaning his clothes in a way that "no valet in the world can do as well as Sambo when he chooses," Frederick went to get the hotel register in which all guests were obligated by local law to write their names, home addresses, and occupations. The police checked the registers every day and guests were supposed to make their entries accurately. But Drysdale blithely dismissed this requirement and told Frederick not to bother him with such details and to register him under any name and occupation that he chose.

Frederick was entirely willing to play with Drysdale's biography, as he did with his own when it suited him. Frederick's years of successfully serving clients in half a dozen countries on two continents had made him into an excellent actor and judge of character. He had also gotten to know human nature too well to take entirely seriously all the moral pieties that laws and social norms were meant to reflect. Instead of putting his trust in abstract principles, Frederick invested in private relations; and he could be very generous with his affections.

Taking the black-covered book to a mantelpiece in the room, Frederick began to write in it with an expression that Drysdale characterized as showing "that he was going through a severe mental struggle," an implausible description that says more about Drysdale's racially inflected projections than about what proved to be Frederick's adroit and ironic flattery. Asking "wheder dat'll do, Sah," Frederick handed the book to Drysdale, who sheepishly realized that the valet had "rather turned the tables" on him. He had registered him as "Hon. G. W. Ingram, residence Washington, occupation United States Senator, last stopping place Paris, intended stay in Monaco two weeks, intended destination Cairo, Egypt."

To his discomfort, Drysdale realized that he would have to back-pedal because "such false pretenses might lead to awkward complications"; moreover, he would have to find some way to retreat gracefully after saying that he did not care what Frederick wrote about him.

"Has my friend registered yet?" he asked.

"No, Sah . . . I'se jest goin' to his room now, Sah."

"Very well, then," Drysdale told Frederick. "You need not trouble him. This description you have written will answer for him very nicely, and I will put my own name and 'pedigree' beneath."

Thus it was that Drysdale's young English friend received what Drysdale, with his rather cumbersome wit, chose to characterize as "the greatest honor of his life"—being transformed "for the moment into an American and a Senator."

Like any valet or waiter, Frederick would have wanted to ingratiate himself with his patrons by assuming a deferential mien and manner, both because the job demanded it and because his income from tips depended on it. However, in his subsequent encounters with Drysdale, who spent about a month at the Hôtel de Paris before resuming his leisurely journey along the Mediterranean coast, we also get glimpses of Frederick's poised self-confidence and of his mastery of local cultural norms, which he understood far better than his patron.

Frederick's assurance and sophistication belied the primitivized portrait captured in Drysdale's articles. When Frederick saw Drysdale and the Englishman crossing the hotel lobby toward the door on the first evening after their arrival, he hastened to intervene to forestall a possible social gaffe.

> "'Scuse me, Sah . . . but was you goin' over to de Casiner, Sah?"
> "No," I told him, "not to-night. We are going over to the café."
> "Oh, I begs your parding, Sah," said he.
> "I was only going to say dat dey don't admit no one to de Casiner in de evenin' 'cept in evenin' dress, Sah, an I thought it might be onpresumpterous for you to go to de door an' not be able to git in. It's all right in de daytime, Sah; but in de evenin' dey requires evenin' dress. 'Scuse me, Sah."

On another occasion, Frederick was able to explain to Drysdale and the Englishman how one gained entry to the Casino, which was off-limits to the local Monegasques: "You has to apply in persing fer de ticket, Sah. . . . But it ain't no trouble 'tall, Sah. All you has to do is to walk in de do', an' dey'll spot you in a minute an' put you on de right track. Dey has won'ful sharp eyes, Sah." To be sure, this is a minor comment about a routine event, but it is also an observation made by a man with an eye for detail, a job well done.

Frederick was unusually blunt about his own abilities in comparison with those of his coworkers, especially the native Monegasques. "Dey has to bring in all dere hotel waiters, Sah," he explains to Drysdale at one point; "dese native dagoes don't know nothing."

Frederick's sense of ease and self-assurance would only have been bolstered by the personal freedom and social acceptance he found in old Europe. His impression that he was better than his fellows at what they all did for a living could have goaded him to seek advancement as well. Indeed, part of Frederick's reason for moving from country to country and job to job was probably that, in addition to satisfying his curiosity, he was searching for a place where he could put down roots and build a career.

Frederick left Monte Carlo for Italy around mid-March 1898. During the next year, he continued his exploration of Europe and, heading this time in a generally eastward direction, toward Russia, traveled to five new cities—Milan, Venice, Trieste, Vienna, and Budapest. Everywhere he went he followed the same pattern and worked in hotels or restaurants for periods of a few weeks to a few months, or presumably just long enough to have a look around and to earn enough money for the next leg of his trip. Frederick's ability to find such work in different cities suggests that he had good letters of reference from previous employers as well as a winning way of presenting himself, which was its own best recommendation.

It was in the spring of 1899 that Frederick first got the idea of going to Russia. Although details are scanty, he appears to have been employed as a valet by a rich Russian, perhaps a nobleman, perhaps of very high rank, who planned to take him to St. Petersburg. He may even have accompanied a grand duke (this was the title given to the sons and grandsons of Russian tsars) who had met him in Monte Carlo and took a liking to him. But entering Russia, unlike the six countries in Western and central Europe through which Frederick had traveled thus far, was not routine. The authoritarian Russian Empire required passports. Moreover, no one could enter the country without also having his passport visaed by a Russian official abroad, something that was not entirely automatic. Frederick began the process of securing all the necessary documents in Budapest, and he completed his passport renewal on May 20, 1899.

In his passport application, Frederick listed his occupation as "waiter" and indicated that he was planning to return to the United States within one year. For this passport—in contrast to his Paris application—he gave his home address as Chicago. His disregard for accuracy suggests that whatever he said was simply a way to forestall suspicions that he might have expatriated himself. The only difference in Frederick's physical description is that he now had a "black moustache" instead of being clean-shaven; he would eventually let it grow to an impressive width. Nothing in the application suggested that Frederick was going to Russia with intentions different from those that had led him to crisscross Europe; in fact, he noted that after visiting Russia he planned to return to France.

Armed with his new passport, Frederick was able to get his required second visa from the Russian consulate in Budapest. However, a visit like this required a brief interview that would have made any black American's head spin. Unlike most of their counterparts in the United States diplomatic service, the Russian staff would not have cared that Frederick had black skin. If anything, his appearance might have awakened their curiosity because people of African descent were rare in Russia. But their lack of concern over race would have been replaced by a different bias that Frederick had not seen manifested elsewhere in Europe in quite as virulent a form—anti-Semitism. Official Russian government regulations required a consular officer to ascertain if an applicant for a visa was Jewish or not. The purpose of this regulation was to restrict the entry of Jews into Russia and to limit their freedom of movement if they were admitted.

In Frederick's case, the matter would have been settled easily. But it is hard to believe that he would not have been struck by the question implying that Jews were, in a sense, the "Negroes" of Russia. He could not have been ignorant of anti-Semitism in Europe during the years he had been there, especially in France, where the notorious "Dreyfus affair"—the prosecution of a Jewish officer in the French army on trumped-up charges—raged from 1894 to 1899. But there is a difference between an outburst of hatred that received some popular support and contravened the laws of the land—as was the situation in France—and a system of official Russian laws and widespread public sentiment that recalled the Jim Crow South.

The comparison can be taken only so far. The Jewish population of Russia had never been enslaved. This is something that Russians had reserved for their own Christian peasants, who were liberated only in 1861, just two years before American blacks were emancipated. Also, the Russians liberated their serfs peacefully, by government decree, and without the horrific bloodshed of the American Civil War. Nevertheless, by applying for a Russian visa, Frederick was for the first time seeking to enter a country where his sense of belonging would be very different from what he had experienced in Europe thus far. In contrast to the other countries where he had been accepted more or less like anyone else, in Russia he would explicitly *not* be a member of a despised and oppressed minority. A black American would have felt this distinction with greater poignancy than most whites of any nationality.

3

NOTHING
ABOVE MOSCOW

Crossing the border of the Russian Empire was unlike anything that
Frederick had experienced before. Foreigners were suspect, and having
their passports visaed abroad was just the beginning. Western European trains could not run on the more widely spaced Russian tracks,
which Russia had adopted in part to thwart an enemy's ability to utilize
railroads during an invasion. As a result, all passengers arriving at the
frontier had to transfer to Russian trains for the trip farther east. But the
stop also gave uniformed officials time to examine travelers' passports
in detail and to search their luggage thoroughly, a process that could
sometimes take several hours. Hapless individuals whose papers were
not in order were sent back on the same train that had brought them.

The government's oversight did not end at the border. In every
place he stayed, Frederick would have to show his passport to the
police, although the hotelkeeper or landlord would usually do this for
him. Also, a visitor who had completed his trip to Russia could not
just pack up and get on a train; he would have to report his intention
to the police and get a certificate from his district superintendent that
he had done nothing to prevent his departure. In Frederick's case,
because he would stay in Russia longer than the usual six-month term

provided by a visa, he would have to deposit his American passport with the government passport office in exchange for a residence permit that he would then need to renew once a year.

Russian customs restrictions on tobacco and alcohol were the same as those in the rest of Europe. But there were also bans on items that struck visitors as odd, such as playing cards, which happened to be under a monopoly that funneled proceeds from sales to an imperial charity. Published materials dealing with a variety of topics could be confiscated on the spot because of censorship laws. Baedeker's popular guidebook suggested that travelers to Russia avoid trouble by not bringing in any "works of a political, social, or historical nature"; and "to avoid any cause of suspicion," they were even advised not to use newsprint for packing.

When Frederick arrived in 1899, the Russian Empire was entering its final years, although few could have predicted how quickly and violently it would collapse. Under the young, weak Tsar Nicholas II the autocratic regime seemed to be slipping ever more deeply into senility. Incompetent, corrupt, and reactionary, it could no longer distinguish between real threats and its own delusions. Radicals were advocating sedition, revolutionaries fomenting unrest, terrorists assassinating high government officials and members of the imperial family. But as the regime tried to defend itself against enemies, it also lashed out at those who could have been agents of its reform—progressive lawyers and newspaper editors clamoring for a civil society, university students avidly reading Western political philosophy, world-famous writers portraying the darkest corners of Russia's life. In between lay the vast majority of the population—largely rural, illiterate, and poor.

Once trains left the Russian border and began their long journey into the country's heartland, visitors were often struck by how the empire's preoccupation with control extended even to the regimentation of its male population. Half the men on the platforms of the major stations appeared to be wearing uniforms of one kind or another—police officers, soldiers, railway men, teachers, civil servants, even students. And few visitors failed to note that time itself ran differently in Russia, as if it too echoed the regime's reactionary policies. Because Russia used the Julian calendar, rather than the Gregorian calendar that was widespread in the West, a visitor crossing into Russia from Austria or Germany in 1899 would discover that he had gone back twelve days in time, so that May 22 in Vienna or Berlin was May 10 in Moscow or St. Petersburg. This discrepancy actually got worse in 1900, when it increased to thirteen days.

Time also seemed to flow differently when visitors were traveling across Russia, because of the vastness of the country. The landscape was generally flat and the scenery monotonous. Passengers heading to Moscow faced a thirty-hour trip of some seven hundred miles after they crossed the Russian border with East Prussia at Verzhbolovo. The train crept along at a soporific twenty-five miles an hour, with long stops at stations. Cities and towns were small, far apart, and mostly uninteresting. Telegraph posts slipped past, echoing the regular clatter of the train wheels. In late May, ponds and streams still overflowing after the spring thaw glistened bleakly in the distance. Forests of white birches and firs that looked almost black interrupted the greening fields that ran to the horizon. There were few roads, and rarely was there anything on a road other than a shaggy-headed peasant riding in a cart behind a plodding horse.

Frederick spent the better part of his first year in Russia traveling to St. Petersburg, Moscow, and Odessa, again working in hotels or restaurants and getting a feel for each city. In the end, he settled in Moscow, and this choice is notable. St. Petersburg, the starkly beautiful imperial capital on the northern edge of Russia that Peter the Great had founded by decree in 1703, looked like a modern Western city, with broad boulevards and grand palaces and ministries that rivaled anything in Paris or Berlin. Most of the city's best restaurants in which Frederick could have worked belonged to Frenchmen and

Germans and had a Western cuisine and atmosphere. Odessa, the major port on the Black Sea that lay a thousand miles to the south, was also a modern, planned city with handsome squares and buildings, tree-lined streets, and a cosmopolitan character. By contrast, Moscow, which lay approximately in between, had grown gradually over eight centuries, like a tree adding rings, and looked like nothing Frederick had ever seen before.

Originally the capital of the early Russian state, Moscow was the country's historical and religious heart. "If ever a city expressed the character and peculiarities of its inhabitants," Baedeker declared, "that city is Moscow." The first sight that struck newcomers was the bulbous golden domes and three-barred crosses on the hundreds of Orthodox churches gleaming everywhere above the rooftops. At the turn of the twentieth century, most of the buildings in Moscow were two or three stories high, with only a handful of taller ones in the center, so churches were visible from afar, and hardly any address in the city was more than two or three streets away from a church. To Western eyes, Russian churches with their bright colors and multiple cupolas reaching skyward looked exotically different. To Napoleon Bonaparte, when he paused on a hill before his army entered Moscow in 1812, the innumerable cupolas and bell towers shimmering in the distance looked positively Oriental.

Once you reached the center of the city, another architectural wonder came into view. On a rise by the Moscow River stood the Kremlin, a giant, redbrick medieval fortress over a mile in circumference with nineteen pointed towers above the swallowtail crenellations on its sixty-five-foot walls. Next to it spread the vast expanse of Red Square, at one end of which the sixteenth-century Cathedral of Saint Basil the Blessed, an extraordinary whirl of brightly colored shapes topped by faceted and striped cupolas, seemed to be twisting itself into the sky. For Muscovites, this ensemble of fortress, square, and church was a revered place and a living connection to a cherished past. The early tsars who had established Moscow's greatness and laid the foundations of the empire were entombed in the Cathedral of the Archangel within the Kremlin's walls. All Russian tsars still traveled from St. Petersburg to the Assumption Cathedral in the Kremlin to be crowned. And it was Ivan the Great Bell Tower in the Kremlin that first proclaimed coronations to the city, the empire, and the world. "There is nothing above Moscow," a Russian proverb says, "except the Kremlin, and nothing above the Kremlin except Heaven."

A newly arrived visitor like Frederick emerging from one of the four main train stations onto the Moscow streets would be enveloped by a rich tapestry of sounds, sights, and smells that were both alien and familiar. The city was a bustling, noisy place. Ringing church bells marked the daily cycles of services, their intricate patterns an analogue to the gaudy splendor of the churches themselves and an indelible part of the city's "soundscape": the quick tinkling of the small bells coursing through the measured tolling of those in mid-range and the deep, slow drone of giants weighing many tons. Horses' hooves beat a sharp staccato as they trotted by; carriage and wagon wheels clattered and thundered over the city's cobblestone streets and squares. Motorcars were just beginning to appear in Moscow when Frederick arrived, and one would occasionally roar down a street, leaving acrid exhaust and rearing, frightened horses in its wake. The first electric tramway had been built in 1899, but Moscow still ran mostly on horsepower. All over the city, barnyard whiffs of manure mingled with the smell of charcoal and wood smoke from the chimneys of thousands of kitchens and samovars—portable brass water heaters for making tea that were fired up several times a day in every household.

The crowds thronging Moscow's central streets were strikingly mixed. Many passersby wore European clothing, or what the simple Russian folk termed "German" dress. Gentlemen in top hats and frock coats; ladies in elegant gowns, trailing scents by Coty or Guerlain; military officers in dress uniforms with shining epaulets—all would have looked at home in Vienna or London. Foreigners were also a common sight in Moscow, and German and French names were everywhere on shop signs in the city center. But side by side with them was old Russian Moscow: heavily bearded peasants in gray sheepskins and bast sandals; Orthodox priests in robes sweeping the ground, their faces bearded, their straight hair topped by wide-brimmed hats; old-fashioned merchants in long-skirted coats, their demonstrative portliness a sign of their commercial success. The unabashed displays of piety on the streets always struck foreigners. Whenever members of the simpler classes passed churches or sidewalk shrines, the men would doff their hats, and all would bow and cross themselves with a broad sweeping gesture—forehead, stomach, right shoulder, left. If an icon was within reach, they would then lean forward, gingerly, to venerate it with a kiss.

Unlike what Frederick saw in Western Europe, not everyone's skin in Moscow was white and not all eyes were round. The empire's Slavic heartland was ringed by countries that the Russians had conquered or absorbed during the past centuries, and two-thirds of the empire lay beyond the Ural Mountains, in Asia. Subject peoples from all over could be seen on Moscow's streets as well: Circassians from the Caucasus, Tatars from the Crimea, Bukharians from Central Asia. Their colorful national dress was a reminder of how far east Moscow lay and reinforced the belief of many Europeans that Russians had, at the very least, an Asiatic streak in them. Of the three great human "races," only the "black" was rare: unlike many countries in Europe, Russia never pursued colonial ambitions in Africa; and unlike many countries in the Americas, it never enslaved people of African descent. Except for occasional entertainers who passed through on European tours, few blacks had any occasion to visit Russia, and hardly any chose to settle there. During Frederick's years in the city, there were probably no more than a dozen other permanent black residents amid a population of well over a million. But because the parade of humanity on the city's streets was so varied, Frederick did not stand out nearly as much as his actual rarity might have led one to expect.

The black Jamaican-American poet Claude McKay experienced this when he visited Russia a few years after the 1917 Revolution and was struck by "the distinctive polyglot population of Moscow." He was also charmed to discover that "to the Russian, I was merely another type, but stranger, with which they were not yet familiar. They were curious with me, all and sundry, young and old, in a friendly, refreshing manner." By contrast, white Americans brought their racial prejudices with them when they went abroad. Emma Harris, a black singer who settled in Russia before the Revolution, was introduced to this fact by Samuel Smith, the American consul in Moscow, whom Frederick also met. After having been arrested in the Russian provincial city of Kazan on an invented charge of being a Japanese spy, she appealed to the consulate for help and Smith's intervention gained her release. But when he saw her after she reached Moscow, he exclaimed, "How strange! We did not know that you are a Negress!" She understood that she might not have been helped if her race had been known, and that she should not count on any further assistance in the future.

As a result of the Russians' attitudes, the few black people who visited or lived in Russia did not encounter any racial prejudice and were free to pursue whatever livelihoods they chose. Frederick would himself acknowledge this years later, when he shocked a tourist who proudly styled herself "a Southern woman from America" by explaining that "there was no color line drawn" in Russia.

This made Russia look very different to black and white Americans. Frederick could exult that in tsarist Russia he was not judged by the color of his skin and was as free—and unfree—as any Russian. However, for a white American who staunchly believed that his country was a light unto other nations and that his citizenship granted him unique liberties, Russia was something else entirely—a reactionary autocracy riddled with obscurantist beliefs, which were, moreover, concentrated most vividly in Moscow's semi-Asian appearance and hidebound religious culture.

On a map, Moscow looks like a wheel. From the Kremlin at the hub, the main boulevards radiate outward like mile-long spokes toward the Sadovoye Koltso (Garden Ring), a continuous band of broad boulevards encircling the core of the city. All of Frederick's addresses in Moscow, and his future business ventures as well, clustered in the same northwestern sector of the city, in the vicinity of Triumphal Square, which was, and still is, a major intersection of the Sadovoye Koltso and Tverskaya-Yamskaya Street, one of the main spokes of the wheel. This area had concentrated in it several of the city's most popular light theatrical venues and is probably where Frederick sought employment when he first arrived.

Little is known about what exactly he did during his first several years in Moscow. He later said that he began as a waiter in a small restaurant, but he also claimed that he worked as a valet and then as a head butler for a Russian nobleman. What is certain, however, is that shortly after arriving he made the momentous decision to start a family.

In 1901, Frederick was almost thirty, and what was left of his youth was fading. He met Hedwig Antonia Hähn early in 1901, about a year after he had settled in Moscow. They married on September 11 at Saints Peter and Paul Evangelical Lutheran Church not far from the Kremlin. She was a twenty-five-year-old German, originally from Putzig, a small town in West Prussia on the shore of the Baltic, and came from a humble background—her father was a telegraph operator. Hedwig was no longer in the first blush of youth either. But she was pretty and thus a good match for Frederick—a bit tall for a woman at five feet eight, with dark brown hair and eyes, an oval face, a high forehead, a fair complexion, a straight nose, and a pointed chin. She was also no prude and did not resist intimacy outside wedlock with the exotic-looking foreigner: their first baby, Olga, was born on February 12, 1902, five months after the wedding. Despite the fact that Frederick and Hedwig came from vastly different worlds, their love for each other proved genuine and she found fulfillment as his wife and as a mother. Olga would be followed in 1906 by a son, Mikhail, whose birth especially delighted Frederick, and then by another daughter, Irma, in 1909.

In their early years together, Frederick and Hedwig lived at 16 Chukhinsky Lane in what could be called a "middle-class," semisuburban neighborhood just outside the Sadovoye Koltso and a convenient twenty-minute walk from Triumphal Square. By then Frederick was earning enough for Hedwig to be able to occupy herself only with "home duties." In contrast to more developed parts of the city on the inner side of the Sadovoye Koltso, the neighborhood where the Thomases lived had the feeling of a provincial town, like many other areas on Moscow's outskirts in those days. There were still big empty lots interspersed with small and large ponds. Most of the houses were one or two stories high and built of wood; only some of the streets were paved with cobblestones while the rest were dirt; streetlights were scarce and used kerosene.

The church records pertaining to the wedding do not make any reference to Frederick's race, but they do contain the surprising revelation that he identified himself as a Roman Catholic, which means that he chose not to attach himself to one of the Protestant churches in Europe that were closer to what he had known as a child. The differences between the Catholic and A.M.E. churches could hardly have been greater in terms of history, geography, power, architecture, art, music, and ritual. Overall, there is little evidence suggesting that any religious faith was important for Frederick. But his choosing Catholicism is nevertheless significant. By identifying with the most venerable and "highest" of the Old World churches he was taking another decisive step on his path of reinventing himself by abandoning American cultural markers for those of a cosmopolitan European.

* * *

It did not take long for Frederick to find a job commensurate with his skills and experience. In 1903, he began to work as a maître d'hôtel at Aquarium, an entertainment garden occupying several park-like acres just west of Triumphal Square, at what is now 16 Bolshaya Sadovaya Street. Aquarium was a focal point of Moscow's lively nightlife for a clientele drawn from the more genteel and prosperous classes of society, especially those who were not put off by the frivolous nature of the garden's entertainments. It retained its aquatic name even after the fountains, grottoes, and artificial streams flowing into a pond with goldfish that had existed there in 1898 were long forgotten.

Frederick's employer, Charles Aumont, was a Frenchman. He had rebuilt the garden in a style intended to make visitors feel that they were arriving somewhere grand and magical: a giant white colonnade topped with sculptures greeted them at the entrance, and a marble staircase bathed in electric light led into the garden. A magnificent building decorated with carved cupolas, columns, and arches meant to evoke a Moorish palace housed a restaurant on the left. In the depths of the garden was a spacious concert stage. Bands in pavilions played fashionable tunes; people strolled along gravel walkways among trees strung with bright lights; vendors offered snacks and souvenirs from booths; barkers invited passersby to try their hand at bowling and other games. The garden provided a chance to get away from the noise and bustle of the city streets, to see and to be seen, to have some fun, perhaps to enjoy a brief flirtation or even a dalliance. A modest fee allowed a customer to enter the Aquarium grounds at dusk and to stay there until the garden closed in the early morning.

More expensive tickets gave entry to a large enclosed theater on the grounds that featured lavish productions of fashionable operettas and comedies imported directly from Vienna, Paris, London, and Berlin. The subjects were invariably lighthearted, the plots quick-paced, and the humor often risqué. The theater's private rooms were also available, curtained in a way that shielded those inside from public view but not from the stage. In the early 1900s, the most famous customer for these was the biggest name in Moscow—Grand Duke Sergey, the tsar's uncle and the city's governor-general. Younger grand dukes sat openly in first-row orchestra seats. After the performance at the enclosed theater was over, patrons could continue their evening by moving to the "café chantant." This was a different, open-air theater that included a restaurant where customers would sit at small tables facing a stage and order food and drink while they watched, or ignored, a variety show of twenty or thirty acts in quick succession —everything from trained animals to acrobats to operatic singers.

Aumont was a very successful, talented, and ruthless business-man, and Frederick learned a great deal from him (including how not to behave). For owners of establishments like Aquarium, sales of food and especially of drink were major components of their income, and cynical observers of Moscow nightlife often complained that the variety shows were really just magnets for successful restaurants. The managers of the gardens certainly did what they could to link the two. Many of the song and dance acts featured attractive young women whose primary talent was projecting their allure to a largely male audience. But the enticements did not stop there. According to the norms of the time, a client seated in the restaurant who was particularly taken with a performer—and who had the money and the courage—could send her an invitation to join him at his table after she had taken her turn onstage.

The exploitation of chorus girls and other female performers was one area where Aumont sinned but Frederick did not. Frederick became personally involved in the fate of one such young woman in 1903. Natalia Trukhanova was a sweet-faced actress with dreamy eyes and a voluptuous figure who aspired to a career on the stage of the celebrated Moscow Art Theater, which had recently launched Chekhov's plays and had become the center of a revolution in Russian theatrical practice. But she did not succeed, was in desperate need of money, and—following a friend's advice—applied for a job at Aquarium. Aumont liked her and hired her on the spot to perform in light comedies. He also offered her a monthly salary that exceeded her wildest dreams and, glossing over some of the fine print, urged her to sign a contract at their first meeting.

She did not realize what she had gotten herself into until she finished her first performance and was preparing to go. Her costar ran into her dressing room and began to upbraid her in a loud, harsh tone for not knowing the ropes: "Have you lost your wits? They're going to start asking for you in the private rooms any second! And you want to relax? You want to earn your bread without working? No, missy! That won't work here! Please be so kind as to sit and wait in your dressing room until you're called. One of the maîtres d'hôtel will fetch you." A few minutes later, one of them did appear—"the negro Thomas" as Trukhanova referred to him. He announced very politely that a party was asking for her in private room 18 and that everyone there was entirely decent and sober. She obediently followed Frederick to the door, and thus began what she called her yearlong "path of sorrow," working every night like a "real geisha."

Her fate would have been worse were it not for Frederick and the other maîtres d'hôtel, who looked out for her like "tender nurse-maids," as she put it. Trukhanova described how, whenever she was entertaining customers in a private room, one of the maîtres d'hôtel would take care to place a bottle of her "personal" champagne in front of her. This was actually a rather foul-tasting mixture of mineral water colored with tea, but it looked like the real thing and allowed her to avoid drinking anything alcoholic. And if a client happened to pour some wine or liquor into her glass, the maître d'hôtel who was keeping an eye on the room would immediately swoop in and remove it. Trukhanova reciprocated and won the affection of the Aquarium's restaurant staff by donating her commissions to the general pool for tips. Her distaste for her work was so strong that she would also not keep anything that her clients bought for her and saw "every flower, every piece of fruit" as "defiled." Frederick noticed this and remembered it in a way that touched her deeply. On New Year's Day, January 1, 1904, he presented her with an enormous bouquet from the grateful staff and began his speech by announcing: "Not a single one of these flowers comes from the restaurant, and the ribbon is . . . straight from Paris!"

The success that Frederick quickly achieved at Aquarium made it seem as if he had become master of his own fate by settling in Russia. But there were subterranean historical forces at work in his adopted country, even if they were initially hardly noticeable to people like him caught up in their daily lives. They erupted for the first time scarcely five years after he arrived and did so with a violence that would show the fragility of the life he had built for himself—indeed, the fragility of his whole surrounding world.

On the night of February 8, 1904 (N.S., that is, by the New Style calendar), the imperial Japanese navy launched a surprise attack on the Russian Pacific fleet lying at anchor in the outer harbor of Port Arthur in China, "thus accomplishing the original Pearl Harbor," as an American historian put it. The two countries' imperialistic ambitions in Manchuria had come into conflict, and the Japanese naval attack that launched the Russo-Japanese War proved to be only the first of the military disasters that the giant Russia would suffer at the hands of little Japan during the next year and a half. The Japanese besieged and eventually captured Port Arthur itself, then defeated the Russian army in Manchuria. Finally, between May 27 and 29, 1905, in the Battle of Tsushima Strait, the Japanese annihilated the antiquated Russian fleet, which had sailed for over half a year and had traveled nearly twenty thousand miles from the Baltic to the coast of Japan. The president of the United States, Theodore Roosevelt, brokered a peace conference between the belligerents in Portsmouth, New

Hampshire, in August 1905—none too soon for Russia. The country had already been experiencing revolutionary turmoil for months. The war that began six thousand miles to the east of St. Petersburg had initiated upheavals that shook the Russian Empire from top to bottom, leaving cracks that would help to bring it crashing down a dozen years later.

As an erstwhile American citizen, Frederick was in a strange position because of the war and the events that followed. Some decades earlier, during and after the American Civil War, Russian-American relations had been amicable; the United States was grateful for Russia's support of the Union. There were also mutually profitable political and commercial relations between the two countries, including Russia's momentous sale of Alaska to the United States in 1867. However, as the twentieth century approached, American public opinion began to turn against Russia for two dominant reasons—abhorrence of the tyrannical absolute monarchy and revulsion against Russia's treatment of Jews. Indeed, during the Russo-Japanese War, the United States sympathized with Japan, and New York bankers made large loans to Japan in the hope that this would help to defeat Russia.

Frederick was thus making a life for himself in a country that was increasingly being vilified in the land of his birth. Another ironic twist was that not only were Jim Crow laws continuing unabated in the United States, but a newer animus had appeared against the Chinese, whose entry into the country and ability to acquire citizenship were blocked by explicitly racist federal laws. The Russians thus considered the Americans hypocritical, and vice versa. When President Roosevelt's administration transmitted a petition to the Russian government protesting against widespread anti-Jewish pogroms, the Russian ambassador to Washington complained that it was "unbecoming for Americans to criticize" Russia when blacks were being lynched and Chinese beaten up on the streets of the United States.

The disastrous war with Japan could hardly have come at a worse time for the Russian Empire. As the twentieth century opened, waves of turmoil had begun to spread across the country. Workers struck against onerous conditions in factories; students demonstrated for civil rights; peasants in the countryside tried to seize land from the nobles. Committees of citizens sprang up demanding broad-ranging reforms in political life, the economy, and education. The Socialist Revolutionary Party resurrected its "Combat Organization," which carried out a series of spectacular assassinations—two ministers of the interior in 1902 and 1904, and then, in February 1905, Grand Duke Sergey, former governor-general of Moscow and visitor to Aquarium (where Frederick may well have met him), who was literally blown to bits inside the Kremlin.

What subsequently became known as the "First" Russian Revolution erupted shortly after the New Year in 1905, when a strike by a hundred thousand workers paralyzed St. Petersburg. On January 9 (January 22 in the West), a day that would reverberate throughout Russia and around the world as "Bloody Sunday," troops fired on peaceful demonstrators. Outrage against the tsar and the government swept the country and further fed the revolutionary turmoil, prompting new massive strikes, uprisings among peasants and national minorities, and even rebellion in the armed forces. Finally recognizing the magnitude of the opposition, Nicholas II issued a manifesto on October 17/30 that guaranteed civil liberties and established a legislative body called the Duma. The Russian Empire had taken a major step toward becoming a constitutional monarchy, although many of these early promises and achievements would be undone by the emperor and his ministers in the following decade.

Despite the October Manifesto, which was meant to calm the country, the revolutionary upheavals grew stronger. Moscow was the scene of the greatest violence, exceeding even that in St. Petersburg. On the evening of December 8, 1905, what became known as the "siege" of the Aquarium Theater took place. More than six thousand people gathered for a huge rally and to hear orators in the theater, which was a popular meeting place because it was not far from the industrial quarter where many of the most militant revolutionaries worked and lived. Troops and police surrounded the building and the grounds but the siege ended relatively peacefully.

The following day things got worse. On Strastnaya Square (now Pushkin Square), closer to the city center and a fifteen-minute walk from Aquarium, a crowd of peaceful demonstrators inadvertently provoked a jittery unit of dragoons, whose berserk response was to fire several artillery rounds at the civilians. Many Muscovites who had previously not had any sympathy for the revolutionaries were appalled and enraged. People began to build street barricades out of anything that was handy—fences, doors, telegraph poles, iron gates, streetcars, placards. Aquarium was in the middle of it, and barricades went up just outside the entrance. Skirmishes between revolutionary militiamen and troops flared up throughout the city. The American ambassador in St. Petersburg, George von Lengerke Meyer, sent a coded telegram to Washington: "Russian nation appears to have gone temporarily insane; government practically helpless to restore law and order throughout the country; departments at sixes and sevens; also crippled by postal and telegraph strike. Only the socialists appear to be well organized to establish strikes when and wherever they like."

By far the worst fighting in Moscow took place in the Presnya district just outside the Sadovoye Koltso, a half-hour walk from where Frederick and his family lived. The government was finally able to crush the rebellion by December 18. During its course, some 700 revolutionaries and civilians were killed and 2,000 were wounded. The police and military combined lost 70 men. These numbers were far lower than what foreign newspapers reported initially, but more than enough to justify horror abroad and despair and outrage at home.

The reverberations from those days lasted for years. In 1906, 1,400 officials and police officers, as well as many innocent bystanders, were killed by the Socialist Revolutionaries. In 1907, the number climbed to 3,000. The following year, 1,800 were killed. The scythe swung in the opposite direction as well, and during the same period

the imperial regime arrested and executed several thousand terrorists and revolutionaries. But all this would later seem like a trickle
in comparison with the rivers of blood that started to flow after the
Bolshevik takeover in 1917.

What happened to Frederick and his family during these days
of chaos and mayhem in Moscow, if they were there? Like hundreds
of thousands of others throughout the city, they probably huddled
indoors much of the time, away from windows, venturing out only
to find a food shop that was open or to catch rumors about what
was going on.

But it is also possible that they saw little or none of it. On December 26, 1905, the American ambassador to St. Petersburg sent a
report to the secretary of state on the status of American citizens in
the capital and in Moscow and attached lists of all those known to
be living in both cities. The totals are surprisingly small—only 73
in St. Petersburg and 104 in Moscow. For Moscow, the list had been
compiled by Consul Smith, but Frederick and his family are not on
it. There is no doubt that Smith knew both Frederick and Hedwig:
he had met them at least twice, when he signed their passport applications in May 1901 and again as recently as July 1904.

In fact there is some evidence that Frederick did leave Moscow for a period during the Russo-Japanese War and the 1905
Revolution—specifically, sometime between November 1904 and
September 1906. As he explained to American diplomats more than
a dozen years later, "In 1905, I was on my way to San Francisco
and stopped in Philippine Islands, Manila, when Russo-Japanese
War broke out. I was accompanying a Russian nobleman as inter-
preter." He also told an American tourist a more detailed variant
of the same story.

Was this the truth or invention? If Frederick was trying to persuade the diplomats that he was a loyal American despite having
lived abroad for twenty-five years, what good could it have done
him to make up an aborted trip to San Francisco with a stop in the

Philippines (which had recently become an American colony)? As it happens, there is evidence pointing in the opposite direction. Frederick had family ties to Berlin through his wife. It is possible that he moved there temporarily to escape the violence in Moscow; it is also possible that he went there to open a restaurant. However, after World War I, with Germany defeated and widely reviled, it would not have been in Frederick's interests to acknowledge any connections to that country, especially when dealing with American officials. Nevertheless, judging by the fragmentary evidence available, Berlin is the more likely version.

Although Aquarium had survived serious damage, Aumont had been frightened by the violence and destruction he witnessed during the revolution. His self-indulgent business practices also caught up to him, and by early 1907 bankruptcy was looming. Aumont decided to escape to France (he stole his employees' money when he left), and Aquarium fell on hard times for a number of years.

Frederick needed a new job, and the next one he got marked his emergence into the topmost ranks of his profession. Among Moscow's many celebrated restaurants, one stood out because of its age—it dated from the beginning of the nineteenth century—and its fame. Yar Restaurant, or simply Yar, as Muscovites called it, was considered by many connoisseurs to be the finest in Russia and one of the best in all of Europe. Jobs in Yar were coveted by waiters not only because of its prestige but because of the generosity of many of its famous and wealthy clients. That Frederick became a maître d'hôtel there, probably starting in 1908 if not before, is testimony to how far he had come in Russia. By then he had probably already developed his glib, if often grammatically flawed, command of spoken Russian. His French would have been useful with some patrons, but he would need to communicate readily in Russian with most of the others as well as his employer and the restaurant's staff.

Yar was located on the northwestern edge of Moscow. To be near his new job Frederick moved his family from the calm of Chukhinsky Lane to 18 Petersburg Highway, which was the main road to the imperial capital about 350 miles to the northwest. Although two miles farther out from the city center than Frederick's old neighborhood near Aquarium, Yar was well situated in terms of attracting clients. Directly across the highway, on the edge of Khodynka Field (where over a thousand people had been trampled to death during a celebration commemorating the 1896 coronation of Nicholas II, a tragedy that many took as a bad omen for his reign), were the Moscow racetrack and the airport of the Moscow Society of Aeronautics. During the early years of the twentieth century, airplanes were a new craze in Russia, as they were elsewhere around the world. Muscovites saw their first airplane on September 15, 1909, when the French aviator Legagneux demonstrated his Voisin biplane at Khodynka Field. Thousands thrilled at the sight, and spectators flocked in ever-increasing numbers to subsequent displays of aerial acrobatics. Yar was happy to provide champagne and other potables to celebrate exhibitions of hair-raising stunts by the spindly aircraft, as well as to mourn the victims of their disastrous crashes.

When Frederick began to work at Yar the owner was Aleksey Akimovich Sudakov, who had bought the restaurant in 1896 and nurtured it to its great success and fame over the next twenty years. Sudakov was an absolute perfectionist and would not have given Frederick a visible and responsible position without being certain of his professionalism and polish. Despite the obvious differences between them, there are also several striking parallels between Frederick's life path and Sudakov's. Sudakov was born a peasant in Yaroslavl province and went through a demanding apprenticeship as a lowly assistant waiter before becoming a manager and finally buying a small restaurant of his own. This background is not unlike Frederick's origins in black, rural Mississippi and his work in big city restaurants and hotels. Both men succeeded only because of their own talents and because they had learned all aspects of the restaurant and entertainment business from the ground up.

But it was not only Sudakov who could serve as a mentor—there also was Aleksey Fyodorovich Natruskin, the "king" of Yar's staff, as Sudakov himself described him. Natruskin was the senior maître d'hôtel when Frederick worked there and had held this position without interruption for thirty years. As such, he was Frederick's immediate superior and would have played a role in honing his already advanced skills, either actively or by example. Well known to several generations of Yar's loyal customers, Natruskin was much admired and respected by them for his ability to balance his dignified manner with the utmost attention to their desires and tastes, a combination that they found very flattering (and that many later remembered as Frederick's salient traits as well). Natruskin's calculated skills were well rewarded by the clients he charmed and made feel at home. Visiting grand dukes gave him jeweled gifts as mementos while businessmen and others tipped him lavishly in cash. By the time he retired, he had saved 200,000 rubles, the equivalent of several million dollars in today's money, which he used to buy an investment property in Moscow. There was much in his life and career that Frederick would imitate; there was also much in it that he would surpass.

As might be expected in view of Frederick's success in working with such exacting colleagues, the relations among them were rooted not only in pragmatic considerations but also in mutual respect and even affection. There is evidence for this in the grandest event in Yar's twentieth-century history—an event that Frederick helped orchestrate—the celebration on December 19, 1909, of Yar's reopening following a major reconstruction. The day was filled with many remarkable tributes to Sudakov, and Frederick joined the five other senior employees in composing and signing a memorable one of their own (in Russian, of course). Identifying themselves as Sudakov's "closest assistants and collaborators," they proclaimed that they "saluted" him as "an energetic and conscientious proprietor" and "bowed down" to him as "a person of rare humanity." They assured him of their "genuine affection," not only because of his "skillful management," but also because of his "sensitive soul, which responds to all that is honest and good." They concluded their tribute by wishing Sudakov "Many Years" ("Mnogaya Leta"), which is actually the name of a Russian Orthodox hymn asking God to grant the celebrant a long life. Proclaiming the hymn's title at the end of congratulatory remarks such as these would traditionally serve as the prompt for singing it, and the six signers of the address almost certainly did so, together with many of the others present.

To Western eyes and ears it might seem odd that a famous restaurant's reopening would be accompanied by an expression of religious faith. After all, Yar was a place where people went to overindulge in food and drink, and to have their passions stirred by Gypsy choirs and comely chorus girls. But a prayer service in a place like this was entirely in keeping with Russian norms of the time and demonstrates the extent to which religious rituals and beliefs penetrated all aspects of social life, and at all levels of society (even though there was always a minority that complained about the unseemliness of such mixing). The service in Yar also illustrates the easy coexistence of transgression and forgiveness in the Russian consciousness—not as hypocrisy but in the sense that contrition would always be able to expiate sin, and the passions, if properly guided, could lead to spiritual salvation. In later years, one of Yar's most notorious fans, the sinister religious mountebank Rasputin, would become a visible emblem of this duality.

What was Frederick like at his job? Fred Gaisberg of the American Gramophone Company saw him in action a number of times at Yar and was struck by his sophistication and charm. Gaisberg came to Moscow to persuade the internationally celebrated Russian operatic bass Fyodor Chaliapin to sign a long-term recording contract. What impressed Gaisberg was not only that Frederick knew "every noble-man and plutocrat in Moscow" but how "he was always perfectly dressed and would personally welcome his patrons with a calculating eye in the vestibule." Frederick's skill at figuring out quickly where the client stood on the ladder of celebrity and how much money he was likely to spend, and remembering what food and drink he had enjoyed during previous visits—all of which required an unusually retentive memory and a knowledge of people—was one of the reasons he had proved exceptionally successful at Yar. The other was that he was very accommodating, and Gaisberg underscored that Frederick "was a general favourite everywhere, especially amongst the ladies, who made a pet of him." Moreover, implying that Frederick at Yar, like his peers in other famous Russian establishments, had set new standards for memorable hospitality, Gaisberg concluded that "Paris, Berlin, Vienna, Budapest—none of them could compare in my opinion with St. Petersburg and Moscow if one wanted carefree night life."

A maître d'hôtel's skills would be exercised routinely in any good restaurant that attracted a well-heeled clientele, but at Yar there were times when such skills were challenged and pushed to the limit. One reason was Moscow's cultural norms, especially among some of the rich and successful members of its merchant class, who valued the ability to demonstrate bravado or unbridled passion in a way that would make people notice and remember their Russian "broad nature." The other was the reputation Yar acquired as a favorite destination for especially extravagant sprees. The result was some truly memorable escapades. An American writer, Roy Norton, visited Yar around 1911, when Frederick was still working there. Although Norton had already spent some time in Europe studying the be-havior of "spendthrifts" in various countries, he quickly concluded that Russians were by far the most extravagant, and that Yar was the place in Moscow where one could see them at their best. Norton was especially impressed by one such reveler who decided that it would be fun to play football in the dining room with hothouse pineapples, which were selling in Moscow that winter for around 44 rubles, or $22, each: around $1,000 in today's money. He ordered a whole cartload and proceeded to kick them all around, smashing china, overturning tables, and spilling imported champagne. His bill from the proprietor, who approached him with a smile, was supposedly 30,000 rubles, or around $750,000 in today's money. Frederick told Norton that there are "probably an average of fifty bills a month, paid for one evening's entertainment, that will average seven thousand five hundred rubles each."

Within a decade of Frederick's arrival in Russia, his life was looking very bright. He had a lucrative position at a famous restaurant and his family was about to grow once again: Hedwig was expecting their third child. Irma was born on February 24, 1909, and baptized at home on March 31 by a pastor from the Saints Peter and Paul Church. Frederick's happiness over Irma's arrival was poisoned, however, by the debilitating effect that her birth apparently had on Hedwig's health. As the Thomas family's oral history suggests, Frederick's subsequent distance from Irma was due to his seeing her as somehow responsible for the loss of his wife, whom he cherished deeply. Irma's tragic fate and the way she suppressed any recollections of her family past when she grew up also imply that a chasm had developed between her and her father—a situation that darkened her entire childhood and that she was never able to overcome.

There is no direct evidence regarding the nature of Hedwig's illness after Irma's birth, although there was much that could have happened to her. Despite improvements in hygiene and the growing use of birthing hospitals in early-twentieth-century Moscow, childbirth was still beset with potential dangers for both the baby and the mother, with puerperal fever leading the way and a troop of other ghastly complications following. Hedwig died of pneumonia, with the additional complication of blood poisoning, on January 17,

1910, at the age of thirty-four, and was buried at the Vvedenskoye Cemetery of Foreign Confessions in Moscow, also known as the "German Cemetery."

Olga was almost eight when her mother died and thus just old enough to understand some of what this meant. But Mikhail was only three and Irma not yet one, so for them their mother's death was a confusing and distressing event that they could not fathom; also, they would not remember her. Hedwig's death was Frederick's first close personal loss since his father's murder in Memphis. He would continue without Hedwig, of course, but the uncomplicated harmony of the family life he had built with her is something he would never know in quite the same way again.

Frederick's most urgent task after Hedwig's death was to find a way to care for his children. His income at Yar was more than sufficient for him to hire the domestic help he needed, and the obvious solution was to find an experienced nanny. His choice fell on Valentina Leontina Anna Hoffman, and it would prove to be a fateful one. "Valli," as she was often called, was twenty-eight years old and came from Riga, the capital of Latvia, a small province on the Baltic Sea that had been part of the Russian Empire since the eighteenth century. Her surname and the fact that she knew German as well as English—in addition to Russian, of course—suggest that she belonged to the Baltic region's dominant German population and was educated. Judging by surviving photographs, she was a plain and rather large woman; and given subsequent developments, her appearance played a role in how Frederick treated her.

While working at Yar, Frederick had also begun to prepare for the next major step in his life, one that must have been in the back of his mind for years. The tips he received at work continued to be generous and he was accumulating a sizable sum in savings; in fact, he now had more money than ever before in his life. The time was right to decide what to do next—continue like Natruskin until retirement, which was the safe route, or take a calculated risk like

Sudakov and invest in a business of his own. Frederick decided to follow Sudakov's—and his father's—example and to bet on his own skills and energy.

The business risks that Frederick faced could not be separated from the bigger ones threatening the entire country, although the energy with which he pursued his personal ambitions suggests that he thought Russia would somehow get through it all. The Revolution of 1905 showed the fragility of the Russian Empire's social and political system, and what happened then could happen again. Although terrorism had declined from 1908 to 1910 in comparison with previous years, over 700 government bureaucrats and 3,000 civilians were murdered during this period (these deaths included the shocking assassination of the powerful prime minister Peter Stolypin in 1911). Strikes by workers demanding political and economic reforms dropped in 1910 to their lowest level in several years, with only some 50,000 workers participating in 2,000 mostly small job actions. But this relative lull was hardly a sign that the country's underlying problems had been fixed, despite an economic boom that began around 1910. Strikes increased the following year and would grow to crisis proportions by 1914 as the government continued to suppress workers with blind, stupid brutality. An especially notorious incident occurred in 1912, when troops fired on thousands of peacefully demonstrating gold miners in Siberia, killing 147. The Duma demanded a full investigation, but little came of it. By this point in the country's history, nothing could dispel the impression that the imperial government was dangerously, even catastrophically, adrift.

However, these threats flickering and rumbling in the distance did nothing to dampen Muscovites' enthusiasm for revelry. Many observers noted that people in the city began to seek pleasure with increasing frenzy as the century's second decade began. Frederick saw how others around him were making money and was ready to start doing so as well.

4

EARLY FORTUNE

In November 1911, Moscow's devotees of nightlife got some exciting news: Aquarium was going to reopen the following spring under
new management. After Aumont had absconded with his employees'
money four years earlier, the place had changed hands more than
half a dozen times in a complex sequence of rentals and subleases.
Some entrepreneurs had good runs initially, but even though the
property was one of the biggest and most desirable green spaces in
the city, their success never lasted long. To journalists who followed
Moscow theatrical life, it seemed as if Aumont had laid a curse on
anyone who tried to resurrect Aquarium after him.

An additional surprise was the self-confidence of the unlikely
trio that took over the place, none of whom had been a player in the
high-stakes game of Moscow nightlife. Two were Russians—Matvey
Filippovich Martynov, a businessman, and Mikhail Prokofyevich
Tsarev, a former barman who had risen to maître d'hôtel at Aquarium
under a previous manager. The third was Frederick, who was very
familiar to Yar's habitués, and who was now calling himself "Fyodor
Fyodorovich Tomas."

Launching into this business venture was another major step in
Frederick's process of reinventing himself. To become an entrepreneur, he had to give up the security of a very well paying job and to

put his hard-earned money and family's welfare at risk. But there was a deeper change as well. By adopting a Russian first name and patronymic, he was changing the very terms by which the world knew him. This also proved to be more than a gesture of accommodation for the benefit of Moscow's business world; it became part of Frederick's identity even in his own family. Two of his grandchildren, who now live in France, did not know his American first and middle names. They believed that "Fyodor" was the only name he ever had because this is how their father, Frederick's first son, had always referred to him in his family oral history.

Running Aquarium was a large, ambitious, and expensive project. The property had been neglected in recent years and needed extensive repairs. At least initially, Frederick and his partners intended to cover the costs by pooling their own savings. Of all the tasks facing them, the most urgent was to book the kind of entertainment that would dazzle Muscovites on opening night and keep them coming back all summer long. Accordingly, in February 1912, when the city's freezing weather and snowdrifts made spring seem very distant, Frederick left for Western Europe to recruit variety theater acts for the coming season. It was typical that he wanted to oversee the crucial process of selection himself rather than entrust it to his partners or to talent agencies. The trip also shows how he quickly emerged as the leading member of the partnership, especially regarding issues of artistic taste. It helped as well that he knew foreign languages, since the others did not.

For about six weeks, Frederick traveled by express trains with a secretary and an assistant to Vienna, Berlin, Paris, London, and other major cities to see as many different programs as possible, in the best theaters. Because variety theaters were an international business, Russian entrepreneurs like him had to compete with their foreign counterparts for the most popular acts and stars. This required putting on a performance of one's own—an ostentatious display of wealth, which implied that the theater director was not only rich but in a position to offer generous contracts to potential clients. An entrepreneur would therefore typically telegraph ahead to reserve large suites in famous hotels, such as the Grand on Vienna's Kärntner Ring or the Ritz in Paris on the Place Vendôme. He would arrange to have the suites lavishly decorated with bouquets of flowers that would impress desirable stars at lunches and private meetings. Finally, he would have to dress and act the part of a rich, worldly sophisticate.

During his first recruiting trip to Europe, as well as the others he made in subsequent years, Frederick did not spare any expense and booked the best acts he could find for Aquarium's variety stage. He went so far that a journalist in Moscow who got wind of what some of the performers were being paid began to complain that it was too much—presumably because it might lead to a price war among Moscow's entrepreneurs. Two black American singer-musicians, George Duncan and Billy Brooks, who worked for Frederick while on their swing through Russia, remembered that he always tried to impress audiences with acts that were big, often involving five to twenty-five performers. Duncan and Brooks even joked that because there were no limits to what Frederick would be willing to put onstage, he would have gone along even if someone wanted to "work twenty or more elephants." They acknowledged sadly that although they had always prided themselves on their own performances and stage settings, and that when the curtain went up their act looked "big all the way," "Thomas' acts with whole carloads of scenery, made us look dwarfed."

Frederick and his partners launched Aquarium's new season on April 28, 1912, when the daytime temperature in Moscow finally began to reach the upper fifties. The city's cold, continental climate made people so eager to get out-of-doors that they were willing to start even when it was still chilly during the day and the temperature dropped nearly to freezing at night. It had been a feverishly busy, expensive, and exhausting five months of preparations, but now all was ready. The first groups of variety stage performers that Frederick had engaged in Western Europe, and others from various Russian cities, had arrived safely in Moscow. The garden had been redecorated with new construction, paint, and numerous flower beds; the restaurant was reorganized; a new staff had been hired. The well-known Saburov theatrical troupe, which had begun to perform in Aquarium years earlier under Aumont, was preparing to start its season of light comic plays and musicals in the enclosed theater. Posters announcing Aquarium's opening and listing the performers had gone up throughout the city, and advertisements appeared in the big newspapers and magazines. All that remained was to open the gates and see who came.

From the first day, people began to stream into the garden. Within a month, it was clear that the season was going to be a success. By summer's peak, the new managers could scarcely believe their eyes. The box office for the open theater, where the variety acts performed, had to put up a SOLD OUT sign most nights; Saburov's farces played to packed houses; all the tables in the café chantant were still booked after midnight. Several journalists who covered Moscow theatrical life quickly pointed to "Mr. Thomas" as the member of the "triumvirate" most responsible for the garden's sensational success; indeed, the partnership soon began to be referred to as "Thomas and Co." A reporter who hid behind the pseudonym "Gamma" praised "Mr. Thomas' good taste" for the acts he booked abroad, and characterized the program he put together on the open theater's stage as nothing less than "brilliant" (even if he criticized some of the garden's other entertainments). His summary conclusion is the one that mattered most: "Aquarium has become the favorite place of Muscovites and has left Hermitage"—which was the other big entertainment garden in the city and Aquarium's only real competitor—"far behind."

These two establishments would in fact continue to compete in future years, but although Hermitage was always very successful,

Aquarium garnered more attention—and earned more money—because of Frederick's skillful management and eye for novelty in entertainment. And although Muscovites had a rich array of fashionable restaurants, cafés, variety theaters, dramatic theaters, operas, concert halls, and cinemas vying for their attention, Aquarium's celebrity never faded once "Thomas and Co." took over.

From the first night that Aquarium opened, one of the keys to its success was Frederick's ability to provide a range of entertainments that catered to various tastes and pocketbooks. Prominent among these was the pervasive atmosphere of sexual license. It was not that Frederick or his partners promoted prostitution on Aquarium's grounds; there was plenty of this readily available elsewhere in Moscow, including streetwalkers on nearby boulevards. Suggestive performances were also far from the only thing that appeared on Aquarium's different stages. Nevertheless, the garden quickly became a kind of eroticized zone where those who were so inclined could easily and cheerfully suspend proper morals. Conducive to this were the park-like setting and the feeling of being apart from the city, the spicy performances by attractive showgirls who were also available to mingle with patrons, a leisured clientele in search of dissipation, and the fact that journalists liked to play up the garden's libertine atmosphere in their reporting.

A frequent visitor to Aquarium captured well the ambience of pleasure and permissiveness that characterized a typical warm summer evening. A refreshing light breeze greets you when you enter from the heat and noise of the street; many small lamps that look like fireflies sway on the trees; the moon—a large, light-filled sphere—floats above; flags cheerfully wave over the kiosks and the stages. The crowds promenading on the sand-strewn paths make a rustling noise like waves gently washing onto a beach. The beckoning sounds of an orchestra come from a stage across the way, its footlights surrounded with a rainbow display of flowers in crystal vases. You see the happy and excited smiles of women clad in light summer dresses, their flashing eyes, their thirst for love, for happiness, for wine, "or ... maybe just for money," the visitor concludes with practiced cynicism. The crowd greedily watches the acrobats on the open stage and guffaws at the vulgar jokes of the comedians. Nearby stands an obvious libertine. He is wearing an elegant tuxedo with a boutonniere in his lapel and a bright red handkerchief sticking out of his breast pocket. His eyes narrow as he watches a big-haired, big-bosomed blonde pounding out a march on a piano, something very bouncy "and Germanic." A minute later, he is gazing lustfully at a svelte young woman onstage, a spear thrower barely out of her teens. Then he whispers a playful invitation to a woman who is standing next to him "to come and spend this short summer night with me." A bald, wrinkled little old man passes by with a dazzling young woman on his arm; she throws her fiery gaze at all the men she encounters, inviting them to follow. Multiple attacks on the old man begin and half an hour later he is alone and on the watch for a new "victim" while the dazzling young woman, with a pink-faced student by her side, is causing a row at the entrance, where she is stridently demanding an automobile. Staid, faithful Muscovites and their wives stand for hours by the open stage on spots they claimed and will not abandon even during intermissions. For their "fifty kopek" entrance fee, they want to soak up as many sights as possible, and they will leave only when the fireworks are over.

Aquarium's atmosphere naturally had an especially powerful attraction for young men, whether they were Russians or visiting foreigners. Several months after the garden's opening, R. H. Bruce Lockhart, a boyish-looking twenty-five-year-old Scot who had recently arrived in Moscow to take up the post of vice-consul at the British consulate, and who would go on to an adventurous career and a knighthood, made a memorable visit there with an English friend, George Bowen. They had never been to Aquarium before, but they knew of the place because of how famous it had become that summer, and also because their consulate often had disagreements with "the negro Thomas" who "presided over" it, as Lockhart phrased it, regarding "the engagement of young English girls as cabaret performers." Frederick may have been a novice at running Aquarium during its first season, but as his encounter with Lockhart shows, he was anything but inexperienced when it came to resolving a messy situation that involved passion, jealousy, suicide, and the police.

Lockhart and his friend understood very well the moral gradations of the entertainment venues that were available at Aquarium, which Lockhart summarized as "a perfectly respectable operette theatre, an equally respectable open-air music hall, a definitely less respectable verandah cafe-chantant, and the inevitable chain of private 'kabinets' for gipsy-singing and private carouses." One night, already well primed by a boozy dinner elsewhere, they naturally chose the café chantant and took the best box. Despite their "exalted state," they were initially bored by a string of unappealing acts. Then suddenly the lights were dimmed and everything changed.

The band struck up an English tune. The curtain went up, and from the wings a young English girl—amazingly fresh and beautiful—tripped lightly to the centre of the stage and did a song and dance act. Her voice was shrill and harsh. Her accent was Wigan [i.e., from Lancashire] at its crudest. But she could dance, as Moscow had never seen an English girl dance. The audience rose to her. So did two young and suddenly refreshed Englishmen. The head-waiter was summoned. Pencil and paper were demanded, and then after bashful meditation—it was a new experience for both of us—we sent a combined note inviting her to join us in our box. She came. Off the stage she was not so beautiful as she had seemed ten minutes before. She was neither witty nor wicked. She had been on the stage since she was fourteen and took life philosophically. But she was English, and the story of her career thrilled us. I expect our shyness and our awkwardness amused her.

However, Lockhart and Bowen were not able to continue their interesting conversation uninterrupted. A waiter walked in with a note for the young woman, who read it and asked to be excused for a minute. Shortly thereafter, the young men

> heard high words outside the door—a male Cockney voice predominating. Then there was a scuffle and a final "blast you." The door opened and was hurriedly shut, and with flushed face our Lancashire lady returned to us. What was the matter? It was nothing. There was an English jockey—a mad fellow, always drunk, who was making her life a burden and a misery. We expressed our sympathy, ordered more champagne, and in five minutes had forgotten all about the incident.

But they were not allowed to forget for long, because an hour later the door was thrown open again.

> This time Thomas himself appeared, followed by a policeman. Outside the door was a mob of waiters and girls with scared faces. The negro scratched his head. There had been an accident. Would Missie go at once? The English jockey had shot himself.
> Suddenly sobered, we paid our bill and followed the girl to the shabby furnished rooms across the road where the tragedy had taken place. We were prepared for the worst—scandal, possibly disgrace, and our almost certain appearance as witnesses at the inquest. For both of us the matter seemed terribly serious. In the circumstances the best course seemed to be to take Thomas into our confidence. He laughed at our fears.
> "I will make that ol' right, Mistah Lockhart," he said. "Bless yo' heart, the police won't worry you—or the English Missie

either. They's sho' used to tragedies like this, and this one has been comin' fo' a long time."

Several days passed before Lockhart and his friend could relax and accept that Frederick had been right. In the end, they learned something that he had known at least since he worked at Yar (where romantic dramas also unfolded regularly)—Russian police and other officials showed deference to anyone who had rank or social standing, and such deference could always be "reinforced by the concrete of hard cash." Frederick's years of experience as a waiter, valet, and maître d'hôtel before he took over Aquarium had made him an expert on reading his clients' desires and fears. By the summer of 1912, he had also become a master of all the written and unwritten rules of running a successful business in Moscow, a business that employed scores of people and entertained thousands every week.

The summer of 1912 was also when Frederick first became rich. In September, when the season was starting to wind down, a reporter managed to ferret out the final tally of how much Aquarium's partners had earned. It was a remarkable 150,000 rubles net profit, or the equivalent of about $1 million each in today's money. In less than a year, Frederick had launched himself on a trajectory that would scarcely have been imaginable to blacks, or to most whites for that matter, in Mississippi or anywhere else in the United States, and that put him into the first ranks of Russia's theatrical entrepreneurs.

From an American perspective, it is also nothing less than amazing that Frederick's race was never an issue as he rose to prominence in Moscow. Even the highly opinionated journalist "Gamma" made only a single, oblique reference to Frederick's skin color (and the other commentators in the Moscow press did not mention it at all). Gamma tried to be witty, invoking ancient Roman history and identifying "Mr. Thomas" with no less a figure than "Julius Caesar," adding that Frederick had "turned black" in Yar and "not in Gaul." The journalist's rather pretentious point was that Frederick's experience at Yar, where he perfected the skills that allowed him to "rule" in Aquarium, was similar to Caesar's conquest of Gaul, which preceded his becoming dictator of Rome. Frederick's "blackness" is thus neither an explicit racial category nor connected to his American past; it is, instead, a metaphor for superior experience and skill, as well as a simple identifying trait.

Around this time several Chicagoans visited Aquarium—which they characterized as "one of the institutions of Moscow"—and were so "astonished" by Frederick's "prosperous" and "diamond bedecked" appearance, as well as by the fact that his mixed-race children were "now at school in one of the leading academies of Russia," that they felt compelled to report their discovery to a local newspaper once they got home. Frederick also demonstrated to them one of the reasons for his success by charming them with his personal attention and reminiscences about their city, including the Auditorium Hotel, in which he had worked twenty years earlier. "Good evening, Mr. Blank," he said addressing each by name. "I can give you better tables if you will do me the honor of moving. How were things when you left Chicago?"

The success and sheer size of Aquarium might have seemed enough to keep Frederick busy, even with his two partners sharing the load. Running the place was also a year-round job, so that as soon as the first season was over he had to start preparing for the next one. In September 1912, he went on the road again, this time to the major Russian cities St. Petersburg, Kiev, and Odessa, to recruit new variety acts for the 1913 summer season. Simultaneously, he was also making plans to open a "Skating-Palace" on the Aquarium grounds that would operate during the colder weather.

But Frederick's ambitions reached farther than Aquarium. His first success had whetted his appetite for more. That fall, rumors began to circulate in Moscow's theater world that he was in discussions regarding a new business, one he would run by himself. The failure of a theater with an attached garden right in the city's center provided the target.

"Chanticleer" had just ended a disastrous season under the management of Stepan Osipovich Adel, an entrepreneur who was an old hand at running theaters into the ground and ruining his employees. When Frederick revealed that he was going to take it over, Muscovites in the entertainment business cheered the news. "This one plays for keeps," a magazine editor proclaimed about Frederick. "He'll know how to create a big, solid enterprise." In a vivid sign of how thoroughly Frederick had become assimilated into the city's life in personal and not just professional terms, a Moscow journalist declared that "F. F. Tomas" had become "our favorite." Several of these encomiums were accompanied by a flattering photograph: Frederick gazes at the viewer with calm self-possession, one arm resting comfortably on the crook of a walking stick; he sports a dapper hat, an elegant suit with a boutonniere, and a big bushy mustache.

Frederick decided to rename Chanticleer "Maxim" after the famous belle epoque restaurant in Paris (the name was popular for cafés chantants in cities throughout Europe), and immediately began to plan renovations. When Muscovites went to the theater in those days, no matter if it was to see serious performances of music and drama or light genres such as operetta, comedy, and vaudeville, they expected to feel that they had arrived somewhere out of the ordinary. Unabashed luxury was the norm (except at some artistically avant-garde theaters), and this meant elaborate displays of rich fabrics, gilt, soaring ceilings, glittering chandeliers, and ornate plaster decorations. Frederick did not stray from this formula, and by mid-October 1912 the interior of Maxim was ready and the list of performers complete. When the black Americans Duncan and Brooks saw the place in all its refurbished glory, they were struck by how everything in it was "gold and plush. When you went inside the door you would sink so deep in carpets that you would think that you would be going through to the cellar."

Anticipation among Moscow's pleasure seekers was high when advertisements announced the October 20 opening. One magazine even tried its hand at a jingle to capture the mood: "To Maxim's I will go/With friends to see the show." But a snag suddenly developed and forced Frederick to put off the opening for several weeks.

A complication that affected Maxim was the property's location at 17 Bolshaya Dmitrovka Street, between Kozitsky Lane and Glineshchevsky Lane: three churches were located nearby. (None of these survived the Soviet antireligious campaigns of the 1930s.) The Russian Orthodox Church saw theatrical performances as inherently frivolous and impious and therefore considered it highly improper to have theaters of any kind close to places of worship. Church hierarchs also insisted that theatrical performances throughout the city be suspended during major religious holidays, even if the theaters were nowhere near churches. Moscow's secular authorities generally sided with the church, although there was some flexibility in how and when religious policies were enforced. The previous entrepreneur, Adel, had faced difficulties and restrictions because of the surrounding churches during the few seasons he tried to run Chanticleer, and now it seemed that Frederick's turn had come.

In a case like this, everything depended on personal connections, deep pockets, or both. The Moscow city governor, Major General Aleksandr Aleksandrovich Adrianov, who also had a prestigious appointment at court in St. Petersburg as a member of His Imperial Majesty's Suite, was officially a pillar of the establishment. He supported the church zealously and at times ordered the Moscow police to prohibit theatrical performances during major Orthodox holidays. Frederick's desire to open a café chantant in the neighborhood of three churches thus potentially put him at odds with one of the most powerful officials in the city. But the fact that Frederick succeeded after only a brief delay, and that Maxim subsequently became one of the city's most successful and popular nightspots until the revolution, indicates that someone pulled strings on his behalf. In fact, rumors about this appeared in Moscow's press less than a year after Maxim opened. The "someone" was not named but was characterized as "influential" and as spending his nights "rather often" in Maxim until seven in the morning. This person was also rumored to be important enough that his activities were of some interest in St. Petersburg itself, which was beginning to look askance at the matter. This is the kind of situation that would have been kept strictly secret in imperial Russia, and there is no public evidence that city governor Adrianov himself was the influential person in question. Nevertheless, his involvement remains a possibility, as does that of someone else of high rank in the city administration, or in the police (the person in question was also clearly big enough not to be easily touchable).

Be that as it may, Frederick's problem was soon made to disappear, and when Maxim finally opened on November 8, 1912, it was a major event in Moscow nightlife. Crowds of people showed up—from well-known devotees of all such openings to regular folk looking for a new place to have fun—and marveled at how the interior was done up with "great luxury." In contrast to the somewhat more democratic Aquarium (although the gatekeepers there were actually still quite strict about whom they would let enter), in Maxim Frederick had decided to aim squarely at Moscow's moneyed classes. He stressed that it was a "first-class variety theater" with a "European program" and promised patrons "Light, Comfort, Air, Atmosphere, and a Bar"; the idea of being served fanciful mixed drinks at a counter was still a novelty in Russia in those days. After the variety show in the theater, patrons were invited to continue with a "cabaret"; there were also private rooms. The evenings began at 11 p.m.; the new establishment's focus was clearly on what was considered to be entertainment for sophisticated adults.

Maxim's location may have been problematic from the point of view of the church, but it was nothing if not brilliant in terms of visibility and public access. This was doubtless why Frederick went to the effort of working around the city's zoning policies rather than

looking for a property elsewhere. But he also had to show some ingenuity because of the kinds of shows he put on. Bolshaya Dmitrovka
Street is one of the spokes of the Moscow "wheel" radiating from the
Kremlin, and number 17 was, and is, only a fifteen-minute walk from
Red Square. It lies in the same district as the city's most celebrated
theaters of high culture, including the Moscow Art Theater—forever
associated with Chekhov's plays—and the Bolshoy Theater, one of
the great houses for classical ballet and grand opera in Europe. Given
this prominent neighborhood, Frederick realized that he would have
to find some way to tone down Maxim's reputation for putting on
risqué acts, but without abandoning them altogether.

The ruse he used was to throw a skimpy verbal veil over part
of his enterprise while advertising the rest openly. Not long after
the November debut, he began to place ads in which he announced
that Maxim was, of all things, a "family variety theater." But he also
made clear that after the variety program was over, patrons could
see the famous "Maxim cancan quartet" straight from the Moulin
Rouge in Paris. This made it seem as if husbands could bring their
wives to the earlier evening performances at Maxim without blush-
ing ("family" certainly did not mean children in this case), while
everything bawdy, such as the notorious Parisian kick line with its
raised skirts, yelps, and flaunted pantaloons, would appear onstage
only later.

There were even more risqué performances available, although
these were still very tame in comparison to what "adult" entertainment means today. Frederick created a "theme" space in Maxim, an
intimate and dimly lit "Salon Café Harem," as he called it. It tended
to attract mostly rich men, who reclined on low settees, smoking
Egyptian cigarettes or Manila cigars while sipping Turkish coffee
laced with Benedictine, and watched with sated eyes the bare midriffs
of Oriental "belly dancers" writhing on the carpeted floor.

However, even if the ads proclaiming Maxim to be a "family
variety theater" were sufficient to placate the authorities, who must

have watched Frederick's activities with eyes half shut, they did not fool everyone. One commentator with a professional interest in Moscow's nightlife thundered that this new café chantant was "shameless" and had reached "the heights of outrageous debauchery" right after its opening. He also heaped sarcastic praise on it for being as successful in fostering a "family" atmosphere as were some of the city's notorious public baths. And he concluded by wondering how a place such as Maxim could be allowed to exist when some smaller establishments, which were like "innocent infants" in comparison, were closed by the authorities.

This was an intentionally naive and provocative question; the only real mystery was whom exactly Frederick paid and what it cost him to be "allowed" to stay open. Was it enough to treat the "protector" in question to an occasional lavish evening on the house? Or did a fat envelope also have to change hands? As Frederick would demonstrate repeatedly in future years, he had no compunctions about circumventing laws and regulations to protect his interests, especially when it would have been naive, or out of step with the unwritten norms of the time, not to do so.

The extraordinary effort that Frederick expended that spring and early summer, when he was unable to get much sleep because Aquarium stayed open until dawn, must have weakened his resistance, and in June he fell ill with a severe case of pneumonia. For more than two weeks, he was bedridden at home and his life was at risk. Although he recovered, his lungs were weakened, and this condition increased his chance of contracting the dreaded disease again.

Frederick's illness was also an unhappy reminder of how his wife, Hedwig, had died from pneumonia two and a half years ago. This event had destabilized his family life in a way that he was still trying to resolve at the same time that he was launching the Skating Palace and Maxim in the fall of 1912. By then, Valli Hoffman had been the children's nurse for several years and, because Frederick was very busy, had primary responsibility for raising them.

It did not take Frederick long to see that the children had grown very attached to her; they even started calling her "Auntie." Her interest in him also became apparent. She was around thirty, an age that made her a spinster. Frederick was no longer young either, but he was a vigorous and attractive man who could be extremely charming. He had also become rich and showed every sign of becoming even more successful in the future. By contrast, and in light of how their relationship played out, what Frederick felt for her was probably just affection born of gratitude and familiarity. He may also have imagined that stabilizing his family's life by remarriage would let him focus even more intently on his expanding business affairs. Their wedding took place on January 5, 1913, in the Livonian Evangelical Lutheran Church in the town of Dünamünde on the outskirts of Riga, Valli's hometown. A commemorative photograph of the new family appears to capture the relations between them: she looks pleased, almost self-satisfied, whereas he seems thoughtful and wary.

Frederick now had the means for his family to live well. After returning to the city center from Petersburg Highway, he moved his household twice in the same neighborhood, not far from Aquarium, before finally settling into an impressive eight-room apartment (number 13) at 32 Malaya Bronnaya Street. This handsome, modern, six-story building, which towered over its neighbors, was built in 1912 and had been designed by a fashionable architect. Directly across the quiet street is a famous park called Patriarch's Ponds, which is to this day one of Muscovites' favorite spots. Frederick also did not skimp on educating his children. In Russia on the eve of World War I, even in a major city like Moscow, only about half of the children of elementary school age received any kind of education. The situation was far worse in the provinces, and although the quality and extent of public education were improving rapidly at the time, illiteracy was still widespread among the lower classes. People with means usually relied on private schools, and Moscow had several hundred to choose from—most quite small, judging by their total enrollment of only some seven thousand pupils. This is the path that Frederick chose. He could even have sent his children to one of the schools sponsored by foreign organizations, such as Catholics or Evangelical Lutheran Germans. All of his children learned a number of foreign languages in addition to Russian and two eventually attended universities in Western Europe; at home they spoke mostly Russian.

Frederick's businesses required so much attention that he spent little time with his children. Despite this, Mikhail, who was his father's favorite, recalled Frederick as a loving but very strict parent. One especially vivid event from his childhood was the time, when he was very young, his father tried to instill a sense of responsibility in him by staging a dramatic beating. Mikhail had falsely accused a servant of taking an apple that he had in fact eaten himself, and Frederick, wanting to teach his son a lesson, threatened to punish the servant even though he knew perfectly well who the culprit was. He went so far as to strike the old man several times. Mikhail not only confessed but remembered the lesson for the rest of his life.

The promise of familial stability that Frederick and Valli's wedding seemed to offer proved short-lived. In his role as the primary talent scout for Aquarium's variety acts, Frederick was constantly thrown into the company of attractive young women. Although the "casting couch" was hardly Hollywood's invention, and directors of Russian theaters and cafés chantants were to some extent procurers because they hired female performers with an eye toward having the women entertain male guests offstage as well as on, there is no evidence that Frederick ever abused the power he had over women, either in Moscow or later.

But true love was another matter. Around the time he married Valli, Frederick met a young, beautiful, sweet-tempered German woman named Elvira Jungmann. She was a dancer and singer who had enjoyed considerable success on the variety stages of Western Europe before she came to Moscow to perform. Her appeal and popularity were great enough to be celebrated in a series of publicity postcards issued around 1910 by the Georg Gerlach Company in Berlin, which was famous throughout Europe for producing reams of photographs of personalities from the world of entertainment for the fans who coveted and collected them. Some of Elvira's postcards were quite risqué for their time and depict a very pretty woman with luxuriant hair down to her buttocks wearing tights, dance slippers, and a form-fitting bodice that shows off her curvaceous figure and remarkably thin waist. But she appeared in other, more demure guises as well, including an American cowgirl costume for an act that she performed on Maxim's stage in 1912. This might seem very unlikely for Russia at the time, but Buffalo Bill Cody and his Wild West shows had in fact toured England and the Continent with great success at the end of the nineteenth century, and by the early twentieth cowboys, as well as Indians, were already very popular in Europe. Elvira was also better educated than one might have expected for a variety theater performer: in addition to her native German, she was fluent in English, knew French, and picked up Russian so well that some natives did not notice she was a foreigner. Less than a year after Frederick married Valli, his affair with Elvira was well under way. She gave birth to their first son, Frederick Jr., on September 10, 1914 (she would call him "Fedya," the diminutive endearment of "Fyodor"); a second son, Bruce, quickly followed in 1915. Even though they did not marry until 1918, Elvira embraced domesticity and became Frederick's loyal companion for the rest of his life, for better and especially for worse. The consequences of their affair would be dramatic and lasting for everyone in the family.

Neither the initial successes of Aquarium and Maxim nor the tensions in his personal life slowed Frederick's ambition to keep increasing the size and reach of his businesses. Starting in the early summer of 1913, rumors began to spread through Moscow's theatrical circles that the two most successful new entrepreneurs of the preceding winter and summer seasons, "F. F. Tomas and M. P. Tsarev," were planning a series of bold new business ventures. First, they bought out their third partner, Martynov, for 55,000 rubles, which would be more than $1 million today. Then, they reconstituted themselves as a two-man firm with the aim of bringing under one business umbrella the three properties they had been managing both separately and together—the Aquarium complex, Frederick's Maxim, and Tsarev's Apollo (a popular variety theater and restaurant in Petrovsky Park on the city's outskirts, near Yar). This move represented their first step in trying to become the biggest popular entertainment company in Moscow. The second one would come a year later, when they would incorporate themselves as the "First Russian Theatrical Stock Company," an innovative concept in Russian popular entertainment. When the financial details of the new company were announced in January 1914, they were impressive: total capitalization was 650,000 rubles, the equivalent of $12 million today, consisting of 2,600 shares priced at 250 rubles, or about $4,600, each. The new company's plans were equally ambitious, and included opening, both throughout the Moscow region and in other cities, new theaters for drama, opera, operetta, and movies—which were all the rage in Russia at this time, as they were everywhere else around the world. The new company would also include additional investors, a group of Moscow capitalists to whom Frederick and Tsarev would answer as elected directors. That the partners were able to find businessmen to provide the capital they needed to expand is testimony to their success in Moscow's money circles and to Frederick's complete acceptance by them. Had the Great War not intervened, they might well have succeeded.

* * *

As the fame of Frederick's properties spread, they became obligatory stops for foreign tourists, including even the occasional American who decided to add Russia to his European vacation. This is what attracted a pleasure seeker with the jazzy name Karl K. Kitchen, who identified himself as a "Broadwayite," and who was touring European capitals with the express purpose of sampling their nightlife during the winter of 1913–1914. When he came to Moscow, a Russian friend suggested that the first place they should visit was Maxim, which, Kitchen was pleased and surprised to learn, was "presided over by an American." He had no idea what was in store for him.

Kitchen's friend did not think it necessary to warn him about whom he was going to meet. And Kitchen's reaction after visiting Maxim is a reminder, if one were necessary, of why Frederick was never tempted to return to the United States.

"'Thomas's' is indeed presided over by an American," Kitchen recalled later, "and a blacker American I never saw in all my life":

> "Mr." Thomas is a "cullud" gentleman who came to Russia some years ago as a valet to a grand duke. His Highness took such a fancy to him that he started him in business, and to-day "Mr." Thomas is the proprietor of one of the largest and finest restaurant music-halls in Russia. He expressed himself as delighted to meet a New Yorker and offered to show us his establishment— which saved us ten roubles entrance fee.

As the owner and host at Maxim, Frederick was used to being part of the show. By claiming to have been a personal servant of a son or grandson of the tsar of all the Russias, Frederick was implying that he had been close to and richly rewarded by one of the most important men in the land. This was a far more intriguing story than that he had worked his way up from the restaurant floor, especially if he was telling it to a visiting white American whom it would be amusing to shock.

Frederick could not have failed to recognize the note of disapproval in Kitchen's reaction to him, which Kitchen preserved in his memoir by putting ironic quotation marks around "Mr." and by parodying Frederick's black southern accent. But Frederick remained genial throughout the visit, showing that as master of an impressive domain he could ignore slights from a white American who was ultimately of little consequence.

Kitchen, by contrast, was dazzled by the size of Maxim's building and especially its main restaurant, which he noted could seat several hundred people and was filling up even before the evening's performance had begun. He also found the crowd to be "stylishly dressed," although he quickly added that it was "far from distinguished in appearance." What he actually meant by this is that he disapproved of the mix of ethnicities that he saw. "'See that little feller over there,' said 'Mr.' Thomas, pointing to a short man with an Oriental cast of countenance. 'He's a Persian silk merchant—one of the best sports we have in Moscow; always orders champagne by the dozen and spends five or six hundred roubles every time he comes in here.'" For Frederick and the Muscovites, money and personal flair trumped ethnicity or race, with the glaring exception of Jews, as far as many Russians were concerned.

Whether Kitchen realized it or not, Frederick was not only showing off but also subtly rubbing Kitchen's face in his own bias. Surveying the stage in the café chantant, Frederick casually remarked, "The performance won't be very good to-night": "One of the grand dukes is givin' a party at his Moscow palace and I'm helpin' him out, jest as a friend. I've sent half my talent there, but I likes to help out these Russian gentlemen, especially if they is grand dukes. They is great sports and spend lots of money with me." These are the kinds of glittering connections that were bound to impress any tourist, and especially Americans who had no domestic equivalents to the mystery and glamour of royal "blood."

Frederick guided Kitchen through Maxim's other spaces as well, thus giving the visitor a good sense of how the establishment was designed to keep customers entertained and spending money all night long.

> The cabaret room was empty, "Mr." Thomas explaining that it did not open until 2.30 A. M. The tango room was also deserted —not until 2 A.M. would the first dance begin. There were forty or fifty people in the dimly lighted Turkish room, where a Hindu orchestra was playing, and as many in the American champagne bar, where only bubble stuff at thirteen and fourteen roubles ($6.50 and $7) a bottle is served.

This price would be several hundred dollars per bottle in today's money, so the Persian merchant must have spent thousands each time he visited. No wonder Frederick called him one of the best "sports" in the city.

Frederick's easy grace in dealing with a character like Kitchen reflects his self-assurance as well as the pleasure he took in his own success. But foreign tourists were not the only ones he attracted. Frederick was equally smooth when dealing with what he saw as the preposterous claims of someone who wanted a piece of his hard-won profits. Some of the problems he had faced, like the one involving church zoning, required effort and ingenuity; the one that followed was more like waving off a buzzing nuisance.

In December 1912, the Russian and French Societies of Dramatic Writers and Composers signed an agreement about intellectual property rights that was scheduled to take effect on October 30, 1913, just around the time when Frederick was rushing to reopen Maxim for his second winter season after rebuilding the interior. Previously, theater directors in Russia and France had done whatever they wanted with music and works created abroad. The new agreement was supposed to end unauthorized use and plagiarism. Because Parisian styles and fashions ruled in Russia at this time, the French had much to gain and were especially eager to have the agreement enforced with regard to one of their most valuable exports—popular music.

In Moscow, the agent of the French society was an energetic, fussy, but not very intelligent or successful Russian lawyer by the name of Grigory Grigoryevich Konsky. This was potentially a very lucrative assignment for him because the city had a good number of venues that performed a lot of the latest French music and because he would get a percentage of any royalties he managed to recover for his patrons. Konsky doggedly pursued Frederick over a five-year period. However, the prey proved to be much wilier than the hunter.

In early April 1913, five months before the agreement was even officially supposed to take effect and just when the summer season was starting, Konsky began to make the rounds of the prominent theaters and restaurants in Moscow where popular French music was usually performed. His first, exploratory conversation with Frederick, whom he approached as the most important member of the Aquarium partnership, did not go well. Frederick began by feigning inexperience. He pleaded that he was a novice at directing a variety theater and could not risk angering his partners by setting a precedent and being the first to pay royalties openly. He did not deny the validity of the French claims but suggested a cunning solution: perhaps the best way to handle the payments would be if he made them secretly and without signing a contract.

Konsky could not accept this offer because it amounted to subverting the international agreement by substituting cash under the table for legally mandated fees. Frederick had obviously decided that he could "play" with Konsky rather than pay him. He tried to shift Konsky's attention away from himself by suggesting that the lawyer should approach Aleksey Akimovich Sudakov (the well-known and respected owner of Yar and Frederick's former employer) to set the example of cooperating with the new law.

This ploy worked initially in distracting Konsky, but in the end he got nowhere with Sudakov either. Veteran entrepreneurs like Sudakov were accustomed to making free use of French music, plays, and operettas and naturally balked at suddenly having to pay for the right. Undaunted, and still following Frederick's advice to pursue someone prominent, Konsky next turned to Yakov Vasilyevich Shchukin, the owner of Hermitage Garden, Aquarium's rival. Shchukin initially agreed to pay something, but then abruptly changed his mind and put off paying, ostensibly because the spring season was cold, his garden was empty, and no money was coming in. Nonetheless, Konsky was very encouraged by the initial promise, and believing that his plan was working he went back to Frederick to ask him if he and his partners would sign a contract now that Shchukin was leading the way. As Konsky reported to his superior in St. Petersburg, "Thomas replied that given the importance and authority of Shchukin, Aquarium would negotiate without a doubt."

Frederick's response excited Konsky greatly because he thought that all the dominoes were lining up just as he had hoped. "You can imagine the effect this would produce!!!" he exulted. Konsky expected that he could get Frederick alone to pay the French society around 2,500 rubles a year (several tens of thousands in today's dollars), which would give him a commission of 200 to 300 rubles, the equivalent of several months of his regular income. He would receive more when the other owners paid up.

Konsky did not realize that he was still getting the runaround. The owners of the prominent Moscow establishments may have been competitors in some respects, but they also seem to have colluded with each other against the hapless lawyer. Despite the promises and assurances they gave him, they continued to play with him—changing their minds, setting new conditions, putting off meetings, making him run back and forth among them. Owners of some of the city's other theaters signed contracts and paid, as did some of their brethren in

St. Petersburg, but most of the biggest ones procrastinated, continued to bargain, or paid Konsky only a bit here and there.

By the end of the summer, the lawyer finally realized that it would "be impossible to come to an amicable agreement with Thomas." He explained to his employer that he had "exhausted all means" available to him and that he intended to take the steps necessary "to start a scandal"; later he escalated this threat, saying he would "start a war." Konsky's rhetoric betrays a personal and vindictive edge: in addition to still wanting the fees, of course, he clearly hoped that a big, noisy trial would punish Frederick for all the trouble he was causing.

By this point, Konsky understood that he was not dealing with a novice and described Frederick to his superior as "one of the premier restaurateurs not only in Moscow but in all of Russia"; he also noted that Maxim was actually doing bigger business than the venerable Yar. But realizing who his opponent was also unnerved Konsky. He saw that Frederick was not "afraid of a lawsuit," that it could take two or three years to mount the case against him, and that other owners in Moscow who were resisting making payments were probably taking their lead from Frederick. Nevertheless, Konsky continued to fuss and to scheme. He started gathering evidence for a lawsuit, sent Frederick notarized "cease and desist" orders, and even found a musician who had left Maxim on bad terms and who agreed to provide, for a fee, a list of all the French pieces that were being performed there.

All this also came to nothing and Frederick never paid Konsky a kopek. Then, in the summer of 1914, the Great War broke out and life in Russia and Europe began to change irrevocably. France and Russia were allies, but in the face of the vast historical storm that had begun, Konsky's little case faded over the next few years and eventually disappeared, together with the entire world that it represented. All that it produced is a paper trail, now preserved in a French archive, that provides an intriguing portrait of the indomitable Frederick Bruce Thomas in action.

*   *   *

Frederick's successful life in Moscow, and infrequent dealings with officials at the American consulate, made him immune to American racial politics. But he was not indifferent to the situation of blacks in the United States. In the fall of 1912, at the same time that he was making plans for Aquarium's second season and launching Maxim, he decided to bring a black man to Moscow who has been characterized as "the most famous and the most notorious African-American on Earth" during the early years of the twentieth century. "Jack" Johnson, the heavyweight boxing champion of the world, occupied the pinnacle of what was then one of the world's most popular spectator sports. Frederick's invitation to Johnson was not only a smart business move meant to attract customers to Aquarium during the slow winter season but also an extraordinary transcontinental attempt to extend a helping hand to a fellow black man who was in serious trouble, and whose career Frederick followed closely.

Born in 1878 to former slaves in Galveston, Texas, Johnson had won dozens of fights against black and white opponents by the early 1900s. He was clearly a contender for the world championship, but because of the color line in boxing, white champions initially refused to enter the ring against him. Johnson persevered and in 1908 demolished the white heavyweight champion Tommy Burns. American whites in particular were outraged by the result and began to howl for a "great white hope" to beat Johnson back down to the position that they believed his race was meant to occupy. This led to what came to be called the "fight of the century" on July 4, 1910, when Johnson destroyed James J. Jeffries, a racist white boxer who had retired as the undefeated heavyweight champion of the world six years earlier, and who reentered the ring "for the sole purpose of proving that a white man is better than a Negro," as contemporary accounts put it. The victory Johnson won against Jeffries was enormous in all respects. The winner's purse was $225,000, about $5 million in today's currency. Critics who had disparaged Johnson's previous wins were stunned into silence. When news of the victory reached blacks across the country, they poured into the streets in jubilation. The backlash from outraged and humiliated whites was swift: riots exploded in twenty-five states and fifty cities. The police intervened to stop several lynchings, but two dozen blacks and several whites died, and hundreds more were injured on both sides.

Johnson's prowess in the ring was not all that infuriated many white Americans. The boxer was a flamboyant showman who loved fine clothes, fast cars, and—what was most incendiary at the time— fast white women. When Jeffries failed to show Johnson his "proper" place, racist whites turned to the "law," which was their next best weapon during the Jim Crow era. On October 18, 1912, Johnson was arrested in Chicago because of his open affair with a nineteen-year-old white prostitute named Lucille Cameron. He was accused of violating the federal Mann Act of 1910, which banned the transportation of females across state lines "for immoral purposes." Johnson managed to escape a trial by marrying Lucille—the marriage prevented her from testifying against him—although this also led to renewed fury across the country and more energetic attempts to ruin him financially and to jail him.

Frederick first approached Johnson just a few days after he had been arrested, and this was no coincidence. A year earlier, Richard Klegin, an American promoter of sporting events in Europe, had tried to start a boxing club in Moscow with Frederick's help. At that time, the imperial government opposed the idea because Russia had never had Western-style prizefights before, and Klegin returned to the United States, but without giving up all hope. He left his proposal "in the hands of Mr. Thomas, owner of the Aquarium Gardens in Moscow," as an American newspaper phrased it, just in case the government's attitude changed. It did change around October 20, 1912, and the timing was perfect—so perfect, in fact, that it is tempting to speculate that Frederick may have had something to do with it. This was just two days after Johnson's arrest, an event that had been reported immediately in scores of newspapers around the United States and quickly picked up by the foreign press in Europe and elsewhere. Frederick cabled Klegin to tell him about the government's decision to allow boxing matches and to suggest that they organize "a great tournament" that would start in Moscow on January 1, 1913. It would last a week, and the final "battle" for the heavyweight championship would be between Johnson and Sam McVey, a black American heavyweight then popular in Europe. All the bouts would be held at Aquarium, which could make arrangements to seat ten thousand spectators. Klegin, in turn, immediately wired Johnson's manager with a concrete offer from Aquarium: this included a certified check for $5,000, three round-trip tickets to Russia, a chance to win a $30,000 purse in a match against McVey, and one-third of the proceeds from the film that would be made of the fight. In today's money, all this would be a very nice deal—an up-front fee of around $150,000; another $750,000 if Johnson won, as was expected; and even more from the film. The offer caused a sensation in the United States, and newspapers from coast to coast publicized it because of Johnson's notoriety and celebrity, the large sums involved, and the remote and exotic locale. Newspapers also noted that the offer came from Aquarium's black American proprietor, who was described not altogether accurately as a "negro named Thomas" from Chicago. Johnson quickly accepted and announced that he was anxious to go to Moscow. Thanks to Frederick, Russia was now beckoning to Johnson as a refuge from American racism.

However, despite repeated efforts, Johnson was unable to leave the United States until the summer of 1913, so Frederick was forced to postpone all his grand plans. Johnson then toured several other European cities for close to a year before finally arriving in Russia in mid-July 1914. When he did meet Frederick, they hit it off right away: "Thomas and myself became close friends and we made our headquarters in his park," Johnson recalled. The two black men had similar origins and had triumphed in two very different white worlds. They shared another similarity as well. As Johnson illustrated vividly in his memoirs, both were fond of tall tales that enhanced their present or embroidered their past and that underscored the extent to which both were showmen.

> As the war approached, our host [Frederick] became engrossed in Russian war preparations, for he was a factor of some importance in Russian political and commercial circles. He was a confidential agent of Czar Nicholas, and I was greatly surprised to learn that he was taking part in military councils and other phases of the war preparations. High military officers made their headquarters at hotels and restaurants in his park [Aquarium] and it was while I, members of my party, and several army officers were dining together in one of these restaurants that we learned that war had become a reality. As we sat at the table some of my military friends were summoned to the telephone, told that war had been declared, and instructed immediately to join their units for hurried mobilization.

This is mostly fiction with a sprinkling of fact, and it is difficult to disentangle Johnson's inventions from Frederick's. There is no doubt that army officers liked spending time in Aquarium, drinking champagne, and ogling the chorus girls, and that some would also have enjoyed meeting and dining with the black American champion. There is also no doubt that Frederick had acquaintances among influential Russian businessmen and, possibly, politicians. But although Frederick may have been known and liked by such men because he was a genial and broad-minded host, he was certainly not a confidential agent of the tsar or a player in the Russian political arena (also, there were no hotels in Aquarium, just living quarters for some of the staff).

Johnson's career might have developed quite differently if Frederick's plans for him in Russia had been realized. Johnson had run a successful saloon in Chicago, the Café de Champion, before he was run out of town. Nothing prevented him from doing the same in Moscow, perhaps with Frederick as a partner, and without any of the problems that continued to dog him when he was touring Western Europe, or that resurfaced after he returned to the United States. It is regrettable that he and Frederick were unable to spend more time together, but by the end of July 1914 the world around them was about to go mad.

When war was declared on August 1, 1914, Johnson realized that if he stayed in Moscow, he would be cut off from the rest of Europe by the fighting that was about to break out along Russia's long border with the German and Austro-Hungarian empires. Frederick helped him to leave in a hurry, although Johnson had to abandon much of his luggage on the way. But he did not forget Frederick and managed to keep track of his friend from a distance, through the maelstrom of Russia's collapse in the Bolshevik Revolution of 1917 and Frederick's hairbreadth escape to Constantinople in 1919.

5

Becoming Russian

For fifteen years, Frederick had lived in a kind of charmed circle in Russia that allowed his talents to develop largely unaffected by strikes; assassinations; executions; the revolutionary turmoil that convulsed the country in the aftermath of the war with Japan; or the arrests, pogroms, and repression that followed. Even when the forces of history took on flesh and blood in Moscow's streets, Frederick could stand on the threshold of his music- and laughter-filled world, his arms open in welcome to the crowds seeking respite inside. Money was all one needed to enter Aquarium and Maxim, and no matter what was going on outside there were always people who had enough. It is a paradox that the politically unstable and depressing period in Russia after the war with Japan was also marked by rapid improvements in industry, agriculture, and the economy in general. More people were making more money than at any other time in Russian history. Before the summer of 1914, there was no reason for Frederick to think that this would ever change.

On June 28, 1914, in Sarajevo, the capital of Bosnia, a small Balkan state that was part of the Austro-Hungarian empire, a teenage Serbian member of the Black Hand terrorist organization assassinated the heir to the Hapsburg throne, Archduke Francis Ferdinand, and his wife. The assassin, Gavrilo Princip, believed that he had struck a blow against Austrian domination of the South Slavic peoples. In fact, his pistol shots set off a new kind of war that would engulf Europe as well as parts of Asia and Africa; draw in the United States; and destroy the German, Austro-Hungarian, Turkish Ottoman, and Russian empires. Millions of lives would be lost and irrevocably changed in a dozen countries, including Frederick's in distant Moscow.

In 1914 the major European powers were entangled in two alliances that pitted the Central Powers—Austria-Hungary and Germany—against the Triple Entente: France, Great Britain, and Russia. On July 28, one month after the archduke's assassination, the Austro-Hungarian empire declared war on Serbia, claiming that the Serbian response to a harsh ultimatum had been unsatisfactory. Russia automatically backed Serbia for a reason that was largely sentimental —a belief that the two countries shared the same "blood and faith." Germany then declared war on Russia on August 1 and on France on August 3. On August 4, after Germany invaded Belgium while attacking France, Britain declared war on Germany. On August 23, Japan entered the war on the side of the Entente, and on October 29, the Ottoman Empire attacked Russia. Italy joined the Entente in 1915, as did the United States in 1917. The world had never before seen a war that was as vast, destructive, and unnecessary.

Within two weeks of the war's beginning Frederick made the fateful decision to step out of his charmed circle. The way he chose to do this not only was remarkable in itself but may have been unprecedented in the experience of black Americans in Russia: he asked to become a subject of the tsar. Frederick did so in response to several threats that rose around him when the war began and that he could not have avoided by continuing to maintain his purely paper-based American citizenship. In the short term, his dramatic action would succeed and he would prosper for several more years. But he could not have foreseen that his decision would rebound upon him later, when he was most vulnerable and the threats against him were far more serious.

On August 2/15, 1914, Frederick composed a petition to the minister of internal affairs in St. Petersburg requesting citizenship for himself and his family. (The imperial capital would soon be renamed Petrograd because the original name, which was actually derived from the Dutch, sounded too "Germanic" to Russian ears newly sensitized by war.) This petition was first vetted by the governor-general of Moscow, Major General Adrianov, and then forwarded by him to the minister on December 19, 1914. Adrianov would certainly have heard of Frederick's role in Moscow's nightlife, and probably knew him personally. He sent the petition off with the necessary supporting documents and a cover note in which he referred to the petitioner as "Fridrikh Brus (Fyodor Fyodorovich) Tomas," a "negro citizen of the North American United States," and added, "There is no opposition on my part toward the satisfaction of Tomas' petition." (Probably for reasons of cultural inertia, Adrianov had automatically converted "Frederick" into its Germanic form, "Friedrich," which was more familiar to him.)

Frederick's petition is such an unusual document that it deserves to be quoted in full. In the heading, he refers to himself in a way that underscores his hybrid identity—"Fyodor Fyodorovich Tomas (Frederick Bruce Thomas), citizen of the United States of America." He then signs the document with his American name transliterated into the Russian alphabet. An English translation cannot do full justice to all the bowing and scraping in the original.

> Your Excellency, I have the honor to humbly address a request to You:
> To most loyally petition His Imperial Majesty the All-Russian Sovereign Emperor about accepting me and my family into Russian citizenship. I have been living in Moscow for 17 years and

have become so accustomed to everything Russian and grown to love Russia and Her Monarch so much that I would carry with great pride the exalted title of Russian subject.

I am married to a Russian and my children study in Russian schools.

I attach a permit issued by the Office of the Moscow Governor General and my national American passport.

Moscow, 1914, August 2.

Frederik Brus Tomas

One clear way of measuring how far Frederick had traveled in his life is to juxtapose his avowal of love for Russia and its tsar with his birth on a farm amid the roadless forests, swamps, and cotton fields of Hopson Bayou, Coahoma County, Mississippi.

Frederick's reference to having lived in Moscow for "17 years" is off by two, and is typical of other inaccuracies and inventions in the documents that accompanied his petition to the minister of the interior. The heart of the petition is a form on which he had to provide answers to a series of questions that were then certified by the superintendent of police in the district where he lived. Here Frederick told the truth when necessary, exaggerated where possible, and burnished his past when he could get away with doing so. An example is his claim that he spoke and read Russian well, which was only a half-truth; although he could communicate readily in Russian, he made many grammatical mistakes. To enhance his education, he replied that he had completed studies at "an agricultural school" in Chicago. Presumably, this sounded better than saying he had worked as an errand boy, a waiter, or a valet.

The notoriously inefficient Russian bureaucracy revolved around the all-powerful tsar and moved sluggishly at the best of times; it slowed even more after the war began and numerous problems accumulated on the front lines and in the rear. It took until May

2, 1915, for the minister of the interior to send all the new petitions for citizenship (there were only 112) to the Imperial Council of Ministers. After the council approved them on May 14, they were presented to the tsar at his summer palace in Tsarskoe Selo outside Petrograd. The following day, Nicholas II wrote on the document—in blue pencil—"Agreed." Frederick had officially become Russian on May 15/28, 1915. His race had been mentioned several times in the paperwork but it never became an issue.

Despite Frederick's seeming candor, his application was a calculated and well-timed move with a hidden agenda. On June 24/July 7, 1914, about five weeks before he filed his petition and four days before Princip fired the shots in Sarajevo, Frederick had gone to the American consulate in Moscow to renew passports for himself and his "official" family—Valli and the three children by Hedwig—because the ones he received in 1912 had recently expired. Frederick of course signed the renewal application, as he had always done before, despite its statement that he was only "sojourning" in Moscow "temporarily" and that he intended to return to the United States "in two years." In other words, when international affairs in Europe seemed relatively normal, Frederick saw no reason to change his nationality. It was not until a month later, after war had been declared and its consequences for him became apparent, that he suddenly discovered his "love" for Russia and the tsar (although there is every reason to believe that by 1914 he had indeed gotten very "accustomed to everything Russian"). If there had been no war, Frederick would have continued to live and work in the special space that he had found for himself between the real Moscow and his "virtual" American citizenship.

Frederick made other evasions as well, and one was especially daring. At the same time that he sought the protection of Russian citizenship for one set of reasons, he tried to conceal what he was doing for another. The maneuvering this necessitated between his

purely personal interests and his prominent role as a Moscow entrepreneur could not have been easy. His duplicity would remain
hidden to this day from everyone except, presumably, Elvira; possibly Olga; and the author of this book. The Thomas family's oral
history does not allude to the matter, and this implies that even his
oldest son, Mikhail (who later modified the spelling of the surname
to "Thomass"), did not know about it.

Frederick concealed from the American authorities that he had
decided to become a Russian citizen. The Moscow governor-general's
office and the Russian Imperial Ministry of the Interior did not inform the Americans either. As a result, neither the American consulate general in Moscow nor the embassy in Petrograd nor the State
Department in Washington, D.C., ever found out that Frederick
Bruce Thomas had officially expatriated himself. This would have
two remarkable consequences. Four years later, in Odessa, during
what were some of the most perilous days of his life, he would be
able to save himself and his family by concealing that he had formally
surrendered his American citizenship. And in 1931, three years after
his death, his two youngest sons, who were born in Russia, would be
recognized as Americans on the strength of their father's (nonexistent)
American citizenship and only because the State Department did not
know that he had given it up in Moscow.

Another extraordinary move on Frederick's part is that he concealed his Russian citizenship from his wife Valli. On July 27, 1916,
well over a year after Frederick and his three oldest children had been
accepted into the Russian fold, Valli applied to renew her American
passport, which had been issued in July 1914. Her application was
approved and she was informed that she had been "duly entered on
the Consular register, and that her national passport has been forwarded to the Department of State at Washington to be substituted
by a fresh one." Valli could not and would not have done this if she
had known that Frederick had expatriated himself because, as she
realized, her American citizenship was entirely dependent on his.

The attestation that Valli received from the consulate in 1916 also corroborates that the American authorities did not know Frederick was a Russian citizen. Valli's application underscores as well that Frederick had effectively abandoned Irma, who is listed on the form as Valli's "daughter" (in future years, Irma would refuse even to talk about her father).

Why would Frederick have bothered to apply for Russian citizenship? Against his will and despite his best efforts to resist such things, he had been swept up by a new, European stream of history and had to defend himself from its consequences as best he could. When Austria-Hungary began to menace Serbia in July 1914, Russia responded with an explosive mixture of patriotism and belligerence. In Moscow on the nights of July 14/27 and 15/28, for example, demonstrations broke out in several central locations, with thousands of people repeatedly singing the Russian imperial anthem, "God Save the Tsar," demanding that it be played over and over again by orchestras and bands summoned out of restaurants; shouting "Long live Russia and Serbia"; and angrily denouncing Austria-Hungary and Germany. When on the first night large crowds started heading toward the consulates of both countries with the intention of demonstrating their defiance more forcefully, mounted police intervened to prevent it. Within a year, however, hatred of the Central Powers grew to such an extent that when anti-German riots broke out in Moscow, the police did nothing to stop them and German nationals began to be rounded up and expelled from the city.

For as long as he had lived in Moscow, Frederick had numerous and close family connections to Germans and Germany. His ties were hardly an exception, however. Baltic Germans were numerous in European Russia and played a major role in all aspects of the empire's life, especially the civil service and the military. Economic, cultural, and political ties among Russia, Germany, and Austria-Hungary had also been long-lived and extensive. In 1913, almost half of all foreign goods imported into Russia were German and 30 percent of Russian exports went to Germany. Perhaps the most visible embodiment of Russian ties to Germany was Alexandra—the tsaritsa, or empress— who, like a number of her predecessors, was born a German princess. All such associations became poisonous after August 1, as did the tsaritsa herself: her loyalty to Russia would become deeply suspect during the war. Frederick's decision to take Russian citizenship would thus go a long way toward defusing possible accusations of Germano-philia (and he would start claiming Elvira was Swedish).

Simultaneously with filing his petition for citizenship, Freder-ick began to take part in extravagant public expressions of Russian patriotism. At the end of August 1914 (N.S.), news reached Moscow of a major battle taking shape in East Prussia between massed Rus-sian and German forces. Named "Tannenberg" by the Germans, it ended several days later with the utter destruction of two Russian armies and the suicide of one of the disgraced commanders. Fred-erick and Tsarev responded to the unfolding events by organizing a benefit evening at Aquarium on August 16/29, with all the proceeds from the garden's entry fees and sales of theater tickets going to the wounded, thousands of whom were starting to pour into Moscow and other cities in the Russian heartland. Publicity from evenings like this earned Frederick a lot of goodwill.

Nightlife in Moscow went on, although nothing about it could remain quite the same against the background of the Great War, which kept unfolding with grim relentlessness. On the Russian front, the fighting took on a character very different from how it was being conducted in the West. After an initial, rapid, wheeling advance through Belgium into France in August and early September of 1914, the Germans were stopped just thirty-five miles outside Paris. It was the fatal Russian incursion into East Prussia, ending in the Battle of Tannenberg, that had helped save the French capital. Thereafter, for much of the rest of the war, the western front congealed into brutal trench warfare with relatively little movement but hecatombs of deaths along a curved line that ran from the English Channel to Switzerland. In the east, the war was more wide-ranging and mobile, and even more bloody. After Tannenberg, in early September 1914, Russian armies four hundred miles to the south attacked the Austro-Hungarian province of Galicia, seized an important fortress, laid siege to another, and captured over a hundred thousand prisoners. For much of the war, this province would be the site of massive retreats and advances by both sides, with horrific losses every time the scythe of war changed the direction of its swing.

However, not all evidence of the war's carnage came from dispatches about events hundreds of miles away. As the mobilization of Russia's enormous army grew—it would eventually reach 15 million men—actors and other theater workers in Aquarium, Maxim, and other venues began to be called up. Men in military uniforms appeared everywhere in Moscow—on the streets, in theaters, and on streetcars. Refugees escaping the battles on the empire's western frontier started to arrive as well; masses of the wounded filled hospitals and clinics; trainloads of Austrian prisoners of war passed through to points farther east.

But the biggest change for those in businesses like Frederick's was prohibition. Although never announced as the official law of the land, as it was in the United States in 1920, Russia's "dry law" began as a series of restrictions on sales of alcoholic beverages during mobilization leading up to the war and ended with the tsar's "wish" that the sale of alcoholic beverages be stopped throughout the empire for the war's duration. The actual regulation of sales was left to the discretion of local governments, although all of them rapidly signed on. Moscow was the first to restrict sales by restaurants in accordance with their classification; then came Petrograd, and finally the rest of the country.

At first, the effects appeared to be dramatic. Some Russian and foreign observers concluded that the country's population had genuinely embraced sobriety. The army's mobilization seemed to take half the expected time because the recruits were not drunk when they showed up, as they had been during the war with Japan. "Drunkenness vanished in Russia," proclaimed the *New York Tribune*; "there never has been anything like it in the history of the world," reported an excited Englishman living in Moscow; "one of the greatest reforms in the history of the world," exclaimed another. The Russian Duma, or parliament, received an official request from the United States Senate for information about the practice of prohibition, and an American delegation traveled all the way to the provincial city of Samara to investigate matters there.

But—as Grand Prince Vladimir of Kiev is reported to have proclaimed as far back as the tenth century—"Russia's joy is to drink," and the old habits quickly reasserted themselves. The highly unpopular ban quickly dissolved in an ocean of evasion, corruption, and bootlegging, just as it would in the United States a few years later. With his decade and a half of experience in Moscow's restaurants, cafés, and bars, Frederick would not have been surprised.

Russians began to take steps to avoid the restrictions even before they were fully in place. In mid-November 1914, for example, an American in Petrograd saw thousands of men, women, and even children lining up outside liquor shops as early as 4 a.m. during a driving snowstorm because that was the last day when they could buy wine and beer before prohibition took effect. In Moscow after prohibition, residents had only one legal method of obtaining any alcoholic beverage, whether it was vodka or wine—with a doctor's prescription, in a limited amount, and one time only. However, what was supposed to be a controlled trickle soon became a flood as the "medicinal" spigot was wrenched open by bribes; illegal stills and moonshine production began to proliferate as well.

If you had money and knew where to go in Moscow, you could buy anything. Frederick's well-heeled clients expected nothing but the best, and it was his ability to satisfy them during prohibition that made him a millionaire several times over in the short span of three years. In upscale places like Aquarium and Maxim, the owner's normal practice was to pay off the police officials in charge of enforcing the ban on liquor sales. Such bribes could be substantial. For example, a certain Richard Fomich Zhichkovsky, the police superintendent in the district where Aquarium was located, and whose palm Frederick doubtless greased, accumulated enough money to be able to buy an automobile for the two mistresses he had, as well as a pair of horses and a two-seater motorcycle.

Some eating and drinking establishments in Moscow took the trouble to maintain outward appearances by serving alcoholic beverages in pitchers or in bottles that had originally held fruit drinks and mineral water. Waiters also brought vodka to the table in teapots, and clients drank it out of porcelain cups. But other restaurants flouted the law and sold everything openly. Because of shortages, prices skyrocketed and bootlegging became highly profitable. In 1915, a bottle of French champagne in a fancy café chantant could cost as much as $1,000 in today's money. The sale of vodka had been a Russian government monopoly prior to prohibition, earning the imperial treasury enormous sums. Part of these huge profits also started to pour into private hands as distillers now sold their bootleg vodka at several thousand percent over the cost of the raw ingredients, and with no government middleman. Even Nicholas II was reputed to have ignored the prohibition he initiated and continued to enjoy his cognac with lemon, although, in a concession to the times, when he and members of his retinue visited the front, they eschewed crystal glasses for silver cups.

The result of this freewheeling atmosphere was that a year after the war began, word spread in Moscow that Frederick was enjoying an "unheard of success" in Aquarium and "harvesting laurels and silver rubles" in "colossal" amounts. What made this possible, in spite of the soaring prices of drink, was the new money that appeared in Russia because of the war and the new, frenzied atmosphere of Moscow's nightlife. As soon as mobilization began, well-soaked send-offs for officers became obligatory in the better restaurants. Such occasions, with bravura regimental marches booming from the orchestras, were clearly not the time to skimp on toasts to the victory of Russian arms over the "hordes of Teutonic barbarians." Later, as reports of appalling losses began to accumulate, a nervous and febrile note crept into such celebrations, but they also became more urgent.

As the war ground on, new sorts of moneyed clients started to appear in the fashionable and expensive establishments as well. Some were in the military, although they were "heroes" of the home front rather than of the front lines—quartermasters who had successfully skimmed tidy sums from the torrents of supplies that passed through their hands; military doctors who sold exemptions from the draft to the sons of rich families. And then, as in all wars, there were swarms of businessmen making money hand over fist from contracts to supply the army with everything from boots and canned meat to high explosives. Maxim especially reconfirmed its status during these years as "The Favorite Place of Muscovites," a slogan that Frederick adopted in his numerous advertisements.

In January 1915, in the dead of a bitterly cold winter, Muscovites' attention became riveted on another massive swing of the scythe of war in Galicia. The Austro-Hungarian armies launched a counteroffensive in the Carpathian Mountains against Russian forces. However, the attack failed miserably and by March the advancing Russians had captured the enormous fortress Przemyśl, thus potentially aligning their armies for a march through the mountain passes toward Budapest and Vienna, the twin capitals of the Hapsburg Empire.

There were also dramatic events to the south that Muscovites followed with a mix of anxiety and excitement. A second front had opened for Russia at this time, in the Caucasus Mountains and on the Black Sea. The Ottoman Empire was an old enemy that had recently allied itself with the Central Powers. Two months after the war began, Turkish warships shelled cities on the south coast of Russia, including Odessa. The great prize that beckoned in this part of the world was Constantinople. If Russia could take this ancient city, to whose Byzantine Christian past the Russians felt a visceral tie, it would have free passage from the Black Sea through the Turkish Straits to the Mediterranean, and from there to all the oceans of the world. (In fact, in a secret treaty planning the partition of the Ottoman Empire after the war, France and Great Britain formally promised Constantinople and the Straits to Russia.)

Muscovites responded to the news from both fronts with an outpouring of patriotic generosity. In early February, leaders of the city's theaters organized a campaign they called "For the Russian Army, from the Artists of Moscow." Frederick played a visible role in the weeklong series of benefit concerts and performances to collect gifts for the troops, and Maxim was mentioned prominently in the press. The campaign began with a solemn prayer service in the enormous, white marble Christ the Savior Cathedral south of the Kremlin. (Stalin dynamited it in 1931, using much of its decorative stone to line the walls of Moscow's new subway stations; it was not rebuilt until 2000.) The week ended with a gala show in the Great Hall of Moscow's Nobility Club, located on Bolshaya Dmitrovka Street near the Bolshoy Theater, during which performers from all of Moscow's theaters and circuses appeared onstage. The campaign was a resounding success and won the actors and the theaters that sponsored them a great deal of public appreciation.

Frederick would need this and any other goodwill he accumulated when two months later he got into trouble with the city authorities. In April 1915 Maxim was shut down, ostensibly for letting in Moscow high school students and law students from Petrograd. As in the case of selling alcoholic beverages despite prohibition, there was too much profit to be made to take age and other legal restrictions overly seriously: fines and closures were often just the cost of doing business. Frederick certainly did not break stride because of the temporary problems with Maxim, whose winter season was coming to an end anyway. Rather, as a journalist reported, he continued to "prepare energetically" for Aquarium's summer season, which was only a few weeks away. The coming spring was also heralded by a joyous event in his personal life—the birth on April 25 of his and Elvira's second son, whom they gave his father's middle name, Bruce.

However, other threats loomed. Frederick's prominence and success attracted not only greedy officials looking to wet their beaks but also envious competitors who wanted to humble and hurt him. That same April Frederick came under attack from Andrey Z. Serpoletti (whose real surname was Fronshteyn). He was the pugnacious editor of a Moscow theatrical journal, also a variety stage satirist, and was always looking out for the interests of his fellow performers— as well as for opportunities to settle scores with old enemies. He complained that directors of variety theaters were adding to their soaring profits from illegal liquor sales by cutting the salaries of the actors they hired and targeted Frederick specifically, making fun of his broken Russian.

If this initial attack of Serpoletti's was relatively mild, the one he initiated a year later was dangerous, especially in the intensely xenophobic atmosphere that had developed in Moscow by that time. What Serpoletti wrote in the guise of a malevolent short story is also the only unequivocal attack that Frederick was subjected to *as* a black man in Russia. However, it is noteworthy that even in this case he was not attacked primarily *for* being black.

Trying to be witty, Serpoletti first throws some silly camouflage over Frederick's name and business, and then provides an encoded summary of Frederick's biography, which he obviously knows well. This "citizen," as Serpoletti pointedly calls him, who was "despised" in his native "Egyptian Colonies" (these are allusions to Frederick's application, his African blood, the status of blacks in the United States, and the nation's origin as English colonies), came to Russia from Paris as a lackey; "got fat" on Russian bread; benefited from Russians' good nature; made a lot of money; and became a captain in a restaurant, a maître d'hôtel, and finally the owner of an entertainment garden. Serpoletti's main point is that despite such humble origins and "undeserved" success—which Serpoletti bitterly envied—Frederick "puts on airs because of his position" and assumes a "negro-dully-arrogant" ("negrityanski-tuponadmenno") attitude toward Russian artists, whom, moreover, he calls "pigs." Then comes Serpoletti's final, vicious thrust—an accusation that was as dangerous to make in Russia during World War I as was calling someone a "communist" in the United States in the 1950s: Frederick is "great pals with foreigners in general and with Germans in particular." Despite all this scaffolding, the reason for Serpoletti's animus is clear: Frederick supposedly preferred to hire foreign performers for Aquarium and Maxim rather than native Russians (including Serpoletti and his protégés).

Frederick successfully countered this accusation by continuing to demonstrate his Russianness at every opportunity, to the extent of assuming a leading role in a grand patriotic demonstration that began in Moscow on May 19, 1915, just a few days after his application for citizenship had been approved. This was a momentous time in the Russian conduct of the war. A German advance in Galicia inflicted huge Russian casualties, and a retreat that had been orderly at first degenerated into a "mad bacchanalia" all along the front, with troops fleeing their positions and hundreds of thousands of civilian refugees also streaming east. The combined German and Austro-Hungarian advance lasted five months. By October 1915, the Russian armies not only had lost everything they had won but had been pushed back one hundred miles and forced out of what had been Russian Poland since the end of the eighteenth century.

In Moscow toward the end of May, however, the full extent of the developing catastrophe was still not clear and, in an atmosphere of buoyant patriotism, the Moscow Red Cross planned a three-day event that was named "Tobacco for the Soldier." May 19 began with several thousand actors and other performers from variety theaters across the city gathering in Aquarium's garden, which Frederick and Tsarev had made available as a staging area. Participants formed into a long parade and left the grounds at 4 p.m., heading down Tverskaya Street toward the Kremlin. Leading the procession were actors from Aquarium riding in decorated wagons and dressed in the national costumes of the countries of the Entente. Then came numerous other groups, vehicles, and floats. Participants numbered in the thousands and attracted huge crowds.

As the lead elements of the parade began to enter Red Square, an outdoor prayer service led by a bishop assisted by a multitude of priests began at Lobnoye Mesto—a raised, circular stone platform traditionally used for imperial proclamations. The icon of the Iberian Mother of God—long venerated by Muscovites as "wonder-working"—was brought from its nearby chapel to the platform, as were other icons and religious banners from St. Basil's Cathedral a few dozen yards away. Wounded soldiers from Moscow's hospitals gathered around, accompanied by their nurses. The remainder of the vast square between the soaring redbrick walls of the Kremlin and the ornate facade of the Upper Trading Arcades filled with tens of thousands of people—the men's heads bared; women on tiptoes straining to see, some holding their children up—while the bishop, priests, and deacons intoned prayers for the army's valiant warriors, for the emperor and his "august family," for all faithful Russian Orthodox Christians during this time of dreadful travail. A reverent hush spread over the crowd. The gold brocade raiments of the churchmen gleamed in the afternoon sun as wisps of sweet incense wafted from their swinging censers and the hymns of the deep-voiced male choir rose, fell, and rose again. At the end of the service, the enormous crowd broke into singing "God Save the Tsar" and repeated it over and over again. The actors from Aquarium who had led the parade stayed together as a group by the monument to Minin and Pozharsky, two seventeenth-century Russian national heroes in the war to liberate Moscow from the Poles.

After the service, the parade returned to the Aquarium garden, with the troupe of its actors again leading the way. That evening and during the next two days, special performances to benefit the soldiers took place in theaters all over the city; hundreds of volunteers also took up collections on the streets, in stores, and in restaurants. Frederick and Tsarev themselves worked the crowds in Aquarium with collection cups in hand and were singled out for special praise several times in newspaper and magazine reports.

A native son of Russia could not have done more to demonstrate his loyalty. Frederick's actions were seen by hundreds if not thousands of Muscovites and were known to many more, including the city's leading citizens. He had also inscribed himself convincingly in the tradition of philanthropy for which Moscow merchants and businessmen were famous throughout Russia. Whatever vengeful designs Serpoletti might have had against the black former American could not pierce the armor of goodwill that Frederick created around himself.

Frederick demonstrated his Russianness with uncannily accurate timing; a week later Muscovites revealed the inevitable other face of patriotic fervor—hatred of the enemy and paranoia regarding outsiders. For many, the calamitous retreat of Russian forces in Galicia seemed inexplicable without sabotage or treason on the home front. Anti-German and then broadly antiforeign riots erupted in the city in late May. Hundreds of stores were sacked and entire streets were set ablaze. One horrified Englishman recalled seeing grand pianos being pushed out of the fourth-floor windows of Zimmermann's famous music store on Kuznetsky Most, Moscow's toniest shopping street, and crashing to the sidewalk with a doleful ringing sound as pages of sheet music swirled in the air like flocks of white birds. Some of the mobs swarmed partway up Tverskaya Street, which led to Aquarium. The financial and social costs of the riots were huge: damage was estimated at what would be about $1 billion today. There was also a heavy political cost: the mostly lower-class rioters had gotten a taste of taking the law into their own hands and using street violence to show their frustration with the government's conduct of the war. Few observers realized it at the time, but Moscow's "anti-German" pogrom was a harbinger of far worse things to come.

By the first anniversary of the war, Frederick and his adopted homeland were starting to move in different directions. Russia had lost a million men killed or wounded and another million captured; all evidence showed that the country had been woefully unprepared for a war of this length and magnitude. Blundering through historical events that he could not understand, much less control, Nicholas II in September 1915 dismissed the army's commander in chief, Grand Duke Nicholas, who was not only a professional soldier but his uncle. The tsar assumed command of all the Russian forces himself, even though he had no military experience. Elsewhere, the British attempt to support and resupply Russia by forcing the Turkish Straits and opening a passage to the Black Sea ended in disaster. In one of the many ironies of the time, a hero of the Turkish defense at Gallipoli was Colonel Mustafa Kemal, later to become the savior of his country and arbiter of Frederick's fate.

But Frederick remained unaffected by these problems and was making so much money that he began to search for new ways to invest it. His vehicle of choice was real estate. During the summer of 1915, news had begun to spread that the Ciniselli Circus in Petrograd was going to be put up for auction. This was an exciting possibility, because for all of Moscow's economic and cultural importance, it was still the country's second city. Ciniselli Circus was a prestigious and potentially very lucrative venue. It was the oldest permanent building of its kind in Russia as well as one of the most famous in all of Europe. It was also very popular with the cream of Petrograd society, from the imperial family on down.

The auction was scheduled for December 7 and Frederick traveled to Petrograd to take part in it. A motley array of other major players also participated, including Fyodor Chaliapin, the famous operatic bass whom Frederick had met at Yar several years before, and who was represented by an agent. The stakes were for the highest of rollers: bidding would start at an annual rent of 60,000 rubles (approximately $2 million today) and all participants had to provide a deposit of 30,000 rubles to show they were serious.

The minimum was quickly left behind. An entrepreneur from Petrograd bid 73,000 rubles; another one from Moscow offered 76,000; then Frederick topped him with 78,000. But someone quickly offered 80,000 and Frederick decided that he was out. It is possible that he had gotten wind of something underhanded in the entire affair. Several months later, when the old leaseholder unexpectedly emerged as the winner, rumors began to circulate that the auction had been rigged from the start.

But Frederick still had money to invest and turned his attention to the south and to Odessa. He went there initially to search for new acts to put on Aquarium's and Maxim's stages. Because the war had made it difficult to travel to and from Western Europe, the only ready source of new talent was what could be found in other Russian cities. Odessa was polyglot and cosmopolitan and had a very lively theatrical life. On the eve of the war, its population was 630,000, a third of them Jewish and thirty thousand of them foreigners, including Greeks, Armenians, Germans, Romanians, Italians, and many others. During two trips in February and July 1916 Frederick booked a variety of catchy acts—a singing duet, a female impersonator, an actress who was a local star, a ten-year-old moppet who belted out Gypsy romances—and also negotiated with entrepreneurs who wanted to lease his Aquarium theater for the following season. Frederick must have liked the city itself very much, because during his second trip he also bought a fancy villa there for 100,000 rubles, around $3 million in today's money.

The climate was a bit milder in Odessa than in Moscow, but the city's chief appeal was its location on the shore of the Black Sea. With its wide, straight, tree-shaded streets and elegant stone buildings, it would not have looked out of place on the Mediterranean. In Frederick's time Odessa was an important commercial center and despite its distance from the two capitals was neither quiet nor provincial. Fashionable hotels and restaurants, elegant shops, popular cafés, and several theaters attracted an urbane and moneyed crowd to its famous thoroughfares. Sailors from exotic ports mixed with the city's criminals in the raucous, beer-smelling dives near the commercial harbor. On the city's outskirts, the banks of the lagoons were dotted with villas facing the shimmering expanse of the sea. In 1916, Frederick could not have anticipated the role that Odessa would play in his life in just two years.

During the war's second year, its effects were becoming harder to ignore in Moscow. The city started to be overwhelmed by trainloads of wounded soldiers being evacuated from the European and southern fronts. As with most other Russian military preparations, the number of hospitals proved to be inadequate, and the authorities were forced to look for private property that could be requisitioned until dedicated new facilities could be arranged. Yar was closed to the public for nearly a year and its restaurant transformed into a hospital, with the tables replaced by neat rows of cots occupied by meek and stoically suffering, mostly peasant soldiers. Military commissions also examined Aquarium and Maxim with a view toward using the spacious theaters as clinics or storage depots for medical supplies. But Frederick was characteristically deft in the deals he made, and only part of each of his large properties was taken over for military needs in 1915 and again in 1916.

Other wartime impositions on entrepreneurs began to accumulate as well. Starting in late 1915, fuel and electricity shortages forced the commander of the Moscow military district to announce that all theaters would have to observe shorter hours, starting at 8 p.m. and ending at midnight. New taxes to support the war effort, and coercive "donations" to the official imperial charities, known collectively as "Empress Maria's Department of Institutions," were also imposed on theatrical entertainments. In some cases, taxes were estimated to be as high as 30 percent of an establishment's gross income.

The news from Petrograd was also becoming progressively more unnerving and there was a growing sense that the empire's center was not holding. Nicholas II was at the army's headquarters in Mogilyov, four hundred miles south of Petrograd, and effectively removed from direct control of his government. Russia's nascent parliament had tried to build on the genuine surge in patriotism accompanying the outbreak of the war and could have mediated between the government and an increasingly anxious public. But because Nicholas was unwilling to consider any form of cooperation with it, he left a dangerous power vacuum in the capital. It was partially filled by his wife, Tsaritsa Alexandra, a narrow-minded and credulous woman, who intervened in government affairs while being herself under the influence of Grigory Rasputin, imperial Russia's extraordinary evil genius. As a result, during the year and a half following Nicholas's departure from the capital a process that came to be labeled "ministerial leapfrog" took place: in quick succession, it gave Russia four different prime ministers, five ministers of internal affairs, three ministers of foreign affairs, three ministers of war, three ministers of transport, and four ministers of agriculture. A few were competent; most were craven and inept.

As the country's mood darkened, a febrile atmosphere began to creep into the entertainments and distractions that were sought by civilians and military men. On the eve of the war, a new dance craze had emerged from Argentina, leaped to Paris, and swept around the world—the tango. Its popularity in Russia was so immediate and so great that Frederick, who was always alert to novelty, decided to capitalize on it by refurbishing large spaces in his theaters and naming them after the dance, leading a journalist to proclaim that Maxim had become Moscow's "kingdom of the tango." During the war, the tango's popularity increased, with some professional dancers and singers adding macabre overtones to its elegant, stylized eroticism. One couple became famous for their "Tango of Death," in which the man, who was otherwise impeccably dressed in evening clothes, had his face made up to look like a skull. It was a melodramatic echo of the lurid news arriving from the fronts, as were such other popular tunes as "Wilhelm's Bloody Tango" (named after the German kaiser) and "The Last Tango," in which a jilted lover stabs the woman to death.

The emotional abandon that Russians sought from the tango during the war, and the elation that they got from vodka and wine, found a new blood relative in drugs, especially cocaine. In certain urban circles cocaine became the path of choice to euphoric oblivion in the face of the hopeless problems swirling all around. And it quickly emerged as an emblem of decadence, of failing national spiritual health: the tides of battle on the fronts ebbed and flowed; ministers and courtiers intrigued; profiteers schemed. For many, daily life was becoming more difficult, and for others it seemed pointless.

"Cocainomaniacs," as the addicts came to be called, were a common sight in Moscow's theatrical world, and Frederick grew to know one of the most famous very well. Aleksandr Vertinsky, who performed in Maxim and would work for Frederick in Constantinople as well, became wildly popular at the end of 1915 for his songs of resignation in the face of life's sadness and pain, as well as for their complement—escapist longing for exotic locales. A well-known example of his repertoire is "Kokainetka," or "Little Cocaine Girl," which dates from 1916 and laments "a lonely and poor young woman/Crucified on Moscow's wet boulevards by cocaine." (Later he would stage a dance on a related theme—the "Hashish Tango.") On stage Vertinsky dressed as Pierrot, the sad, naive clown of the Italian commedia dell'arte, whose heart is always broken by Columbine. His face powdered a deathly white, his eyes and eyebrows exaggeratedly made up with tragic black, and wearing crimson lipstick, he looked like a haunted character from another world.

By 1916, Frederick's and Russia's fates had diverged dramatically. Aquarium and Maxim were still thriving and money was pouring in. But his new homeland was succumbing to myriad diseases that were eating away its insides and that no one knew how to slow, much less cure. The country was bleeding men. Popular support for the disastrous war had plummeted and revolutionary agitation against the imperial regime was growing. Shortages of fuel and foodstuffs worsened. Workers struck against the high cost of living; strikes included those in such critical industries as the giant Putilov munitions factory in Petrograd, which was the largest in Europe and employed 30,000 men, the Nikolaev naval shipyards on the Black Sea, and the Donbas region in the Ukraine, with 50,000 coal miners. The authorities responded brutally by drafting the physically able and arresting and prosecuting the rest. When labor shortages led the government to conscript several hundred thousand Muslims in Turkestan and Central Asia to work in military factories near the front, a rebellion broke out and troops had to be dispatched to put it down by force, resulting in thousands of deaths.

But the most grotesque sign of the empire's sickness was Rasputin, the self-styled "holy man" who, for nearly a decade, had had a cancerous grip on Tsaritsa Alexandra and, through her, on Nicholas II and the rest of the government. A semiliterate, cunning, and libidinous peasant, he combined greed with primitive mysticism and a beguiling manner that attracted sycophants and hypnotized the gullible. The empress was a painfully shy and haughty woman whose life was dominated by piety, spite, and frantic worry about the health of her only son, Tsarevich Alexis, the heir to the throne and the most famous hemophiliac in history. As witnesses attest, it was Rasputin's uncanny ability to calm the boy during episodes of life-threatening bleeding that made his mother believe in the "holy man's" healing powers, and to follow his advice on everything else as well.

Rasputin's notoriety in Russia and around the world inspired some contemporaries to invent meetings with him in order to spice up their own life stories. Jack Johnson succumbed to this temptation, according to a memoirist who also went on to claim that Frederick introduced Johnson to Rasputin—and at a court ball in Petrograd, no less. This could never have happened, as documentary evidence proves. But Frederick did know well several people who had to deal with Rasputin's scandalous behavior in Moscow, when he came from Petrograd to close a tawdry business deal. On the night of March 26, 1915, Rasputin and his entourage went to Yar, which was still owned by Frederick's old boss and mentor Aleksey Sudakov. The "holy man's" escapades were legion, but on this occasion he managed to outdo himself. He was already drunk when his group occupied a private room. They ordered dinner, more drink, summoned a choir, and launched into a noisy revel. As always, Rasputin was the center of attention: he ordered the choir to sing his favorite songs; made the chorus girls do "cynical dances," as the police report subsequently put it; performed Russian folk dances himself; and dragged some of the women onto his lap. Not forgetting his role as a "holy man," he also scribbled notes urging them to "love disinterestedly" (meaning that they should yield to him because their love would be sanctified). When Sudakov heard what was going on he fell into a panic and tried to persuade other patrons that it was not actually Rasputin carousing upstairs but an imposter passing himself off as the notorious "friend" of the imperial family. Rasputin got wind of this and was so incensed that he started to prove his identity in the most unbridled ways possible—hinting obscenely about his relations with the empress, bragging that she had personally sewn the caftan he was

The old jail (L) and the old Coahoma County Courthouse, Friars Point, Mississippi, where Lewis Thomas successfully bid on a farm in 1869, and where he and his wife, India, pursued numerous legal actions in subsequent years. (Courtesy Flo Larson, North Delta Museum, Friars Point)

The Auditorium Hotel, Michigan Avenue, Chicago, where Frederick Thomas first worked as a waiter, c. 1892, now Roosevelt University. (*Auditorium*)

Frederick Bruce Thomas, c. 1896, probably in Paris. (L, NARA II. R, courtesy Bruce Thomass)

The Kremlin and Saint Basil's Cathedral on Red Square, Moscow, as Frederick Thomas saw them, c. 1900. (Library of Congress)

View of Tverskaya Street, Moscow, c. 1900, one of the main streets in the center, showing the preponderance of low buildings and horse-drawn transportation.

Yar Restaurant in Moscow, one of the most famous in Russia, where Frederick Thomas worked as a maître d'hôtel and assistant to the owner, after its reconstruction in 1910.

Grand Entrance to Aquarium Garden, Moscow, c. 1912, when "Thomas & Co." took it over. (author's collection)

Frederick Thomas shortly after his marriage on January 5, 1913, to his second wife, "Valli," with his children by his first wife, Hedwig—Irma, 4 years old, Olga, 11, and Mikhail, 6 ½. The other men may be his new wife's relatives. (NARA II)

Frederick Thomas (1st row, 2nd from R) with actors in Moscow's Aquarium Garden. (*Stsena i arena*, May 29, 1914)

"F. F. Tomas" on the eve of opening Maxim in Moscow, October 1912.
(*Var'ete i tsirk,* October 1, 1912)

Elvira Jungmann, c. 1910, a German performer who became Frederick
Thomas's mistress in Moscow and later his wife. (author's collection)

Advertisement for Maxim with "Fyodor Fyodorovich Tomas" as part of the attraction, and a list of domestic and foreign variety acts, including an "Original American Negro Trio Philadelphy [sic]." (*Stsena i arena,* November 4, 1915)

Advertisement for American heavyweight boxing champion Jack Johnson's exhibition fights in Moscow two weeks before the start of World War I: "'Aquarium' Directors F. F. Tomas and M. P. Tsarev, Appearances Beginning July 15 [O. S., July 28 N. S.], The World's Invincible Boxer, JOHNSON." (*Stsena i arena,* July 15, 1914)

View of the historic Stambul quarter of Constantinople, much as Frederick Thomas saw it when he arrived in 1919.

Galata Bridge, Constantinople, view from Stambul toward Galata and Pera, the European quarters of the city. (Library of Congress)

Illustration of what Frederick Thomas's first venture in Constantinople in 1919—the Anglo-American Villa, also known as the Stella Club—looked like: an open air stage with a dancer, a bandstand to the left, and civilian and Allied military clients at tables. (*Al'manakh nashi dni/Almanach nos jours*, no. 10, c. 1920.)

MAXIM-STELLA

(next to the Cine Magic, Taxim).
Manager: F. Thomas.
The only real Anglo-American establishment in Constantinople

Varieties, Dancing, Five O'clock Teas, Dinners and Supper.

Real American Jazz-Band under the Jazz master Mr. Keech of the "White Lyres."
Matiness on Wednesdays, Saturdays and Sundays.

The Management have the supreme honour to have been granted permission from British G.H.Q. for British officers and their families to dance in its establishment every day.

Advertisement for the famous nightclub Maxim in Constantinople in the British military newspaper *Orient News* (April 2, 1922), announcing an American jazz band and the special status that the establishment had been granted by the British occupational forces. Frederick Thomas temporarily included the name of his older entertainment garden to ensure that his former clients would make the connection with Maxim.

Frederick Thomas's third wife, Elvira; his oldest son Mikhail; and his sons by Elvira, Frederick Jr. and Bruce, c. 1920, Constantinople. (NARA II)

wearing, and, finally, dropping his trousers and exposing himself to the young women.

Outrage at Rasputin's behavior and supposed influence played into the hands of his many enemies, and early in 1916 three prominent men, including the tsar's first cousin, murdered him in Petrograd. In their own blundering and bloody way, the three had tried to save their country from one of the malignancies at its heart, although they had misconceived the scope and nature of the task. Corruption had already spread too deeply to be excised by the killing of any single man. But in contrast to the country's ruling circles, the three had at least looked inward, which was the right direction.

During the last months of its life, the Russian Empire was being threatened from two directions simultaneously. The tsar, his ministers, and his top military commanders focused almost entirely on the external danger posed by the Central Powers and were committed above all else to a "victorious conclusion" of the war. As a result, they largely neglected the grave internal threat to the empire's entire social and political order—the disaffection of large swaths of the population, including many troops at the front, the workers, and the peasants. The conditions were ripe for revolutionary groups to exploit the situation and to foment open rebellion.

In the end, the imperial regime's blind pursuit of victory proved suicidal. Six months before the empire collapsed, the Russian army managed to gather itself up for an immense new effort and won its greatest victory of the war against Austria-Hungary, known as the "Brusilov Offensive." In fact, some historians have characterized this as the single greatest military triumph of the Entente against the Central Powers and one of the deadliest battles in world history. But it was a classic Pyrrhic victory. The Russian army suffered such staggering casualties and desertions that it began to disintegrate. More than anything else, General Brusilov's great success underscored the waste of men, wealth, and vast national potential that was Russia's tragic fate during the Great War.

*   *   *

Back in Moscow, Frederick did not see the coming cataclysm. Even though every month it became more difficult to carry on as before because of shortages of food items, alcohol, electricity, fuel, and people, the variety theaters and restaurants were packed and profits kept pouring in. The only adjustments that Frederick made during these troubled times were driven, ironically, by his personal success. To free himself from the daily chore of attending to his properties, he transformed most of his active business interests into passive investments by leasing his theaters to other entrepreneurs. Concurrently, in a move without precedent in Moscow's theater world, he generously rewarded some of his senior employees—the stage manager, the accountant, the head chef, and several maîtres d'hôtel—by transferring day-to-day control of the Aquarium garden's multifaceted operation to them. However, he remained so optimistic about the future that all the leases he signed were for several years and the rents he demanded and received were high.

In fact, Frederick made his biggest investment in Moscow—and thus tied his fate to Russia's more strongly than ever—in the last days of the Russian Empire. He had been scouting properties in Moscow for some time before he finally found one that suited him in terms of location, quality, size, and income. On February 16, 1917, he signed documents that made him the owner of a block of six adjoining buildings, with thirty-eight rental units of varying sizes, on one of the main spokes of the Moscow street wheel, at 2 Karetny Ryad Street. This location is less than a mile from the Kremlin, and, in an ironic twist, was (and still is) across the street from the Hermitage Garden, Aquarium's only rival. He had paid 425,000 rubles, which would be about $7 million today.

In making the purchase, Frederick must have been amused by the unlikely coincidence that one of the former owners—a man with two resonant titles: Prince Mikhail Mikhaylovich Cantacuzene, Count Speransky—had a prominent American connection. In 1899, he had married Julia Dent Grant, the granddaughter of Ulysses S. Grant, commander of the Union armies during the Civil War and eighteenth president of the United States. Julia had in fact been born in the White House during her grandfather's presidency, and after her marriage she lived in Russia with her husband, who was a close aide to the tsar and eventually rose to the rank of general during the war. Who in Hopson Bayou could ever have imagined that a black native son would be involved in a property transaction in Moscow with a family like this?

With this purchase, Frederick completed the process of investing the money that he had made during the war. His focus on real estate reflected not only his desire to put roots even more deeply into his adopted country. His purchase at this moment in Russian history also shows a character trait that he shared with his parents: a conviction that he could prevail.

6

LOSS AND ESCAPE

FEBRUARY 1917

Frederick could scarcely have chosen a worse time to make his biggest investment in Moscow; exactly one week after he bought the apartment buildings from the Cantacuzene-Speranskys the first Revolution of 1917 broke out in Petrograd. On February 23 O.S. (March 8 in the West), hundreds of thousands of striking workers, who had been protesting shortages of bread and fuel for months in the outlying factory districts, started to pour into the city center to demonstrate their anger directly to the authorities. The tsar, who was still at the front, ordered the commander of the capital's garrison to disperse the demonstrators, but the troops were so disaffected that they refused to fire on the crowds. Soon, soldiers and even some officers started to fraternize with the demonstrators and to join them; sailors of the Baltic fleet also mutinied. The insurgents began seizing control of sections of the city and attacking government buildings. On March 11, as the rebellion spread to Moscow and other cities, Nicholas ordered the Duma, which had been pressing him for change, to dissolve. Most members refused, and on the following day they announced the creation of a Provisional Government that consisted largely of liberal and progressive members; more radical elements formed a second center of power—the Petrograd Soviet of Workers' and Soldiers' Deputies. The tsar made a halfhearted attempt to return to Petrograd, but after learning that both of the empire's capitals were in the hands of rebels and that he had no support from his generals, on March 2/15 he abdicated for himself and his son, Alexis, in favor of his brother, Grand Duke Michael. The next day, the latter abdicated in favor of the Provisional Government. As the historian Riasanovsky put it, the three-hundred-year-old Russian Empire died "with hardly a whimper."

Throughout the country, news of the monarchy's collapse was greeted with elation. Sculptures and images of the two-headed eagle—symbol of the monarchy—were torn down everywhere. In Moscow, after some initially tense confrontations between troops and the rebellious crowds in front of the City Duma building near Red Square, the soldiers joined the insurgents and tied red ribbons to their bayonets. Masses of people poured into the streets and squares in the city center carrying red banners in support of the revolution in Petrograd and singing the "Marseillaise." On Sunday, March 25, a giant "Liberty Parade" consisting of several hundred thousand people wound through the heart of Moscow. An American who saw it was much impressed by the orderliness of the procession, the good cheer of the crowds that gathered to watch, the absence of police, and the easy mixing of the social classes. In a sign of the transitional nature of the time, the procession blended the new with the old—banners with revolutionary slogans such as "Land and the Will of the People" combined with prayer at the Chapel of the Iberian Mother of God at the entrance to Red Square. Part of the procession had a carnival atmosphere and the crowds especially enjoyed a circus troupe with a camel and elephant covered with revolutionary placards. Behind them came a wagon holding a black coffin labeled "The Old Order," on top of which sat a grimacing dwarf wearing a sign that read "Protopopov"—the name of the reviled last imperial minister of the interior, who had been placed under arrest by the new regime.

But not all that happened in the spring of 1917 was festive or peaceful, and men of property like Frederick soon realized that the revolution endangered their well-being and livelihood. In Moscow, the police force had been disarmed and disbanded by the insurgents even before Nicholas abdicated. When, as one of its first acts, the Provisional Government announced broad civil liberties, it also granted an amnesty to all political prisoners, including terrorists; in Moscow, some two thousand thieves and murderers were released from prisons as well. A crime wave began in the city, with robberies in the streets and attacks on homes and businesses. The new city militia, composed primarily of student volunteers, proved ineffective, and householders were forced to organize their own associations for mutual protection. This was but an early harbinger of the greater anarchy to come.

Another early decree with fateful consequences for the entire country was "Order Number One," issued by the Petrograd Soviet of Workers' and Soldiers' Deputies, the second center of power in the capital. This soviet ("council") proclaimed that it had the right to countermand any of the Provisional Government's orders regarding military matters, and that every unit down to the size of a company should elect soldiers' committees to decide how it would act in any given situation. This "democratic" order abolished the imperial army's hierarchical command structure, as was intended. But it also sounded the death knell for the army, which, although greatly weakened by early 1917, was still the only organization left in Russia that might have been able to resist the destructive social forces that were now beginning to gather hurricane strength.

By this time, the patriotic upsurge of the war's early phase had been long forgotten. Soldiers wanted peace, and large-scale desertions increased. Some units mutinied against their officers and beat or even shot them. Others began to fraternize with the Germans and Austro-Hungarians across the front lines. However, the Provisional Government remained blind to the reality at the front, and believing it had a debt of loyalty to the Entente persisted in trying to whip up enthusiasm for yet another offensive, with the stated goal of nothing less than "decisive victory." This fatal gap between the ineffectual government and the masses of soldiers, who were largely drawn from the peasantry and the lower classes, was reproduced throughout the country. The peasants had no interest in the war and wanted land reform. Workers wanted better wages, shorter hours, and control over their factories. City dwellers wanted an end to the shortages of food, fuel, and consumer goods. In a hopeful gesture of support for the Russian war effort, first the United States and then the other members of the Entente recognized the Provisional Government within a few days after it was formed. But the new regime failed to win the support of its own people, and that failure would be its doom.

Theatrical life in Moscow started to adapt to the country's new political reality very quickly, but many of the earliest changes were superficial and most activities went on as before, with profits continuing to roll in. The city's new "commissar," who replaced the governor-general, renamed the former "imperial" theaters "Moscow State Theaters." Mikhail Glinka's superpatriotic nineteenth-century opera *A Life for the Tsar* was dropped from the repertory of the Bolshoy Theater. By contrast, with the elimination of the imperial censorship and a marked decrease in the influence of the Orthodox Church on public life, lewd and irreverent plays began to be staged widely. An especially popular genre ridiculed Rasputin and his relations with the imperial family, and included such titles as *Rasputin's Happy Days*, *Grishka's Harem*, and *The Crash of the Firm "Romanov and Co."*

Despite such iconoclasm and the incendiary revolutionary rhetoric resounding everywhere, many venerable tsarist-era institutions continued to function by inertia during 1917, and it is striking that Frederick chose this time to join one of the most archaic. On June 10/23, 1917, he officially became a Moscow "Merchant of the First Guild" and his name was duly entered in the register for "Gostinnaya

Sloboda" (the "Merchant Quarter"), a Moscow place-name dating to medieval times that now referred simply to a specific merchants' association. He had included Olga, his oldest child, who had recently turned fifteen, in his application as well.

The designation that Frederick received had been established in the early eighteenth century and had originally entitled the bearer to some important privileges, such as freedom from military service, from corporal punishment, and from the head tax. The designation was also an honorific and gave its bearers an elevated social status. By the beginning of the twentieth century, however, the designation was little more than an anachronism, although its benefits were not without charm: merchants of the first guild were in principle entitled to attend the tsar's court and wear an official uniform, including a sword. (By the time of Frederick's enrollment this privilege had become academic, of course; Nicholas had been placed under house arrest in one of his former palaces.) Nonetheless, for Frederick this was a sign that he had risen to the top of his profession and that his Russian peers recognized his position. Olga's inclusion demonstrates that he expected her, and probably his other children when they were older, to participate in running the businesses that he had established.

Once again, however, Frederick's timing could scarcely have been worse. By becoming a merchant of the first guild, he was, in effect, proudly confirming that he was a prosperous bourgeois capitalist. Although this class had been an honorable one in old Russia, it would soon become anathema in the growing revolutionary storm. Frederick was on the verge of discovering that he was no longer merely caught in the flow of history; its forces were beginning to turn against him.

Calamitous historical events accumulated rapidly in the second half of 1917. A few weeks after the collapse of the tsarist regime, the Germans decided to aggravate the revolutionary fever that had gripped Russia by shipping Vladimir Lenin, the willful and unscrupulous leader of the radical Bolshevik Communist Party, to Petrograd from Switzerland, where he had been in exile. In the ensuing months, Lenin and his followers did all they could to undermine the weak and increasingly unpopular Provisional Government. They called for Russia's immediate withdrawal from the war, the control of factories by workers, the expropriation of large estates, and the distribution of land to the peasants. All these goals increasingly appealed to the Russian masses, but the Provisional Government could not or would not support them. In July, an attempt by the minister of war, Alexander Kerensky, to launch a new offensive against Germany in Galicia led to an insurrection and the collapse of what was left of the Russian army. At the end of August, there was an attack on the discredited Provisional Government from the right by the army's commander in chief, General Lavr Kornilov, who became involved in a coup conspiracy. The specter of a counterrevolution now rallied the radical parties and the city's workers in support of the Provisional Government, with the result that the attempted coup dissipated. However, the only group that gained from the episode was the Bolsheviks, and by the end of September 1917, they had become the strongest military faction in the capital.

In the summer of 1917 Frederick decided that he would have to come out of his self-imposed role as a passive investor. The political climate was drifting increasingly to the left and he would have to find a way to adapt. His solution was to strike a deal with the Moscow Soviet of Soldiers' Deputies, which was the local version of the Petrograd Soviet that had vied for authority with the Provisional Government ever since the February Revolution. The plan was to establish a new "soldiers' theater" at Aquarium and to stage performances of a kind that had never appeared there before. Rather than light entertainment, the focus would be on famous serious dramatic works, classical music, and operas. The aim of the plan was in keeping with the noblest ideals of the revolution: to democratize access to high culture by educating soldiers, who, as the argument went, had been kept in a state of ignorance by the dark forces of the old regime. Now, they would be exposed to the best, "strictly democratic" works that had been created in Russia and abroad, including plays by Gogol, Tolstoy, Gorky, Chekhov, Schiller, Ibsen, and Shakespeare; operas by Tchaikovsky, Rimsky-Korsakov, and Mussorgsky; and concerts of symphonic and chamber music. An initiative like this was not going to bring in as much money as a French or Viennese bedroom farce, but it was clearly better than leaving the theater empty. Frederick appears to have been the first prominent entrepreneur in the city to align himself with the new order by leasing his theater to an overtly populist, revolutionary group. His reason was surely hard-nosed pragmatism rather than politics. Maxim remained leased to another entrepreneur during the fall of 1917, but without any major changes in its traditional repertory.

OCTOBER 1917

On October 25/November 7, 1917, the Bolsheviks in Petrograd struck. Wearing a disguise, Lenin had slipped into the capital from his temporary refuge in Finland two days earlier and managed to convince his followers that the time had come to seize power. Red troops coordinated by Leon Trotsky, Lenin's ablest assistant, occupied a number of strategic locations in the city. That night, Bolshevik-led soldiers, sailors, and factory workers attacked the Winter Palace, the former imperial residence where the Provisional Government was meeting. The small defense force in the palace, which consisted of several hundred military cadets and elements of a women's battalion, was overcome after a few hours of resistance. The Bolsheviks arrested members of the government; Kerensky, who had become prime minister, had managed to escape earlier in a car borrowed from the United States embassy. The Bolshevik coup against the Provisional

Government succeeded with fewer people killed in Petrograd than after the tsar's abdication in February.

In Moscow, by contrast, there was more serious resistance. On the morning after the Provisional Government fell, Bolshevik troops surrounded the Kremlin and were confronted by cadets from the city's military academies and some Cossacks. Each side accused the other of illegitimacy and refused to back down. The Bolsheviks opened fire first. In the next several days, pitched battles raged across the city between Red units and those few that were still loyal to the Provisional Government. The situation quickly became so chaotic that the city appeared to descend into schizophrenia: people stood in lines to get their bread rations on one side of a square while cadets and Red troops were exchanging fire on the other. An Englishman recalled that railways, post offices, and other public institutions continued to function at the same time that heavy fighting was breaking out all across the city. Despite the danger, he risked venturing out one night and went to see Chekhov's famous play *The Cherry Orchard* at the Moscow Art Theater, which was a few blocks from Maxim, but on the way home he had to duck for cover from machine-gun fire.

Frederick would have had good reason to worry about both of his families' well-being and about his properties. By November 10, streetcars had stopped running and telephones were not working. Banks and businesses closed. Out of fear of being hit by bullets or shrapnel, people avoided leaving their homes except for necessities. Patrols of bellicose Bolshevik soldiers and rough-looking factory workers with rifles slung on pieces of rope began to appear on the city's streets. In apartment buildings, members of residents' committees collected whatever handguns they could find and took turns guarding the entrances against marauding bands of armed men whose allegiance was uncertain; other residents slept fully clothed to be ready in case anyone tried to break in.

By the end of the week, scores of buildings in central Moscow had been badly damaged by rifle, machine-gun, and artillery fire, including some of the most revered cathedrals in the Kremlin itself. As a horrified city dweller characterized it, the damage to Russia's symbolic heart during this fratricidal fighting exceeded what Napoleon's foreign invaders had caused in 1812. An American described what he saw outside his residence in the city center.

> The house we are in is almost a wreck, and the boulevard in front is a most singular and distressing panorama of desolation. The roads are covered with glass and debris; trees, lampposts, telephone poles are shot off raggedly; dead horses and a few dead men lie in the parkway; the broken gas mains are still blazing; the black, austere, smoking hulks of the burning buildings stand like great barricades about the littered yards of the boulevard.

Between five thousand and seven thousand people had been killed. But on November 20, Moscow's Military-Revolutionary Committee announced that it had won and that all the cadets and its other opponents had either surrendered or been killed.

The first weeks after the fighting stopped were an anxious time in Moscow. No one knew exactly what to expect from the Bolsheviks, but the fact that they had seized power in Petrograd by force and had used it indiscriminately throughout the city was an ominous sign. Nevertheless, people in Frederick's world had little choice but to try to live as before, despite the widespread destruction, dislocations, soaring prices, and scanty food and fuel supplies. Maxim had escaped damage in the fighting, and the theater director who had leased it tried to continue with his old repertory—a hodgepodge of melodramas, comedies, lighthearted French song and dance numbers, and, in a gesture to the times, an occasional, ponderously serious play (this unappetizing mix would not survive for very long). Similarly, during the last months of 1917, Aquarium continued serving up its mostly high-minded fare as the official theater of the Moscow garrison. Since both places were still functioning and making money, so was Frederick.

However, as an especially harsh winter descended on Russia, the new regime began to reveal its fundamentally belligerent face, and the danger to Frederick and his ilk became apparent. The Bolsheviks' most urgent task was to secure their grip on power by eliminating all external and internal threats to it. They would eliminate the external threat by getting Russia out of the Great War, and the internal threat by unleashing a new kind of war against entire classes of people they considered their enemies.

In the Bolsheviks' Marxist worldview, the war that had engulfed Europe was being waged by "bourgeois capitalist" powers with selfish economic and geopolitical interests that had nothing to do with, and in fact were opposed to, the genuine needs of the workers and peasants. Thus, immediately after seizing control, the Bolshevik regime offered a cease-fire to the Germans, and on March 3, 1918, the two sides signed the Treaty of Brest-Litovsk. The Bolsheviks agreed to give up one-quarter of what had been the Russian Empire's territory, population, and arable land; three-quarters of its iron industry and coal production; and much else besides. The terms were brutal, but the Bolsheviks were now free to turn their attention to their enemies within.

Their identification of who these were might have struck Frederick as grotesquely familiar. Just as a black person could not escape racist categories in the United States, everyone in the new Soviet state was now defined by socioeconomic class; and despite the seeming differences, the Marxist and communist concept of "class" functioned, perversely, as a quasi-racial label. In the eyes of the Bolsheviks, you were indelibly marked by what you did or had done for a living, and people with money, people who owned property or businesses, as well as the nobility, the clergy, the police, the judiciary, educators, army officers, and government bureaucrats—in short, all those implicated in maintaining or serving the old imperial regime—were on the wrong side of history. An American visitor to Russia at the time described the extreme forms that this attitude took.

The Bolsheviks are out to get the scalps of all "capitalists"—the "bour-jhee," as they call them; and in the eyes of a Bolshevik, anyone belongs to the bourgeoisie who carries a handkerchief or wears a white collar! That is why some of our friends are begging old clothes from servants; rags are less liable to be shot at in the street!

Frederick's origin as a black American would have done nothing to mitigate his class "sins." The Bolsheviks hated the Americans, the French, and the British, believing that the Entente was trying to keep Russia in the war (which was true). And Frederick's past oppression as a black man in the United States was trumped by his having become a rich man in Russia. In the end, he could no more escape how the new regime saw him than he could change the color of his skin.

The October Revolution also changed Frederick's strained relations with Valli, and what had been a stable if awkward arrangement was transformed into a toxic mixture of the personal and the political. In the crazy inversion of Russian norms that the revolution caused, it was as if Valli were a white American woman who suddenly decided that her estranged husband was a "Negro."

Frederick had known for over a year that she had taken a lover. This was a complication because Irma, Mikhail, and Olga continued to live with Valli in the big apartment at 32 Malaya Bronnaya Street; but considering how he had treated Valli himself, Frederick could not have cared all that much. Neither the lover's name nor his occupation before the October Revolution is known, although he must have been an ardent supporter, because he emerged from it as a "Bolshevik Commissar," in Frederick's later characterization. As such, he had become a person of importance in Moscow's new regime, and his involvement with Valli became dangerous. He could back up the animosity she felt for her husband with his political power.

It would not take long for Frederick to be confronted by Valli's wrath. In addition to casting about for ways to accommodate himself to the new regime, he also began to search for a place where his family could escape the threats, restrictions, and shortages in Moscow. Everything suddenly changed when the Bolsheviks signed the Treaty of Brest-Litovsk. In February, the Germans started their occupation of the Ukraine, and by mid-March they were in Odessa. What had been a disastrous loss of territory for the new Soviet regime proved a godsend for Russians with money and others who wanted to escape the Bolsheviks. Despite the fact that until recently the Germans had been a vilified enemy, many Russians now began to see them as the lesser evil. At a minimum, they could be relied upon to restore, in the occupied territory, a more familiar social order than what the Bolsheviks were imposing on the rest of Russia. Frederick could now get Elvira and his children out of harm's way by sending them to the villa he owned in Odessa. Moreover, Elvira was German and had relatives in Berlin, and this would surely be to her advantage with the region's military government.

But finding a place to go was just the beginning of the difficulties that Frederick and his family now had to overcome. The Bolsheviks did not want people to escape their rule, and anyone seeking to leave Moscow had to obtain a special permit. Frederick's own application was peremptorily denied, and that did not bode well for his future. However, he managed to get permission for Elvira and the children by exploiting a loophole that applied to actors and other performers. He claimed that she was still active onstage and had to travel to cities in the south to practice her profession.

Additional obstacles still lay ahead. During the past year, train travel had deteriorated very badly throughout the country: schedules became irregular, tickets were scarce, the rolling stock was ramshackle, and delays because of engine breakdowns were frequent. Getting on a train in Moscow was also no guarantee that you would actually reach your destination. At every station, so many people would try to climb on board that passengers had to fight to keep their places. However, Frederick persevered once again and was able to secure passage for all six. This left only the chore of gathering up the entire group from the two separate households.

On the eve of Elvira's departure, Frederick went to his apartment on Malaya Bronnaya to fetch Mikhail and Irma. Valli was not expecting him. When he walked into the bedroom he was surprised to see that her lover was there with her. The scene left nothing to the imagination: "I ketched her upstairs of my eight-room flat, in baid wid one o' dem commissars," was how Frederick described it to an acquaintance later.

Valli was infuriated by Frederick's sudden appearance as well as by his reason for coming to the apartment. Turning toward her lover, she began to goad him to avenge the humiliations that she had suffered at Frederick's hands for years. This was not an idle threat: commissars at this time carried guns. Moreover, Frederick was not only an adulterous husband but also a class enemy. A hysterical scene followed, as he later described it in a letter: "the Woman forced her Bolshevik Lover to attempt to kill me and only my little Girl and my Son, who was a Child then too . . . saved me from beeing thus killed, because they screamed aloud and the Bolshevik let me go."

During the ensuing confusion and in his haste to escape, Frederick managed to take only Mikhail with him. Irma remained in the apartment, and Frederick would never see her again. Whether she stayed with Valli willingly or was kept by her, and whether Valli kept Irma out of love or calculation, the little girl was the victim of the adults' emotional battle. She would remain a pawn between the two for years after they parted.

Following the grotesque encounter with the commissar, Frederick realized that he had to put as much distance between himself and Valli as possible. This is when the radical revision of family laws, which the new regime introduced only two months after the revolution, played into his hands. In a coordinated series of steps, he divorced Valli, married Elvira, and legalized the status of Fedya and Bruce; thereafter, Elvira always used "Thomas" as her surname. She and the four children then set out on their long, arduous journey to Odessa.

Frederick could now concentrate on trying to figure out what to do with his businesses. All of his actions in the early months of 1918 show that he did not expect the Bolsheviks and their policies to survive the year, even after they had dispersed the Constituent Assembly, a democratically elected body that was supposed to create a new representative government. In January 1918, an armed rebellion of "White" forces against the Bolsheviks had begun to brew in the Don Cossack lands in the southeast. In Moscow that spring, the Bolsheviks had to use artillery, armored cars, and heavy machine-gun fire to dislodge anarchist groups from the city center. There were even Russians who hoped that the Germans would ignore the Brest-Litovsk Treaty and occupy the rest of the country.

Frederick began a series of determined efforts to adapt to the new trends as much as he could and to save what he had created. His lessee had by now abandoned Maxim and Frederick tried to revive its old style and programs. He signed a new lease to rent its theater for a highly optimistic term of five years and an impressive seasonal fee of 105,000 rubles. Despite the fact that Aquarium's winter theater had been taken over by the Moscow garrison, in January 1918 Frederick signed a new deal with the entrepreneur Boris Evelinov to stage operettas and farces in both of Aquarium's theaters during the coming summer. Evelinov paid Thomas a very substantial advance of 175,000 rubles—roughly $3 million in today's currency—a hefty wager that they would be making even more money in the future.

Within weeks, however, virtually all of Frederick's hopes would prove to be chimeras. By March, the Bolshevik regime's wave of theater takeovers reached Frederick and he was forced to abandon his properties. Maxim's main theater was nationalized and given over to a succession of theatrical companies with higher artistic aims than the kind of entertainment in which Frederick had specialized. All that he could recoup for himself was one of the smaller spaces in the building, where he was allowed to open a simple dining room that would provide cheap meals, at three rubles apiece, to theatrical workers and actors who were members of professional unions. This was a precipitous drop for someone who had presided for years over some of the city's most renowned restaurants. The final ignominy came when Frederick was hired as the director of what had been his own theater.

The situation with Aquarium was initially more complicated and confusing, but it ended the same way. After some vacillation on the part of the new regime, Frederick and Boris Evelinov's plans came to naught. The Bolshevik regime, which managed to combine bloodlust with prudery, decided against allowing Frederick and Evelinov to stage their "bourgeois" risqué farces and frivolous operettas.

After this failure, they made one final attempt to find a niche for themselves in the only world they knew and came up with the idea of a summer season of classical ballet at Aquarium. This was in keeping with the "cultural and enlightening" function that revolutionary theater was now supposed to have for the benefit of soldiers and their ilk. It was here that Frederick's well-honed sense of theatricality emerged again, although for the very last time in Moscow. He knew which ballets were popular because short performances by famous ballerinas were staples of the variety stage. Frederick suggested that *Giselle*, a well-known nineteenth-century French romantic ballet, would be a certain success. He was right, and this production of *Giselle* remained on the Aquarium stage for several years after he had fled from Moscow.

The nationalization of Maxim and Aquarium was just the beginning of the changes sweeping through Moscow. Frederick had now gotten caught in an historical rip current that was threatening to pull him under. The country was moving in directions that no one could have imagined. In keeping with Marx's proclamation that a communist revolution signaled the dictatorship of the proletariat and the end of private property, the Bolsheviks systematically dismantled all the social and economic foundations of the Russian Empire. They eliminated former ranks and titles; they gave control of businesses and factories to committees of workers; they decreed that peasants should break up landowners' estates. Foreign trade was made into a national monopoly; banks and church property were nationalized; the old judicial system was replaced by revolutionary tribunals and "people's courts"; education and entertainment were placed under strict ideological controls. Shortly after their coup, the Bolsheviks had established the "Extraordinary Commission to Combat Counterrevolution, Sabotage, and Speculation"—the notorious political police that became known by its Russian abbreviation, Cheka, and that initiated a reign of state terror lasting the entire Soviet period of Russian history. After the Constituent Assembly was disbanded in January, all political parties were declared counterrevolutionary, including those that had originally allied themselves with the Bolsheviks. On January 31, 1918, the government marked a new era by adopting the New Style (N.S.) calendar.

This revolutionary transformation of the country was not meant to be impersonal or peaceful: in Lenin's words, the newly empowered proletariat's mandate was to "rob the robbers." The peasants and workers took this literally and in cities as well as the countryside began a campaign of confiscating and pillaging wealthy homes and estates, businesses, and churches. The boundary between state-sponsored expropriation and armed robbery had disappeared.

Many Muscovites suffered confiscations, thefts, and extortions at the hands of Red troops and the Cheka. Residential properties throughout the city were seized as the new regime saw fit, with owners and tenants often thrown out onto the street and members of the new order moving into their houses and apartments. This was very likely the fate of Frederick's upscale apartment buildings on Karetny Ryad Street, but Valli's commissar could have shielded her in the big apartment on Malaya Bronnaya.

Like all other members of his class, Frederick was at risk of being physically attacked anywhere. Bolshevik soldiers in gray overcoats and shaggy fur hats skulking in dead-end streets and alleyways would target likely apartments and suddenly burst in, ostensibly to search for army officers on the run or for concealed foodstuffs, but often just to rob the inhabitants. Venturing out at night for any reason became especially dangerous. In mid-March on Bolshaya Dmitrovka, just down the street from Maxim, a popular actress was robbed of two expensive fur coats in which she was going to perform that evening. The same month, six armed men walked into the popular restaurant Martyanych and robbed all the patrons of several hundred thousand rubles' worth of money and jewelry. No one even attempted to protest because there was no recourse; if victims tried calling the local police station, they were likely to be told: "They acted on the basis of the law. If you resist—we'll arrest you!"

One of Frederick's business acquaintances, the theatrical entrepreneur Sukhodolsky, was a prominent victim. In early March, a group of fifteen men pulled up outside his home in a well-to-do neighborhood, blocked all the entrances so that no one could escape, drew weapons, and forced their way into his apartment. After ransacking it, they beat up Sukhodolsky and his wife and left with 24,000 rubles and other valuables. The couple were lucky to have survived.

The regime's efforts to redistribute wealth were not restricted to sending out marauding bands to attack individuals in their homes. When the first wave of bank seizures by the Bolsheviks failed to generate the money they wanted ($100 billion to $150 billion in today's currency) to consolidate their power internally and to start projecting it abroad, where they hoped to ignite a worldwide revolution, they turned to the contents of private bank safe-deposit boxes. In Moscow alone by the summer of 1918 they confiscated the contents of 35,493 safes, which yielded half a ton of gold, silver, and platinum bullion; some 700,000 rubles in gold, silver, and platinum coin; 65 million tsarist rubles; 600 million rubles in public and private bonds; and large sums in foreign currencies. This was only a fraction of the total number of safes in the city; the others were cracked later.

By the summer of 1918, Frederick was determined to escape from Moscow. Many people he knew well were leaving for the south, including his former business partner Tsarev, who had rented, for the winter, a theater in Kiev, which was under German occupation. In early June, the Moscow government announced a ban on middlemen in the city's theaters, which deprived Frederick of his job as director of a nationalized Maxim. Cholera and typhus began to spread in the city as health and sanitary conditions deteriorated. In July, fighting broke out when the Socialist Revolutionaries assassinated the German ambassador in an attempt to scuttle the peace treaty with the Germans, and then tried to start an uprising by seizing key positions throughout the city. The Bolsheviks brought in troops and quickly crushed the rebels, but they also exploited the occasion to consolidate their power further. Later the same month, news reached Moscow that Nicholas II and his wife, son, and four daughters had been executed by a local soviet in Yekaterinburg in the distant Ural Mountains.

The only livelihood Frederick had left was the cheap restaurant that he had been allowed to open in part of the Maxim building. Running a restaurant of any kind at this time in Moscow required connections or ingenuity because normal wholesale distribution was in complete disarray. The city was near famine, with rationing of basic foodstuffs and soaring prices on the black market. This is when small-scale entrepreneurs who came to be known as "sackers" ("meshochniki") emerged to partially fill the gap. Crowds of peasants started coming into the city from outlying villages with sacks of locally produced food—flour, baked bread, butter, cereals, eggs—which they bartered for manufactured goods that could still be found in the city's black market, such as head scarves, calico, thread, sugar, soap, and matches. Hungry city dwellers made the same trip in reverse. Bolshevik guards saw the trade as a form of illicit speculation and tried to stop it, but the need in the city was great and the price discrepancies between the city and the countryside were large, making the risks both necessary and profitable. Inevitably, train stations in Moscow became one of the main meeting places for buyers and sellers. This is where Frederick was able to get the provisions he needed for his restaurant and how he was also able to plot his escape from the city.

Frederick fled from Moscow in August 1918, when he learned that he was slated for arrest by the Cheka and that his life was in danger. Some years later, he told the story to a tourist from Texas, who was so impressed that he wrote it up for a newspaper after he got home. He summarized how Frederick's work at his restaurant

> permitted him to go to the station daily as a porter. This he did regularly for about six months and thus disarmed suspicion until, by the aid of a friend traveling under a permit, he was able to conceal himself in a train compartment and escape to one of his villas, outside of the reach of the new Government.

Thomas's trip would have been more dangerous than Elvira's because he was traveling illegally. He could be arrested on the spot by any Bolshevik soldier, official, or member of the Cheka who might want to check his papers, although even without official permission to leave, Frederick could buy any document he needed if he had the cash; in 1918, the going rate for a passport from a police station in Moscow was around 1,200 rubles. After one got onto a train, it was a matter of luck what sort of trip it would be. Frederick was taken in by a friend who may have had his own compartment; this implies that the friend had influence or connections—travelers with neither had to manage as best they could. What happened during the journey south also depended on one's luck. Some trains made it from Moscow to the border of German-occupied Ukraine in only a couple of days, even though there were long stops at intermediate stations. However, other trains heading south were blocked at remote road crossings by bands of armed men who were either Bolsheviks or criminal gangs—it was frequently hard to tell which—and who would open fire on the cars to chase everyone out; they would then loot the passengers' belongings before letting them back on. Conditions on the trains themselves were miserable: they were not only overcrowded but dilapidated and unsanitary; windows were broken; theft was rampant; food and water were hard to get; and stops at stations, which were usually pillaged, failed to provide relief. Young women traveling alone were especially at risk.

Passengers who reached the frontier of German-occupied Ukraine typically felt a mixture of elation and resentment. On the one hand, they were escaping the Bolsheviks. But on the other, the Germans acted like arrogant conquerors and herded disembarking passengers across the border with little wooden switches, as if they were farm animals. Officers checked the passengers' papers at tedious length. In an attempt to stop the spread of typhus, influenza, smallpox, and other diseases, the travelers were sent off for days of quarantine in hideous and filthy temporary barracks before being allowed to continue on their way.

ODESSA

Although the act of crossing the border into German territory immediately removed the class stigma and the threats that had dogged Frederick on the Bolshevik side, new difficulties would have appeared at every step, beginning with his having to insist that he was Russian and not American (he would soon find it necessary to claim the opposite). The United States had been at war with the Central Powers since April 1917 and an American entering their territory would have to register as an enemy alien and would be their nominal prisoner. Frederick's appearance and the way he spoke English would give him away to any German who had ever met other American blacks.

Odessa was also a dangerous place for anyone who was rich or looked rich. When the Germans and Austrians occupied southern Russia, they set up a puppet state in the Ukraine, including Odessa, which they garrisoned with thirty thousand troops. Their presence put an end to the reign of terror against the "bourgeoisie" that the Bolsheviks had unleashed in the city after their October takeover. But not all the Bolsheviks had fled: some went underground instead, plotting how to expel the occupiers and their local allies, and waging a persistent, low-grade guerrilla war that marked daily life in Odessa.

As in Moscow, the Bolsheviks had thrown open all the prisons in Odessa, and several thousand thieves and murderers had spilled out onto the streets. Thus reinforced, the city's notorious criminal gangs—which in their larger-than-life brazenness were comparable to the Chicago gangsters of the 1920s—instituted their own reign of terror against the city's inhabitants, whom they burglarized, robbed, and murdered on the streets, in their homes, and at their businesses.

Odessa was especially dangerous at night. A prominent lawyer who risked walking to the well-known London Hotel late one night counted 122 gunshots from various directions during the twelve minutes that he was outside. Such firing lasted all night long and it was hard to tell who was shooting at whom—Bolsheviks at soldiers or criminals at barricaded home owners.

Expensive villas like Frederick's were typically in outlying, sparsely populated areas and would have been easy prey for thieves. Frederick was also sufficiently well known to have been mentioned in local newspapers when he arrived, together with other notable entrepreneurs and entertainers from Moscow and Petrograd, and this publicity increased his chance of becoming a target. Between Bolsheviks on the one hand, who were still eager to finish settling accounts with the "bourgeoisie," and traditional thieves on the other, he would have found it prudent to move himself and his family to the city center, where there was at least some military protection and safety in numbers.

But even with the threats swarming around them, Odessites were still free in ways that had become impossible in the Bolshevik north. The Germans and Austrians had no interest in establishing a radically different social and economic order and thus largely left the local population to its own initiatives. As a result, the city's residents could pursue all their favorite pastimes and forms of dissipation, which they did with a feverish zeal that contemporaries likened to a feast in time of plague.

During the day, the handsome streets overflowed with polyglot southern crowds. Well-dressed people filled the stores, restaurants, and popular cafés like Robinat and Fanconi, which also doubled as exchanges for crowds of speculators trading currencies, cargoes from abroad, abandoned estates in Bolshevik territory—anything of value. At night, people flocked to theaters, restaurants, cafés chantants, and gambling dens, as well as to dives specializing in sex or drugs. They threw money around as if it had lost all value, trying to grab as much pleasure as they could and to forget the horrors of recent years as well as those still lurking outside. As the champagne corks popped and singers warbled indoors, businesses and home owners alike bolted their iron shutters and locked their entrance doors. The city center took on an eerily empty appearance late at night, as if the entire population had died out. The sudden noise of a crowd leaving a theater or cinema and scattering rapidly broke a silence that was otherwise punctuated only by sporadic gunshots. Cabs were hard to find and drivers demanded enormous fares to venture out, forcing people to take special precautions in case they had to walk any distance. One naval officer recalled being instructed about how to behave: if you saw someone on the street, and especially two or three people together, cross over to the other side immediately and take the safety off your revolver; if anyone follows you, open fire without warning.

This is the world in which Frederick lived for nine months, until April 1919. What did he do in Odessa at this time? Among the refugees were many entrepreneurs and performers from Moscow's theater world whom he knew, including the singers Isa Kremer and Alexander Vertinsky, as well as Vera Kholodnaya—Russia's first star of the silent screen. He also had numerous contacts among Odessa's entrepreneurs and theater owners, with whom he had done business since 1916. It would have been natural and easy for him to get involved in running a café chantant, theater, or restaurant, especially because he had always worked with partners in Moscow, and new establishments were being opened everywhere. It is likely that in addition to his villa Frederick had some money and other assets in Odessa that had escaped expropriation in Moscow. Despite the regime changes in the city during the past year, a number of private banks had managed to stay in operation through the Bolshevik period and would continue to function as late as April 1919. What is certain is that like most other refugees in Odessa he was still "sitting on his suitcases," in the phrase of the time, and waiting for the Bolsheviks to fall or be pushed out so that he could return to Moscow and reclaim what was his.

Everything suddenly changed after November 11, 1918. On that day, at eleven in the morning in a forest near Paris, Germany surrendered to the Allies and the Great War finally ended. Shortly thereafter, as the armistice agreement stipulated, the Germans started to evacuate the territories they had occupied, including Odessa.

Then came news that filled the refugees from the north of Russia with joy. An Allied naval squadron had arrived in Constantinople and was heading for Odessa; the French were going to land an army in the city; White army forces would gather in the resulting enclave to start a crusade against the Bolsheviks, whom the French saw as the Germans' stepchildren and as traitors to the Allied cause. Excited crowds began to gather daily on the boulevards above Odessa's harbor to search the horizon for the ships of their saviors. For Frederick and the other refugees, returning home now seemed just a matter of time.

On December 17, the Allied warships finally reached Odessa. After a local White unit expelled some Ukrainian troops that had briefly moved into the city, an advance guard of 1,800 Allied troops came ashore the same day. On December 18, the first waves of what would be a 70,000-man army, magnificently equipped with all the hardware of modern war—tanks, artillery, trucks, armored cars, and even airplanes—began to disembark from the transports. The enormous quantities of matériel seemed to confirm that the French and other Allies were in Odessa to stay.

People rushed out onto the streets leading to the harbor to cheer the arriving troops as saviors and liberators. After months of anxiety, the joyful unreality of the scene was magnified by the exotic appearance of the soldiers, few of whom, it turned out, actually came from mainland France. Most were from French colonies in North Africa, including black Muslims from Morocco and 30,000 Zouaves from Algeria, whose uniforms included fezzes and picturesque, baggy red pants. There was also a large contingent of tough-looking Greeks in khaki kilts and caps with long tassels.

As the Allied troops continued to pour in, they spread out from Odessa in a semicircle twenty miles long, with the Black Sea at their backs. This was the solid barrier that the French commander in chief, General Franchet d'Espèrey, who was based in Constantinople, promised would allow a White Russian army to grow.

At first, the French occupation invigorated civilian life in Odessa. More people crowded into the restaurants and theaters, there was less shooting in the center, and the speculators were busier than ever. But as the spring of 1919 approached, the situation began to

160 THE BLACK RUSSIAN

deteriorate very rapidly in every conceivable way. The Bolsheviks defeated Allied forces in two major towns some seventy miles to the east, and then started to move toward Odessa itself. The Whites were unable to coordinate their recruitment efforts effectively either among themselves or with the French. By March, the food situation in Odessa had become dire, the city's infrastructure was collapsing, and an epidemic of typhus had broken out. The high commands in Paris and Constantinople concluded that the entire Odessa adventure had been a strategic error and that they had to evacuate the city. On April 6, 1919, Frederick had to escape the Bolsheviks once again.

7

REINVENTION IN
CONSTANTINOPLE

The American consulate general in Constantinople did not have the money or the inclination to provide much practical help to the refugees from Odessa after they finally disembarked on the Galata quay. Frederick initially took his family to the Pera Palace Hotel, which was one of the two best in the city. Staying there was an indulgence that he could ill afford, but it must have been an enormous relief to immerse oneself in the cleanliness and comforts of a good hotel after the filth and deprivations of *Imperator Nikolay* and the degrading quarantine at Kavaka.

The Pera Palace had opened in 1895 on the heights of the city's European district as a modern residence for the passengers of the Orient Express, the fabled train that ran from London, Paris, and Venice (in reality as well as fiction and film), across all of Europe to the Sirkeci Terminal in Stambul. Other than the sultan's Dolmabahçe Palace, the Pera Palace was the first building in Constantinople with electricity, an electric elevator, and hot running water. In its heyday before and after the Great War its famous guests included Emperor Franz Josef of Austria-Hungary; Edward VIII of the United Kingdom; Mustafa Kemal (Atatürk), the founder of modern-day Turkey;

Ernest Hemingway; Greta Garbo; and Agatha Christie, among many others. Lavishly decorated with stained glass, marble, and gilded plaster (recently refurbished to all its former glory), the hotel had wonderful views of the Bosporus and the Golden Horn and was the epitome of the Pera district—a cosmopolitan, Westernized island in an otherwise Turkish Muslim sea.

The Pera Palace Hotel was then one of the main centers of social and business life in Constantinople, and a crossroads for people who had either money or ideas about how to make it. Shortly after he arrived, Frederick ran into an old Moscow acquaintance, the Romanian musician Nitza Codolban, a large-nosed man with slicked-back hair, sad eyes, and a big smile. He was a virtuoso of the cimbalom, an instrument resembling a hammered dulcimer that was very popular in Gypsy music.

Codolban recalled how struck he was by Frederick's passion and eagerness to confront the difficulties ahead: "I'm going to try something desperate," the black man proclaimed, "and I've got a few ideas."

Frederick went on to explain that he was going to start everything from zero. He described how he had overcome far bigger obstacles than the Black Sea to stop now. He also said that he liked this new city, which even reminded him a bit of Moscow.

Frederick then swore to Codolban, as he said he had already sworn to his wife, that he had had enough. No matter what happened in Constantinople, he would never leave. This is where he would die, he declared, after "conquering the Bosphorus nights," in Codolban's florid recollection. "And so, will you join me?" he concluded with his memorable smile.

Much impressed by Frederick's energy, Codolban decided that he would put off leaving Constantinople and, in a reference to their shared past, agreed to work in what he assumed would be a "new Maxim," a nightclub to be named after its famous Moscow predecessor. But Frederick was not ready to move so quickly: "Not a Maxim yet. You have to move slowly with luck," he explained. "I'm going to start with a Stella."

Despite the physical and cultural distance Frederick had traveled, he discovered that Pera suited him surprisingly well. All the Western embassies were located there, as were the most important businesses, banks, fashionable restaurants, bars, and shops. Many of the buildings on the main streets were half a dozen stories high, constructed of light-colored stone, and European in style. The population was mixed; in addition to Turks there were large numbers of Greeks, Armenians, Jews, and people known locally as "Levantines," or natives of European descent. Even though spoken Turkish was unlike anything Frederick had heard before, and its written form in Arabic was unintelligible to him, the language of commerce and the second language of the city's elites was French, which he spoke fluently. This would make life and work in Constantinople much easier.

Frederick also soon noticed some similarities between Constantinople and Moscow because of how both straddled East and West, the old and the new. Despite its European traits and cosmopolitan character, prerevolutionary Moscow often struck visitors as having an Oriental cast due to the unfamiliar architecture of its numerous churches and the traditional garb worn by peasants, priests, and other exotic types. Similarly, in Constantinople the shop signs in French on the Grande rue de Pera, the European district's central thoroughfare, as well as the automobiles, the streetcars, and the men in business suits, all proclaimed "the West." But like the fez (the signature tasseled red hat of the Ottoman Empire) that many of the men wore, reminders that Constantinople was on the border between continents and cultures were never far from sight.

Like Moscow, Constantinople had its own religious "soundscape" that showed visitors how far they had traveled. Instead of a chorus of church bells marking the daily round of services, here it was a single male voice from atop a minaret calling the faithful to prayer five times a day. The muezzin would begin with a mellifluous tenor chant—"Allahu Akbar," "God is Great"—that would draw out into a long, oscillating slide, slowly soaring and descending, like a seagull riding a breeze over the Golden Horn. The muezzin's final words— "La ilaha illa Allah," "There is no god except the One God"—would then fade and dissolve in the crash of the city's background noise: the clatter of cart wheels and hooves on cobblestones, trams banging and squealing, automobile klaxons blaring as drivers raced through narrow streets, vendors shrieking out the virtues of their wares.

Just walking up the steep streets from Galata to Pera was like passing through an ethnic kaleidoscope. Harold Armstrong, one of the many English officers who served in the Allied military administration of the city, captured this impression (even though he viewed it with an Occidental's superciliousness).

> There were long-bearded Armenian priests with rusty gowns and chimney-pot hats, and Greek priests in top-hats with the brims knocked off and dirty shabby boots sticking out from under dingy gowns. There were *hodjas* [Muslim schoolmasters] in turbans, Turks and French colonial troops in fezes. There were slit-eyed Kalmucks, great gaunt eunuchs, Turkish bloods of the Effendi and Pasha [lord and master] class, men with hats on, as in London, men with black astrakan brimless caps on, just as in Teheran or Tiflis. There were women in veils and women in hats, and street vendors and beggars with horrors of open sores and mutilated limbs asking for alms. Some loitered talking and sucking cigarettes. The rest elbowed and rushed, twisted, turned and butted me off the narrow pavements into the complicated medley of vehicles in the road. Everywhere there was confusion, noise and bustle.

A sight that especially astounded many visitors was the city's "hamals," traditional porters who carried enormous loads on their backs, be it hundreds of pounds of coal, a freshly killed beef carcass, or a new bureau measuring twelve by four feet and filling the entire narrow street so that pedestrians had to squeeze into doorways to let it pass.

The Galata Bridge over the Golden Horn that linked the European districts with Muslim Stambul on the other side showed most spectacularly the city's mix of cultures. Visitors would go to the bridge just to observe the great parade of people wending their way across: Turks, Tatars, Kurds, Georgians, Arabs, Russians, Jews; sailors from American warships, Gypsies in tattered robes, Persians in high fur caps. On any given day, one could see a Circassian from the Caucasus in a tunic with rows of cartridge pockets and a sheathed dagger in his belt, a French Catholic Sister of Charity in her billowing black robes, or an old Turk with a bit of green on his turban to show that he had made the pilgrimage to Mecca. The transport on the bridge was as varied as the population: modern automobiles, wagons drawn by horses and oxen, mules hauling baskets, even occasional caravans of camels.

Once across the bridge, however, the crowds and racket melted away. In 1919, Stambul was still the home of old Muslim Turkish traditions, with narrow, quiet, shaded streets; the upper floors of the weathered two- and three-story wooden houses, shuttered and jutting out over passersby, dimmed the light even more. In Stambul life turned inward, and at night the quarter was silent and seemed deserted. But at its heart, concentrated in a space less than a mile long, are Constantinople's grandest and most cherished monuments from the past, and what Frederick saw then, one can still see today. In the middle soars Hagia Sophia, built by the Byzantine emperor Justinian in the sixth century, once the patriarchal basilica of Eastern Christianity, and converted into a mosque by the Ottomans after their conquest in the fifteenth century. Facing it like an echo in stone is the vast, blue-tiled seventeenth-century Mosque of Sultan Ahmed, its rising cascade of domes guarded by six minarets. And on Seraglio Point, jutting into the Bosporus, sprawls Topkapi Palace—a maze of pavilions, galleries, and courtyards that was the residence of the sultans for four hundred years, before the Dolmabahçe Palace was built in the nineteenth century. The glories of the Ottoman past, and remnants of Byzantine architectural marvels, were everywhere in Stambul. Then as now, no visit to the quarter could end without a foray into its Grand Bazaar—a labyrinthine covered market encompassing scores of streets and thousands of shops, all piled high with a riot of goods.

Like the European quarter where Frederick settled, Constantinople's postwar history also seemed fashioned to fit his needs. The Allies began their occupation only days after the armistice, with the British taking control of Pera. The French got Galata, as well as Stambul. The Italians were in Scutari, on the Asian side of the Bosporus. Because the Americans had not been at war with Turkey, they did not administer any territory, but their activities and interests were also concentrated in Pera; in fact, the American embassy and consulate general were only a few dozen steps from the Pera Palace Hotel, where Frederick stayed at first.

The Allies also arrived with plans to stay. They had agreed among themselves to carve up the vast Ottoman Empire, leaving only the core of Anatolia to the Turks, and to divide its mineral- and oil-rich territories by drawing lines across maps without regard to who lived where. The affected areas included present-day Iraq and the Arabian Peninsula, and we live to this day with the consequences of those decisions. Constantinople itself would be transformed into an international city, resembling what Shanghai had been in China since the nineteenth century. To secure their position and to intimidate the defeated Turks, the Allies brought a fleet of several dozen warships to the Bosporus and anchored them off the Dolmabahçe Palace.

Thousands of British, French, Italian, and American officers, soldiers, sailors, diplomats, and businessmen poured into the city, and the nature of commerce in Pera changed accordingly. Many of the military arrivals were single men who brought with them an appetite for wine, women, and song. Such interests were inimical to conservative Turkish Muslim culture, but the liberal, Europeanized districts were happy to satisfy them. And it is doubtful that there was anyone in Constantinople in the spring of 1919 with more or better experience in this line of work than Frederick.

The historical and social forces swirling through the city had thus created another charmed circle, one within which Frederick could try to reproduce the world that had made him rich and famous in Moscow. He would have to deal with the American diplomats and their racism, but Jenkins's acceptance of him in Odessa set a precedent that he could try to build on in the future.

Frederick also had the consolation that for the Turks and other natives of Constantinople, his race was of no concern. The Ottoman Empire had stretched from North Africa to Europe to the Near East and into Asia; it was racially heterogeneous and parsed the world very differently than white America did. A Turk who met Frederick would want to know first if he was a Muslim or not and after learning that he was a Christian would not care at all that he was married to a white Christian woman. In fact, black Africans had regularly risen to high positions at the Turkish sultan's court. The Ottoman language, which was replaced by modern Turkish only in 1928, did not even have a special word for "Negro" in the American sense; it used "Arap," or "Arab," for anyone who was dark-skinned. (The African-American writer James Baldwin would discover that this tradition was still alive in Istanbul as late as the 1960s.) History had uprooted Frederick from Russia very painfully, but the place of exile that it had chosen for him was unique in the world at the time. He had been given a remarkable second chance.

In comparison with the vibrant world of popular Western entertainment that Frederick had known in Moscow and even in Odessa,

Constantinople was a backwater. When he arrived, there were a few elegant European-style restaurants with music in Pera, one or two places with variety acts onstage, and quite a few bars and other drinking establishments that catered mostly to Levantines and to the growing numbers of foreigners, especially military officers. Down the hill near the Galata port, the narrow, foul-smelling streets, which turned to mud whenever it rained, were filled with beer joints and cheap bordellos patronized by sailors and enlisted men; drugs, especially cocaine, were also readily available. Some of these places were so vile that they were put off-limits by the military authorities. The city's traditionally-minded Turkish men shunned Western entertainment and did not drink alcohol or consort with women outside their families; they frequented the ubiquitous coffeehouses instead. Traditional Turkish women did not participate in public entertainments at all and wore veils when they ventured out of the home; they also did not go out into the street after seven o'clock at night. What Constantinople lacked were precisely the kinds of places that Frederick had owned in Moscow—elegant, sophisticated whirls of Western music, entertainment, dancing, drink, and enticing cuisine.

To find the money he needed to start something like this, Frederick turned to partners and moneylenders. Constantinople was a major crossroads for trade between Asia and Europe and teemed with merchants of different nationalities; Greeks and Armenians were especially prominent. Many had profited from the war, and several offered Frederick short-term loans at usurious rates—more than 100 percent interest for six months. Frederick had no choice; he had landed in Constantinople shortly before the beginning of the summer season and could not afford to miss it. Without enough money to buy or rent a suitable building, he decided to open an outdoor entertainment garden, on the lines of his Aquarium, although on a humbler scale. Summers began earlier and lasted longer in Constantinople than in Moscow, so if all went well this venture would go on into the fall; after that he would see.

Frederick was also used to working with partners. By May 15, less than a month after he arrived, he had settled on two—Arthur Reyser Jr. and Bertha Proctor. Little is known about Reyser except that he was Swiss, and that he and Proctor, who was English, shared a half interest in the new venture; the other half was Frederick's. Each half represented a sizable investment—3,000 Turkish pounds (abbreviated "Ltqs"), which would be approximately $50,000 in today's money. Reyser would be a passive partner, not involved in running the business on a daily basis.

Bertha Proctor was something else entirely. A barkeep by profession who specialized in men in uniform, she had made a fortune during the war running a renowned watering hole in Salonika in Greece that was called simply "Bertha's Bar." When the war ended and the British army left Greece for Constantinople, she followed it. Although not exactly a madam, she was remembered very warmly by her many clients as much for her friendly and beautiful bar girls—some of them with colorful nicknames like "Frying Pan," "Square Arse," "Mother's Ruin," and "Fornicating Fannie"—as for her good liquor.

Bertha's experience and connections were excellent complements to Frederick's. In her youth she had been a chorus girl and spent years performing in cabarets on the Continent, so she knew the world of popular entertainment intimately. By the time Frederick met her, she was a fleshy, buxom woman of a certain age, with peroxided, lemon-yellow hair piled high on her head, who liked to sit on a stool behind her bar, placidly knitting, while observing the scene and directing her girls. Her innocuous appearance was deceptive, however. In addition to being a shrewd businesswoman and diviner of men's hearts, she was "a top limey spy," as Lieutenant Robert Dunn, who worked in American naval intelligence in Constantinople, put it. Her job was to eavesdrop on foreigners' conversations and to report anything of interest to British Intelligence. This was an especially productive pastime during the Allied occupation of Constantinople, when the city became "the political whispering gallery of the world," in Dunn's words, and a hotbed of intrigue, rumors, and espionage. Despite her many years abroad, Bertha preserved her thick Lancashire accent: "Look I've coom to ask if it's by your orders that these bloody detectives . . . they've found nawt, lad . . . it's damn disgoosting." With Frederick's Delta drawl, their conversations must have been an earful.

Bertha's popularity with British officers—her prices and women were out of reach for the rank and file—would prove a boon for Frederick, both at the start of his career in Constantinople and later. The two decided to give their venture a name that covered both sides of the Atlantic and called it the "Anglo-American Garden Villa"; it was also known as the "Stella Club." The hybrid name reflected the symbiotic relationship between the two parts of the enterprise: Bertha would preside over her bar while Frederick handled everything else—booking variety acts, hiring employees for the kitchen and restaurant, and dealing with contractors and wholesalers of provisions.

"Bertha and Thomas," as the partners became known, found a large parcel of land on the northern edge of Pera in an area known as Chichli. It was across the street from the last stop of the Number 10 tramway line, which made it readily accessible by public transportation from the center. But the location was also risky, because in 1919 it hardly looked like part of the city. Only half of it was built up, mostly with shabby-looking two- and three-story houses of brick and weather-beaten wood, while the rest consisted of large fruit and vegetable gardens and empty lots that merged into the countryside a short distance away. However, the parcel was relatively cheap to rent and had a scattering of old shade trees as well as a nice view of the Bosporus (the area is now completely built up with apartment buildings that block all street-level views). There was also a roomy house in a corner of the property, which is where Frederick and his family probably moved after leaving the Pera Palace.

By the end of June, the empty lot had been transformed into a mini Aquarium: several simple wooden structures were built; there were pavilions and kiosks, neat gravel paths, and strings of electric lights that made the entire place glow at night. Staff people were hired and purveyors of food and drink lined up. An open-air dance floor occupied a central spot, with a stage behind it and tables for customers facing it. The "Stella Club" was on the second floor of one of the buildings. Advertisements had been appearing in local French- and English-language newspapers for several weeks and on Tuesday, June 24, 1919, the Anglo-American Garden Villa opened.

A new era in Constantinople's nightlife had begun. The establishment offered first-class dinners and suppers in a garden restaurant, an American bar, private rooms, a Gypsy band, and variety acts. For herself, Bertha added that she had "the honour to invite all her British friends to be present"; later she extended a more spirited invitation: "Friends of the Salonica Army, Fall In. We are waiting for you." Frederick also exploited his past celebrity to underscore the attentive personal service and sophisticated cuisine that patrons could expect from him: "Teas, Dinners and Suppers under the special superintendence of the well-known Moscow Maitre d'hôtel Thomas." He would become famous in Constantinople for his signature warmth and the big smiles with which he greeted his customers.

The partners' gamble paid off. The opening weeks of the Anglo-American Villa were very promising, even though expenses were high and the profits were thin. The changeable summer weather was also worrisome. A journalist who admired the place noted sympathetically that "the night winds are decidedly incommodating nowadays for outdoor theatrical performances. At Chichli they blow the stage curtain about and even the curtain doors of the bathing boxes, giving the public a glimpse of [the performers] Mme Milton and Mme Babajane in their preparations." But as the weather improved, the number of customers increased; they were drawn by the unique combination of Russo-French cuisine, pretty Russian waitresses, dancing to the Codolban Brothers Gypsy band, and a cascade of lively variety acts onstage.

Frederick made even bigger entertainment history that summer. On August 31, the Anglo-American Villa announced what would become a key to his future success and renown in the city: "For the first time in Constantinople a Jazz-Band executed by Mr. F. Miller and Mr. Tom, the latest sensation all over Europe." Freddy Miller was an Englishman who did parodies of musical acts and sang humorous songs—his most popular was the stuttering hit "K-K-K-Katie"; "Mr. Tom," a black American, was an "eccentric" dancer with an amusing routine. They were not professional jazz musicians, but their comedy act included some jazz interludes. Their performance was a hit and, with Frederick, they get credit for introducing this quintessentially black American music to Turkey just as it was beginning to conquer London, Paris, Shanghai, Buenos Aires, and everywhere in between. As he had in Moscow, Frederick continued to follow new trends in entertainment closely, and he would import more real jazz to Constantinople in the years ahead. However, even with his nose for innovation, he could not have foreseen how this jaunty music would contribute to the revolutionary transformation of Turkish society that was just beginning.

By the end of the summer, the Anglo-American Villa was pronounced a resounding success by the *Orient News*, the authoritative newspaper of the "Army of the Black Sea," as the British occupiers of Constantinople styled themselves.

Far the best evening entertainment in town is to be found at the Villa Anglo-Americain, Chichli. Mme. Bertha and M. Thomas have succeeded in engaging the finest talent for their stage and attracting the most elegant *monde* to their tables. . . . There is no doubt that the Chichli Villa will continue to give the best vaudeville in Constantinople. That fine hunting ground for artistes, Bucharest, is to be searched by M. Thomas for new talent for the winter season.

But Frederick's new plan to book acts in Bucharest, the capital of Romania, ran into a serious obstacle. To travel, he would need a passport, and to get one he had to apply to the American consulate general. This would be far more complicated and risky than appealing to Jenkins for help in Odessa had been.

Frederick took the plunge on October 24. It was a Friday, the Muslim day of worship, when the city's usual noise and bustle abated somewhat as the faithful prepared to attend services in their mosques. When Frederick got to the consulate general, which was in the middle of Pera and around the corner from the embassy, he met with Charles E. Allen, the vice-consul.

Allen was a twenty-eight-year-old from Kentucky who had worked at a variety of jobs in the United States—high school teacher, principal, railway clerk—before joining the Foreign Service four years earlier. His first postings had been to Nantes, a small city in western France, and Adrianople, a provincial city in western Turkey—neither a very glamorous beginning to a diplomatic career. As Allen's actions would show, he was not well disposed toward the black man in front of him, who arrived trailing stories of riches and fame in Moscow, and with a white wife and a clutch of mixed-race sons in tow.

Frederick had to give responses to questions that Allen then typed onto two forms—a standard "Passport Application" and a much trickier "Affidavit to Explain Protracted Foreign Residence and to Overcome Presumption of Expatriation." The conversation between them was fundamentally dishonest. Frederick did not bother to be very accurate and made a series of big and small mistakes and doubtful statements about his past, including inventing a sister in Nashville who could supposedly vouch for him. But he was much more careful about his future intentions and said that he wanted the passport to go to Russia and France, where he intended to "settle my property interests en route to the U.S. to put my children in school." This was an obvious smoke screen and it is unlikely that

Allen believed him. Frederick had no financial interests in France, although he might have fantasized about moving there because Paris was becoming known for its hospitality toward black Americans. And he could not possibly have wanted to return to Russia while the Bolsheviks were in power and a civil war was raging. Frederick (and Allen) also knew perfectly well that he and his family would be unable to lead normal lives in much of the United States, where Jim Crow was riding triumphant together with a reborn Ku Klux Klan, and where his marriage to Elvira would be widely seen as not only reprehensible but illegal. (Constantinople's English- and French-language newspapers regularly ran lurid articles about American racial policies and lynchings.)

Frederick's biggest problem during his interview with Allen was clearly his decades-long residence abroad, which raised the suspicion that he had expatriated himself. There was little that Frederick could say to mitigate this, but he tried—he claimed that he had intended to return to the United States in 1905, but had gotten only as far as the Philippines. Whether or not Frederick took such a trip is uncertain, although he did mention it to other Americans later and provided some plausible-sounding details. In any event, it would hardly have satisfied Allen's or the State Department's misgivings.

For his part, Allen responded to Frederick with negligence, or worse, and did not fill out several important sections on the forms. These omissions would have been enough to invalidate the application in the eyes of the State Department, had it been sent. But Allen did not even bother to forward it to Washington; he let the documents languish at the consulate general for the next fourteen months. The most likely conclusion is that he had decided to sabotage the application by setting it aside.

Dealing with Allen was just the first of the problems that began to crowd around Frederick that fall. Money was next, and this too would do nothing to improve his standing at the consulate general. Despite the Garden's popularity during the summer season, its income was still insufficient to cover all of the operating costs—food, drink, fuel, housing, and everything else were very expensive in Constantinople—or the loans that Frederick had taken out. When the weather deteriorated in the fall, the Garden's attendance dropped and its financial problems worsened. At first, merchants tried to get what they were owed from Frederick himself. But when he put them off or evaded them, they (believing he was an American citizen) began to bring their complaints to the American consulate general. They did so not only because the city was under Allied occupation, but also because of the so-called Capitulations that gave the United States extraterritoriality in Turkey. This meant that American diplomats had the right to try their nationals in their own courts and according to their own laws rather than in Turkish courts.

The first complaint arrived at the consulate general at the end of November. A Greek subject, George Matakias, reported that Frederick had bought a piano from him for the Anglo-American Villa; when he could not pay for it, he changed the sale to a rental, and still failed to pay what was due. Because the complaint had been addressed to Rear Admiral Mark L. Bristol, who was the highest-ranking military and civilian American in Turkey (he commanded the American squadron of warships sent to Turkey after the war and was also the American high commissioner in the country), the matter landed on the desk of the consul general himself, Gabriel Bie Ravndal. His dealings with Frederick would prove to be somewhat more humane than Allen's, perhaps because of his very different background (he had been born in Norway and grew up in South Dakota, where he published a newspaper and served a term in the state house of representatives before becoming a career diplomat in 1898). Ravndal decided to speak with Frederick in person and got him to agree to return the piano and settle his debt.

However, the other cases that followed did not go as smoothly. In early December, an Italian shopkeeper, Ermano Mendelino, wrote to Ravndal that Frederick owed him 252 Ltqs (around $5,000 today) for wine and groceries and had failed to pay the bill after asking for and receiving an extension. In a direct reference to the Capitulations, Mendelino also accused Frederick of behaving this way because he believed that the Ottoman courts could not touch an American citizen. Ravndal again called Frederick in and tried to mediate between him and Mendelino, but over a year later the Italian had still not been paid. Next came a Bulgarian named Bochkarov who claimed he was owed 34.28 Ltqs for milk that he delivered to the Villa and to Frederick's home. A baker wrote that Frederick owed him 47.93 Ltqs for daily bread deliveries. Another man complained that he had not received the 55 Ltqs he had been promised. A prominent French firm in the city—Huisman, suppliers of furnishings of various kinds—which started doing business with Frederick several days before the Villa opened and delivered goods to him worth 964.95 Ltqs (over $20,000 in today's money), presented its bill to the consulate general. Frederick paid part of this debt, but not until nine months later and only after Ravndal had interceded once again. There were many other such cases to come.

All of this was annoying and humiliating for Frederick, especially in light of the financial security he had achieved in Moscow. It also put him in a false position; although he was quite willing to bend laws when it suited him, he was not the kind of man who would try to swindle tradesmen. But even worse than facing angry creditors who caused scenes at the Villa was enduring the sanctimonious lectures of the diplomats at the consulate. When dealing with them, Frederick found himself transformed from a businessman who commanded dozens of employees into a supplicant trying to placate unfriendly superiors. Shortly before Christmas of 1919, Ravndal admonished him "to arrange all these matters amicably in the very near future. . . . I should like to avoid the annoyance and expenses of court proceedings in these matters but I cannot refuse to take cognizance of suits if such are filed." Frederick's financial problems were becoming an embarrassment to American interests in Constantinople.

His problems were not restricted to the Villa during the difficult fall of 1919. In November he tried to find Olga, his oldest daughter, who had been separated from the family during their evacuation from Odessa in April. Contrary to the hopeful suggestion of the British consul, she had not turned up in Constantinople on any of the other refugee ships from South Russia. Frederick made additional inquiries through the British embassy in Constantinople, and to add weight to his request he deposited thirty pounds sterling with the embassy to cover Olga's passage, should she be found. This was a substantial sum (worth around $4,000 today), and it would not have been easy for him to raise when he could not pay the milk and bread bills for his three sons. The British in Odessa made an effort to find Olga, but without success. It would be several more years before Frederick would learn anything about her fate.

With the onset of Constantinople's cold, wet, and frequently snowy winter, Frederick's business problems got even worse and the prospect of financial ruin began to loom before him. The Anglo-American Villa's optimistically named "Winter Salon" became unusable after the fall season, and the only solution, despite the heavy new expenses this would entail, was to find a heated space. On January 20, 1920, he announced the opening of "The Royal Dancing Club" at 40 rue de Brousse in Pera, a central location in comparison with Chichli, and the site of a previous establishment called the "Jockey Club," a name he also kept. To attract new clients and keep his old ones happy, Frederick tried several innovations. The place was organized as an actual club that people had to join—an arrangement that may have been necessitated by the gambling, specifically baccarat, which went on in an upstairs room. Frederick also stressed ballroom dancing and provided free lessons in the fox-trot, shimmy, and tango by American and Italian "professors." Together with jazz, "dancings"—as such events and the places that fostered them came to be known in Constantinople—would become one of the main reasons for his later success. And like jazz, European-style dancing would also become culturally and politically loaded in Turkey in the 1920s because of the way it broke down the barriers that separated men and women in Ottoman society. Mustafa Kemal would personally encourage this during his aggressive campaign to secularize the country starting in 1923.

Frederick was fortunate that Bertha was still willing to continue their partnership that winter, despite the unpleasant discussions they were beginning to have about unpaid bills. Her bar remained an essential draw for military clients and helped to keep the entire enterprise afloat. A young American who visited one night with a friend, an English major, captured the seductive atmosphere of cosmopolitan wantonness that it fostered.

> Bertha's Bar looked like the lithographs of "Uniforms of all Nations." A monocled French Colonial commandant sat at a corner table. Two handsome girls were with him. Two young men in Italian blue-grey sat along the bar. At another table was a group of mid-Europeans who wore their caps, with the flat, square crown and a tassel, with gravity. A sprinkling of British subalterns, a couple of French sous-officiers de marine, in their rather shabby and inelegant blue, and several young women, completed the picture.
>
> Bertha leaned ponderously forward and put a mammoth confidential elbow on the bar near the Major. . . .
>
> He sipped meditatively.
>
> "Where's Aphro, Bertha," he inquired presently.
>
> Bertha looked at him with a speculative eye.
>
> "She's not here any more," she responded negligently.
>
> The Major did not pursue the subject.
>
> "Melek?" he inquired.
>
> "Her mother is sick in Skutari," said Bertha with precision.
>
> "Nectar?"—the Major turned to his companion—"a lovely Armenian kid," he said.

"Nectar is here," said Bertha.

"Where," asked the Major.

"She'll be here soon," Bertha answered. . . .

Bertha put down her knitting and became confidential again.

"You'll fancy the new little Greek," she said.

"You don't say," said the Major. "Quite new?"

"Yes—from the Dodecanese. She just came up from Smyrna today."

"From Smyrna? M-m-m—that's not good," said the Major. "Pretty big port, Smyrna."

Bertha leaned back and scratched her neck with a knitting needle. She turned her head sidewise.

"Doris," she called. . . .

A slender wisp of a girl appeared in the doorway. She was dressed in a white frock, cut square across the breast and suspended over either shoulder by a little silken strap so that no trace of their marble beauty was shrouded. Neck, shoulders, and head merged with an elegance and justness that seemed artificial, it was so perfect. The head was small, the features regular and exquisitely moulded. Gold hair drawn loosely back and up from the nape of the neck revealed little ears. Eyes were large and blue, the mouth was rosy. Doris' expression was mild and ravishingly child-like.

"*Baccalum* [We'll see], Doris," said Bertha, and took her by the hand to present her to the Major and his friend.

The Royal Dancing Club let Frederick limp through the winter. However, when spring came and he began to plan to reopen Villa Stella, Bertha and Reyser decided that its prospects were too dim and announced they were quitting. This was a serious blow for Frederick. He did not have the money to proceed alone, and the Villa had accumulated debts totaling 4,500 Ltqs, the equivalent of $75,000 today.

This case also landed in the consulate general. Allen and the others were becoming increasingly exasperated by Frederick's financial problems, but they were still constrained in their dealings with him by their belief that he was an American and thus entitled to their assistance. They suggested that he submit to binding arbitration. The process was complex but when he emerged from it his hopes had been rekindled. He not only was free of his former partners but had found a new Russian partner with money, a certain Karp Chernov, who had faith in Stella's long-term prospects. The debts had not disappeared, but as Frederick explained in a handwritten letter to Ravndal, he was doing everything in his power to pay them off in installments.

Villa et Jardin   Constantinople le 10 of July 1920
Anglo-Americain
Chichli No. 312

To His Honorable
the Americain Counsul.

Sir

In answer to your letter of July the 7., I beg to explain, we, Thomas and Tschernoff, gave our word, that we would pay not only the person mentioned, but all our Dettes 4500. (turkish Pounds), in June. We have done our best, the month was cold and rainy, but we managed to cut it down from 4500. to 3000. t. P. The Firm in question has received from 1000 Pounds Dette 700- and Sir, the rest 300. Pounds, will bee settled in 15. days time. Hoping Sir, you will believe, that this explanation and figures are true,

I remain yours
respectfully
Frederick Bruce Thomas.

Frederick was so pressed financially that several days after writing he sent Elvira to the consulate general to speak with Ravndal personally. She was an attractive woman with a sweet disposition and, in the end, her efforts paid off. Ravndal agreed to intercede with the biggest and most insistent creditor and won Frederick some more time.

That spring, two dramatic historical events occurred that seemed to secure Frederick's future no matter where it would play out, in Turkey or Russia. The first was the Allies' decision to consolidate their occupation of Constantinople. On March 16, 1920, the British landed additional troops and established what was effectively martial law. The Allies assumed direct control over all aspects of social, economic, and judicial life in the city, and seized hundreds of private and public buildings to house military and civilian personnel. They also tried to suppress both of Turkey's political wings by arresting scores of prominent representatives of the old Ottoman regime, as well as numerous leaders of the new Turkish Nationalist Movement that had formed around Mustafa Kemal in opposition to both the sultanate and the Allied occupation.

The overall British aim was to force the Turks to ratify the very harsh Treaty of Sèvres, which formally abolished the Ottoman Empire and apportioned much of its territory to the Allies and their protégés. These included the Greeks, who had already invaded Smyrna on the Aegean coast, thus initiating a three-year war with the Turkish Nationalists; the Armenians, who were victims of Ottoman genocide during and shortly after the Great War and now claimed their own state; and the Kurds, who were also clamoring for independence. For the Turks this "second occupation" was a devastating blow to sovereignty and national pride (and a powerful stimulus to throw off the Allied yoke). But for a foreigner like Frederick it was a boon because it moved Constantinople a big step closer toward becoming an internationalized city, one where Western interests—and entertainments—could thrive.

The other development that spring was, if anything, even more promising because it affected the future of Frederick's adopted home-land. On April 4, 1920, the leaders of the White Army in the South of Russia elected General Baron Pyotr Wrangel as their commander in chief to replace General Anton Denikin, who had lost their con-fidence and retired. A more able and charismatic leader than his predecessor, Wrangel reorganized and enlarged his forces and cre-ated an effective Black Sea fleet. The invasion of Ukrainian territory by Poland that spring helped him defeat the Bolsheviks in several engagements and double the territory that the Whites controlled in the south of Russia. The achievement was quickly heralded in Constantinople's newspapers. For a time, it began to look as if the setbacks suffered by the Whites during the past year could be reversed and the Bolshevik regime might fall or be defeated. Were this to happen, Frederick and other exiles could return home and reclaim their former lives and property.

But the influx of Allied troops was not the only change in the city's population in the spring of 1920, and the arrival of other newcomers presented Frederick with an unexpected threat as well as an oppor-tunity. Despite the apparent successes of the Whites in the civil war, waves of evacuees from southern Russia kept crossing the Black Sea, and as a result Constantinople was becoming increasingly Russified. Among the new arrivals were many popular performers, some with experience running their own shows and theaters, and all needing to make a living. Russian restaurants and nightspots began to pop up all over Pera. Many tried to play up the "broad Russian nature" that foreigners found highly seductive—unbridled revelry and passion, although now tinged with a delicious sadness over a lost, glorious past. Frederick discovered that he suddenly had competition.

The biggest threat was a new garden, Strelna, that two famous singers, Yury Morfessi and Nastya Polyakova, decided to open just two short blocks away from Stella, in a strategic location chosen to siphon off Frederick's clients. Their initiative paid off, leading Morfessi to boast that as "'Stella' dimmed," Strelna's affairs "blossomed" and went "blissfully well." The drop in attendance at Stella could have been its end, especially because of all the other financial difficulties that were still hanging over Frederick. Only a bit of skullduggery on the part of one of his performers saved him: she denounced Morfessi to the Interallied Police for staying open after a mandatory curfew, and Strelna was shut down.

In addition to competition, however, the new waves of Russian refugees also brought a valuable resource with them—a substitute for the bar girls Frederick had lost when he and Bertha parted ways. Among the refugees were numerous members of the Russian nobility. Many of the women who belonged to this class had never had to work for a living and had neither professions nor salable skills. At the same time, quite a few of the younger ones were very attractive, had well-developed social graces, and often knew foreign languages, in particular French. The majority were also destitute and willing to take any work they could find. Restaurant owners like Frederick quickly realized their worth. Pretty and graceful young women, in particular blue-eyed blondes who were "princesses," "countesses," or "duchesses," could be a very effective draw for any establishment trying to attract more customers. This was especially true if most of the clients were men who were used to only waiters—male waiters having been the norm in conservative Ottoman society—and it was even more true if the women whom Turkish men usually saw were olive-complexioned, sloe-eyed, dark-haired, and swathed in fabric from head to toe. Thus it happened that the French term "dame serveuse" came to denote a young Russian noblewoman who occupied a tantalizing place in Constantinople's collective male imagination— whether that of a Muslim Turk, a Levantine, an Allied officer, a fellow Russian refugee, or a tourist taking in the city's exotic sights. The thrill a customer would get from being served by a titled woman and the resulting tips were sufficient reason for many of these ladies to exaggerate their birthright, often quite shamelessly: never did any city in Russia have as many women of blue and even royal blood as Constantinople in the early 1920s. It was also inevitable that the ambiguous status of these young women—underpaid and frequently obligated to dine or dance with any male clients who took a fancy to them—made it easy for many to slip into the demimonde.

The style of dress that these Slavic sirens adopted varied from restaurant to restaurant. In one place they would flaunt their Russian boldness: "white Caucasian jackets, high black boots, thin scarves around their hair and heavy makeup." In another, they cultivated a softer, decadent seductiveness, as the singer Vertinsky, who had also arrived in 1920, promised at his nightclub "La Rose Noire": "The serving ladies will whisper to the clients the poems of Baudelaire between the courses. They are to be exquisite, select, delicate and to wear each a black rose in their golden hair." Some wore dainty aprons that made them look like soubrettes in light comedy, an impression that they augmented with their shyness and apologetic manner.

The reactions to them in Constantinople were predictable. A group of thirty-two widows of Turkish noblemen and high officials sent a petition to the city governor demanding the immediate expulsion of "these agents of vice and debauchery who are more dangerous and destructive than syphilis and alcohol." The British ambassador, Sir Horace Rumbold, explained wryly in a letter to Admiral de Robeck, the British high commissioner, that the "little Princess Olga Micheladze" plans to marry "one Sanford, a nice quiet fellow in the Inter-Allied Police. . . . He has money." A tourist visiting from Duluth, Minnesota, gushed that the owner of a restaurant "is an escaped Russian grand duke, and all the waitresses are Russian princesses of the royal family." The latter "were pretty and flirted terrifically. I asked one if she spoke any English and the answer, with a quaint accent, was, 'Sure, I know lots American boys.'" A cartoon in the local British newspaper showed a Turk asking a Russian woman: "Parlez-vous français, mademoiselle?" She replies, "No, but I know how to say 'love' in every language."

At the opposite end of the emotional spectrum, more than one visiting foreigner was moved by the sight of an exiled Russian officer rising at his restaurant table with an expression of somber respect on his face to kiss the hand of the waitress approaching him because they had known each other under very different circumstances in their previous lives. Princess Lucien Murat, a French tourist in Constantinople, had a series of similar heart-wrenching encounters with a number of people she had known in prerevolutionary Petrograd—"Baron S," whom she found working as a street bootblack; "Colonel X," who now manned a cloakroom in a restaurant; and then, at Frederick's bar, her old friend "Princess B," whom she had last seen at a ball in Petrograd "in a silvery dress, with her marvelous emeralds in a diadem on her lovely forehead." "The Princess tells me her lamentable tale, her escape from the Bolsheviks, her flight in a crowded cattle-car." Meanwhile, her "Boss" hovers around—"an ebony black, who, in the old days, kept the most fashionable restaurant in Moscow where, many a time, the Princess dined and danced to the music of the tziganes." Princess Lucien's reaction to seeing her old friend in Frederick's employ is revealing in that it provides a glimpse of a dame serveuse from a point of view other than that of an admiring or lascivious male.

Also revealing, but for reasons of Turkish national pride and what this foreshadowed about the future of the Allied enclave in Constantinople, is the reaction of a sharp-eyed young Turkish patriot during a visit to Stella one warm summer evening. Mufty-Zade K. Zia Bey knew the United States well, having lived there for a decade. Together with his wife and a friend, he decided to sample Pera's nightlife and went to the "café chantant" that was the "best" in the city. When they arrived, Stella was crowded and Zia Bey, who was very proud of his conservative, traditional Turkish values, was immediately put off by its libertine atmosphere, although he was impressed by Frederick's manner.

Every one seems to be intoxicated and the weird music of a regular jazz band composed of genuine American negroes fires the blood of the rollicking crowd to demonstrations unknown even to the Bowery in its most flourishing days before the Volstead Act. Much bejewelled and rouged "noble" waitresses sit, drink and smoke at the tables of their own clients. The proprietor of the place, an American coloured man who was established in Russia before the Bolshevik revolution . . . is watching the crowd in a rather aloof manner. Frankly he seems to me more human than his clients; at least he is sober and acts with consideration and politeness, which is not the case with most of the people who are here.

Zia Bey also bristled at the way everything about Stella reflected the foreign presence in the city and the secondary role that had been forced on the city's Muslim natives: "Not one real Turk is in sight. Many foreigners, but mostly Greeks, Armenians and Levantines—with dissipated puffed-up faces, greedy of pleasure and materialism." Before long, Zia Bey and his wife decided to leave. They relaxed only when they were safely out of Pera, across the Galata Bridge, and back home in "our Stamboul, the beautiful Turkish city, sleeping in the night the sleep of the just; poor Stamboul, ruined by fires and by wars, sad in her misery, but decent and noble; a dethroned queen dreaming of her past splendour and trusting in her future." Zia Bey's attitude represented the numerous threats to the foreign world of which Frederick was a part, although there was no reason for him to be aware of them just yet.

With the prominence of the "dames serveuses" in the minds of Constantinople's male population, it was inevitable that racially tinged insinuations about Frederick's relations with his Russian waitresses would have begun to spread among members of the city's American colony. Some intimated that, like "all Negroes," Frederick was prone to "the greatest sexual excesses" and had "a way of compelling various of his employees to accept his caresses." But in fact, as Larry Rue, a reporter from Chicago who looked into the allegations, put it, Frederick's waitresses considered him to be "the 'whitest' employer around" because he not only treated them with respect but allowed them to refuse advances from anyone, including "numerous British officers" who "protested against this high tone morality."

Frederick did not stop at extending his protective circle around his waitresses and even arranged several galas for their financial benefit, which was very unusual in the world of Constantinople nightlife— such events were typically organized on behalf of star performers or the management. His action was a genuine kindness, although it was also shrewd because it put the young women on special display. This was similar to his decision to donate Stella for "A Great Festival of Charity" on July 24, 1920, on behalf of the "Waifs Rescued by the Suppression of Begging Society." The event had been inspired by one of his star performers, the singer Isa Kremer, and sanctioned by the city's highest authorities—the Interallied high commissioners. Both Kremer and Frederick were praised lavishly for their initiative. This participation recalls his donation of Aquarium as a staging area for patriotic manifestations in Moscow during the war.

Despite the crowds of customers and enthusiastic press reports about Stella during its second season, Frederick was still unable to make ends meet. New creditors kept trooping to the increasingly exasperated diplomats at the consulate general. As the number of complaints mounted, Ravndal's and Allen's tone began to change. Initially, they wrote formulaic but polite requests, but Allen in particular began to sound barely civil: "complaints . . . requiring your immediate attention"; "You will furnish me at the earliest possible moment a statement"; "inform me immediately."

Aggravating the situation was that Frederick became the target of extortionists who masqueraded as creditors and pressured the consulate general to help them get money. In light of Frederick's tarnished reputation, the diplomats took all such complaints seriously. The worst of these swindlers was Alexey Vladimirovich Zavadsky, a Russian who in June 1920 hired a lawyer, enlisted the help of the Russian diplomatic mission in the city (which continued to function on behalf of Russian refugees, with the Allies' blessing, even though the empire it represented had vanished), and claimed that Frederick had owed him over 300 Ltqs in wages since the previous summer. Despite pressure from the American diplomats to pay the man off, Frederick adamantly refused, labeling it "a case of chantage"—blackmail. But he was unable to erase the diplomats' impression that all he did was generate trouble for them.

There was worse to come during the fall of 1920 and the following winter, when his ex-wife, Valli, suddenly resurfaced. Her affair with the "Bolshevik commissar" had ended unhappily and by early September she had managed to extricate herself and Irma from Soviet Russia and get to Berlin. Once there, she immediately set about trying to find and contact Frederick. On September 9, she went to the American Commission's offices and applied for a Certificate of Identity and an Emergency Passport for herself and Irma, explaining that she wanted these in order to join her husband wherever he might be. Berlin was a far from happy place in 1920, with serious food shortages, disastrous inflation, high unemployment, and growing social unrest. Her only hope for a decent life was to gain Frederick's financial support.

In Berlin, the consul took her application and explained official State Department policy; her claim about being married to an American would have to be investigated in Washington. When the answer arrived, it could not have been more disappointing: there was no record of the application that Valli had made to renew her passport in Moscow in 1916 (even though she had proof that she had filed one); it was also impossible to verify any passport application by Frederick or his birth in the United States; accordingly, Mrs.

Valentina Thomas's request was denied. This not only was bad news for her but did not bode well for Frederick either.

Judging by the amount of trouble Valli was able to cause Frederick from afar during the next several years, it was his good luck that she did not receive papers allowing her to come to Constantinople. In early October, even before she got the rejection from Washington, she began to write in English and in German to the American consulate general in Constantinople, and later to the British embassy as well, presenting herself as Frederick's only lawful wife, enclosing photographs of them together as proof of their relationship, besmirching Elvira, complaining of being ill and impoverished, pleading for financial support for herself and his daughter, insisting that he could afford to help them because he was well off, and asking for his precise address.

The task of dealing with Frederick fell to Allen, who forwarded a copy of Valli's letter to Frederick and attached a surprisingly presumptuous demand: "I request you to indicate what attention you will give this matter." The consulate general was now involved not only in his financial problems and his claim to American citizenship, but also in what Allen referred to as his "marital relationships." Frederick was becoming an unbearable burden to the American authorities in Constantinople.

8

THE STRUGGLE
FOR RECOGNITION

In the fall of 1920, Wrangel's White Volunteer Army lost its war against the Bolsheviks, dashing the hopes of Russian refugees in Constantinople that they would be able to return home. Following a cease-fire with Poland in October 1920, the Red Army was able to concentrate its forces in the south and pushed the Whites down into the Crimean Peninsula, until their backs were to the Black Sea. The only escape was by water. In early November, Wrangel began to assemble a ragtag fleet of some 130 vessels—everything from former imperial Russian warships and transports to passenger boats and merchant ships, private yachts, and barges towed by other ships. By November 19, the motley flotilla had finished staggering across the Black Sea and dropped anchor off Constantinople, transforming the Bosporus into a floating archipelago of human misery.

There were nearly 150,000 people on board and the conditions were horrible. All of the ships were overcrowded, some so badly that they listed dangerously. Sanitary facilities had been overwhelmed and water and food supplies were exhausted. Passengers willingly traded their wedding bands and the gold crosses around their necks for jugs of water or loaves of bread that enterprising Turks offered from small boats, which had flocked to the Russian ships. There were large numbers of sick and wounded on board. Many of the refugees had only the possessions on their backs.

The remnants of the White Volunteer Army numbered nearly 100,000 men, with the rest civilians, including 20,000 women and 7,000 children. During the days and weeks that followed, the French interned two-thirds of the troops in makeshift camps throughout the region, including the Gallipoli Peninsula, the site of the disastrous Allied landings during the war. But tens of thousands of others, military men and civilians alike, flooded into Constantinople, where they created a humanitarian catastrophe.

November was already cold; the winter winds were beginning to stream down across the Black Sea from the great Russian plain; and housing, food, clothing, and medical care were all in short supply. The Allied authorities, the American Red Cross, the Russian embassy, and other civic organizations did what they could to help. Some of the refugees were herded into hastily designated shelters—abandoned barracks and other partially ruined buildings—where they endured near-freezing temperatures and starvation rations. Some lucky ones got space in the stables of the Dolmabahçe Palace. But many had to manage as best they could on their own and to survive by their wits. There was no trade or job at which they did not try their hand. Those who knew languages tried to teach them or to work in Allied offices. Others hauled bags of coal and cement on the Galata docks; sold shoelaces and sweets from trays on Pera's streets; spun handheld lottery wheels; hired themselves out as doormen, dishwashers, and maids; or simply begged. Army officers tried to sell their medals to passersby on the Galata Bridge. The writer John Dos Passos saw a one-legged Russian soldier standing in the street, covering his face with his hands and sobbing. Out of despair some officers shot themselves. So many Russian women peddled nosegays in an arcade on the Grande rue de Pera that it is known to this day as "Çiçek Pasaji," "Flower Passage." Anyone who had any money tried to start a business: small Russian restaurants sprang up all over like mushrooms after a rain (as Russians liked to put it). Secondhand shops displayed the luxury detritus of a vanished empire—jewelry, watches, icons, furs—that the fortunate had managed to bring out with them. Classically trained musicians, singers, and dancers organized performances and inspired a taste for Western arts that forever changed the city's cultural landscape. Speculators created an unofficial currency exchange on the steep steps from Pera to Galata. A few made fortunes overnight but lost them the following day.

From the start, there was one thought on everybody's mind: how to get out of Constantinople—how to go somewhere, anywhere, that would be better. Wrangel at first tried to keep his army intact, hoping to return to fight in Russia. But the Allies were not interested in supporting his anti-Bolshevik movement any longer and soon began to disperse his troops and the other Russians in the city to any country that would take them—in the Balkans, Western Europe, the Americas, North Africa, Indochina.

The tragedy affecting his former countrymen played out before Frederick's eyes. That fall, when Stella closed for the season, he had to find another place to rent because the Jockey Club was no longer available. His new winter location in the Alhambra Theater was on a busy stretch of the Grande rue de Pera just a few blocks north of the Russian embassy, a neighborhood that became one of the main gathering places for thousands of Russians who milled about day and night in search of work, food, a place to sleep, news, visas, hope. Most of Frederick's kitchen staff and waitstaff, and many performers, were already Russians. Many more showed up at his door after the massive November evacuation, asking for jobs or help. He hired a few out of kindness but turned away most because his staff was complete. However, no one left empty-handed, even though he was hard up himself. For many years afterward, grateful émigrés across the Russian diaspora who had experienced exile in Constantinople still remembered "Fyodor Fyodorovich Tomas" as "the black man with a broad Russian nature" who never denied anyone a free meal.

The Russians' plight had given Frederick a vivid reminder of how one's place in the world could depend entirely on having the right piece of paper in hand. Although he had fallen ill with pneumonia again at the end of November, and was not yet fully recovered, in late December 1920 he went back to the consulate general to inquire about the passport for which he had applied more than a year earlier. We do not know what excuses Allen gave him to explain the extraordinary delay in submitting the paperwork, or if he even admitted that he had never forwarded it to the State Department. But on Friday, December 24, he finally sent the passport application and the "Affidavit to Explain Protracted Foreign Residence" to Washington. As Allen could not have failed to realize, the application was doomed even before he put it into the diplomatic pouch, because he had left it shockingly incomplete. Nevertheless, as if to be doubly sure that it would fail, Allen also appended a statement that was striking in its dishonesty and malevolence.

Referring to the application as an "abandoned" one (but without explaining how it came to be so), Allen identified Frederick as an "American negro"—a loaded characterization that none of the American officials ever omitted in their correspondence about him—and "a waiter by profession." The latter was Allen's attempt to demean Frederick; if the tables had been turned, it would be like Frederick saying that Consul Allen was a "railway clerk" because he had been one in the past. But not only did Allen obscure the fact that by 1920 Frederick had been a major entrepreneur for nearly a decade; he also tried to make Frederick sound like a parvenu when he claimed that "there is considerable doubt as to whether Thomas is a partner or an employee" in his current enterprise. This too was deeply dishonest. Over the past eight months, diplomats at the American consulate had documented in detail Frederick's relations with Arthur Reyser, Bertha Proctor, and Karp Chernov. In fact, Allen himself handled the money transfer between the two sets of partners and deposited a signed copy of the receipt in the consulate records. And just a month earlier, a subordinate whom Allen had charged with the task of pinning down the precise relationship between Frederick and Chernov reported that they were equal partners. Allen concluded with an especially damning complaint about Frederick that summed up all the diplomats' irritation with him.

> His business ventures in Constantinople have been rather unhappy and he has involved this office in innumerable discussions with persons of every nationality seeking payment for goods delivered to him. . . . His presence is, therefore, a source of continual annoyance to this office . . . and reacts unfavorably on American prestige. I would, therefore, request the Department to examine the documents which I transmit herewith with a view to ascertaining whether Thomas, in view of his protracted residence abroad, has or has not lost his right to protection as an American citizen.

Two weeks later, Frederick's paperwork landed on the desk of Joseph B. Quinlan, one of several dozen clerks in the Division of Passport Control in the State Department. Not surprisingly, he found the case "rather unusual," and passed it on to a superior, G. Gilmer Easley. Whereas Quinlan came from the Midwest, Easley was a Virginian. This may have been why he had no doubts whatsoever about the case.

> This negro has submitted no documentary evidence of citizenship. The Department has no record of previous passports. He has no ties with U.S. and apparently has heretofore taken no steps to assert or conserve citizenship by applying for a passport or by

registering. He has apparently little or no intention to return for permanent residence. Accordingly passport should be refused.

This answer is not only racist in the singular way it identifies Frederick; it is also either a lie or evidence of startling ineptitude. During his years abroad, Frederick had registered with American embassies and consulates, and applied for passport extensions eight times: on the first occasion in Paris in 1896, on the last in Moscow in 1914. All of these documents were duly forwarded to the State Department (and would resurface a decade later; but by then it would be too late). It is doubtful that Easley actually bothered to check these records, or that they would have made any difference to him if he did. He also did not seem to care that the application he was judging was scandalously incomplete.

Fortunately for Frederick, during this first round, Easley's recommendation was reviewed at a higher level and overridden. Allen could not have been very happy with the official response that was sent over his head to his superior, Ravndal, by Wilbur J. Carr, the director of the entire consular service, who wrote on behalf of the secretary of state himself. The response, which arrived at the end of February, was a rebuke, in diplomatically measured bureaucratese, aimed at Allen for wasting everyone's time by not following the instructions that were clearly printed on the forms: Frederick has to submit a complete application; he needs to provide evidence of his citizenship and "of his marriage to the woman represented to be his wife." "He should also state definitely his intention with reference to returning to the United States for permanent residence and as to the future place of residence of his family."

This was bad news for Frederick, although it could have been worse. At least his claim to American citizenship had not been rejected out of hand (as it would have been if anyone in the State Department had gotten wind of his Russian citizenship) and he was, in effect, invited to reapply.

In the meantime, he had to counter the considerable damage that Valli was continuing to inflict on his reputation. When she wrote to the consulate general in Constantinople she included copies of documents supporting her claims, including an official translation of her and Frederick's marriage certificate from 1913. Frederick did not have a single document in support of what he said. As a result, the diplomats, who lived in a world made largely of paper and who had already found Frederick unreliable in other respects, believed her and not him. In a letter to Valli in May, Ravndal referred to Frederick as "your husband," and in one to Frederick written on the same day he referred to Valli as "your wife in Germany."

All this aggravated Frederick's already poor relations with the American officials. He could do little except insist on his version of events. Shortly thereafter, he wrote, in his careful longhand, a detailed response to Ravndal, in which he politely and firmly explained "once more": "I have no wife in Germany, because I have my wife with me here." He continued, "As I wrote to you before, I divorced my former wife in Moscow, because she committed a break of marriage in having a Bolshevik Commissar for her lover for about 2 years." Frederick then explained:

> I divorced this Woman and married my present wife under the Bolshevik Laws, because there were no other Laws, as we were living in the Bolshevik time. Now Sir, I will admit, no Man is supposed to support ones former wife one divorced under such circumstances. What concerns me Sir, I know she is not ill because I have some very near relatives of mine living in Berlin, who inform me exactly about the Life my Child is leading there. As I told you before Sir, my former wife is not the mother of my Daughter Irma, as I had no children at all with her and she only keeps my daughter with her because she thinks I'll support her for the Girls' sake, as I would'nt let my Child starve. Certainly if I had a passport, I would go to Berlin and take my Girl away

with me, but now as it is, I can't move from here; what concerns my Documents, which could prove, that divorcing my former wife and marrying my present wife are facts Sir, I've told you before, that I've been robbed of them in Russia, so that I came here to Constantinople without any papers. Now Sir, begging to excuse me for disturbing you once more with this painful story of mine and hoping, I have well explained everything concerning my connection to this Woman, I remain very respectfully

Frederick Bruce Thomas
Borne in Clarksdale Mississippi

Frederick added the phrase about his birthplace as an afterthought (he used a different pen) to remind the diplomats of his claim to an American passport. However, none of this made any difference; the diplomats did not believe him. The next time one of them wrote to the State Department, he characterized Elvira as Frederick's "free-love companion."

Valli's resurfacing in Berlin with Irma was not the only dramatic twist in Frederick's family life at this time. Olga, his oldest daughter, suddenly turned up in Romania, alive, apparently well, and married, with the surname "Golitzine." On June 13, 1921, she had a telegram sent in French from Bucharest to the American consul general in Constantinople requesting that Frederick be informed of her whereabouts and that she "manque totalement"—"has nothing." Getting the news must have been a joy and a relief for Frederick because he had heard nothing about her for over two years, ever since she disappeared during the evacuation of Odessa. He had been very close to her and on the eve of the revolution was grooming her to help him in his business. Frederick may well have recognized her new surname because the Golitsyns (there are different transliterations) were one of the most famous and grandest of princely families in imperial Russia; it is likely, however, that Olga's husband simply had the same name as this family. Frederick did respond to her plea for help. By 1923 he was sending her 1,500 francs a month, which would be equivalent to several thousand dollars today (things had improved for him by then), and he continued to do this for three years, even after she moved to Paris to study.

Despite his chronic money shortages, Frederick husbanded what he had and insisted on trying to give his family in Constantinople the best life that he could. He bought Elvira new outfits from a local couturiere in Chichli, although he did pass on getting her a fur muff that cost the equivalent of $500. As he told a friendly American tourist, he was having his sons educated "at some of the best schools in the Near East," which in Constantinople meant those that were private and foreign. In the summer of 1921, Bruce was six, Fedya seven, and Mikhail fifteen. Given their father's efforts to reestablish himself as an American, and his claim that he intended to return to the United States and place his sons in school, all three must have attended one of the English-language schools in or near the city; there were several to choose from. However, of the three sons, only Mikhail was destined to complete his education and to do so in Prague, which was to become a haven for young Russians in the diaspora in the 1920s.

At the end of August and the beginning of September 1921, the history of Turkey unexpectedly changed and Frederick's fate changed with it. Some two hundred miles to the southeast of Constantinople, on the arid Anatolian highland near the Sakarya River—a place that seemed very far from the marble halls of power on the banks of the Bosporus—the Turkish Nationalist army that had formed under Mustafa Kemal's leadership won a series of bloody battles against the Greek army that had invaded Turkey with Allied help two years

earlier. The Turkish victory stopped a Greek march on Angora—
"Ankara," as it is now known—the Nationalists' new capital, and
was a turning point in what the Turks came to celebrate as their war
for independence against the Allied occupiers. As a result, Italy and
France dropped their plans to partition Anatolia and withdrew from
the region. A year later, Kemal would force the Allies to abandon
the Treaty of Sèvres, including their scheme to transform Constantinople into an international city, a decision that would affect Frederick
directly. For his victory at Sakarya, Kemal, who had already been
elected president by the Turkish Grand National Assembly in April
1920, was promoted to the rank of field marshal and given the title
"Gazi," "warrior against the infidels"—an honorific that dated back
to the Ottomans.

These distant rumblings of war and changes on the geopolitical map of Turkey reminded Frederick once again that it was time
to seek the shelter of an American passport. Moreover, in recent
months his financial situation had finally started to improve. His
income increased and he had managed to pay off most of his earlier
debts. He had also begun to act more assertively toward his remaining creditors as well as the American diplomats, succeeding even in
mollifying Ravndal at times.

When Frederick went to the consulate general on September
15 to fill out a new passport application he was better prepared.
The official who took his information, Alfred Burri, a New Yorker
by birth, was also far more conscientious than Allen had been two
years earlier. Nevertheless, Frederick still stumbled badly when he
came to the all-important "Affidavit to Explain Protracted Foreign
Residence and to Overcome Presumption of Expatriation." In a
spirit of candor that was as misguided as it was surprising, he admitted: "At the present moment I have a growing theatrical business at
Constantinople and wish to be near Russia where I wish to go to
look after my property in Moscow at the first opportunity." And as
if this were not bad enough, he confessed that though he planned

to make a "business trip" to the United States with his "oldest boy" soon, "I have so large a business in Europe & Russia that I must stay near these for some time to come & will keep my family with me." When Frederick left the consulate general, he may have been satisfied that he had completed an important chore, but he did not realize that he had also made a gift to those in Constantinople and Washington who were eager to deny him the protection he sought.

Burri's assessment of Frederick's case, which he had to forward to the State Department, shows that his feelings were mixed. He acknowledges that Frederick is a very clever businessman and "owns and operates by far the highest class cabaret" in Constantinople. He also sympathizes with Frederick and implicitly distances himself from the prevailing American racial bias.

> Without prejudice it is obvious that a colored man with a white wife suffering no social ostracisms or discriminations over here would not be likely to return to the United States. Furthermore his interests in Russia and elsewhere in Europe, and his fairly popular standing would also tend to keep him away from the United States for years.

But none of this prevented Burri from using Frederick's own words to hang him by concluding "that he will never return with his family to the United States for permanent residence." And Burri's final assessment of the application was devastating: "In my opinion Mr. Thomas is an American born negro, living with a free-love companion, [who] cannot satisfactorily explain his protracted foreign residence so as to entitle him to American protection; and this Consulate General should be instructed to deny him such protection."

Frederick got the passport application out of the way at an exciting time in his life, when he was beginning to make plans for an ambitious new venture that could, with luck, make him rich again. By mid-September the summer season at Villa Stella was winding down. Its Winter Salon could continue to function for a while longer—Vertinsky crooned his decadent songs there to great acclaim in October—but the approach of cold weather meant that Frederick would once again have to move his operation to a properly heated space. What he needed was a place of his own that he could use year-round.

Frederick found it just off Taxim Square in Pera, an area where many amusements were concentrated, near the northern end of the Grande rue de Pera on Sira Selvi Street, and thus, unlike Stella, in the center of the European quarter. The space was actually the basement of a building that housed the "Magic Cinema," one of the largest and most luxurious movie houses in the city. From the theater's elegant, colonnaded main entrance a broad, bright staircase of twenty steps led to a large, well-lit, high-ceilinged hall that could accommodate several hundred people at a time. The far wall had windows and doors that opened onto a broad terrace with wonderful views of the Bosporus (a bonus provided by the steeply sloping terrain where the building stood, which also made it possible to enter the hall from the lower level). Frederick spared no expense in having the space renovated in a luxurious style, with ornate plaster ceilings, richly decorated columns, and polished metal and wood. When the weather warmed up, the terrace would become a spacious garden with gravel paths and cypresses framing the distant views of Asia. He called the new place "Maxim" in a nostalgic nod to its ancestor in Moscow, although its scale was more intimate and it was configured as a classic nightclub rather than a theater: a small stage faced a dance floor that was surrounded by rows of tables; there was also the obligatory American-style bar. For the next five years it would be Frederick's most successful venture in Constantinople. It would also outlive him by another fifty and earn an indelible place in the history of Istanbul nightlife.

Word of Frederick's plan for "a very special amusement rendezvous" first got out in early October and was greeted with enthusiasm by Villa Stella's many fans. Frederick moved quickly and by the end of the month had hired the drummer Harry A. Carter to lead the enticingly named Shimmie Orchestra during the nightclub's first, winter season. Carter, a white American from Minnesota, had been performing across Europe and in Egypt for several years and must have been very good at what he did, because Frederick was willing to pay him handsomely—20 Ltqs for an eight-hour workday, the equivalent of about $3,500 a week today; his contract also included "a first-class dinner" every evening.

Maxim opened on the evening of Tuesday, November 22, 1921. Frederick had designed it to appeal to the upper echelons of the city's Westernized Turks, Levantines, and foreigners, and they responded enthusiastically: the "greatest artistic event in Pera . . . extraordinary tour de force . . . grand luxury . . . modern comfort . . . richness that does not exist elsewhere . . . a fairytale-like atmosphere . . . a real jazz band." And all this was thanks to the "genial director," whose "organizational skills" and "taste for the beautiful" ensured "complete success." There were no superlatives left.

The fame and success that Maxim acquired immediately after opening were due not only to Frederick's talent for serving up an intoxicating mix of first-class cuisine and drinks, hot jazz, beautiful Russian waitresses, and flashy variety acts. He also successfully put himself on center stage as Maxim's public face and animating spirit. Impeccably turned out in black tie, worldly, poised, with a broad smile and a welcoming word for each new arrival—which he could deliver in French, English, Russian, German, Italian, or Turkish—Frederick relished what he had created as much as any of his nightclub's most enthusiastic fans.

It was the rare visitor who did not succumb to his charm or identify it with Maxim itself. "Thomas, the founder, the host . . . the cheerful Negro with the big smile, who thrived in the gaiety, the din of the jazz band, the dazzling luxury, the women, amidst beautifully appointed tables decorated with flowers and crystal," was how a Levantine devotee of Constantinople's nightspots described him. Even a less worldly Turk found himself seduced by the new, electrifying atmosphere that jazz created, although it also overwhelmed him.

> We came into a well-lit basement. This is where the famous Black music was being played. What a crashing of percussion instruments, what a noise, what a cacophony of sound. . . . One fellow was beating on the cymbals with all his might; another, seized with some rage, kept running his fingernails across a thick-stringed instrument, as if he had gone quite mad; while the violin, the piano, and the drum all mixed it up with them. . . . it reminded me of the wild mystical rituals performed by old [African] Arab pilgrims on their way to Mecca. . . .
>
> After a while, the lights were turned down and two performers—a skinny bit of a woman and a muscular man, both of them half-naked, adapting their steps to this madmen's music, kept throwing each other about. Then they stopped, and we clapped our hands and applauded. It was getting late, three o'clock; by now I was no longer in full possession of any of my three senses; neither my head, nor my eyes. . . . I could no longer feel, hear, or walk; in short I was no longer among the living!

Frederick won his patrons over by treating them like members of his own select circle. He was a bon vivant with "a heart of gold," as a longtime fan put it, and often helped people in distress. Fikret Adil, a young journalist, witnessed one such occasion shortly after Maxim opened. It involved one of Frederick's beautiful Russian waitresses, who styled herself a grand duchess, and who had beguiled a rich young Turk into spending all his money on her. The young man's despair was so great that his friends began to fear he might shoot the woman. But then Frederick got wind of the situation and decided to get involved. To everyone's surprise, he discovered that the waitress had fallen in love with the young man; however, since he was now ruined and she had hardly any money left, their future looked bleak. "Then Thomas did something that still brings tears to my eyes," Adil recalled.

Maxim was packed that night. Frederick waited for two Russians to finish their dance number, and after they had taken their bows he walked out onto the center of the dance floor.

> He quieted the crowd down, waving his long-fingered hands as if he was stroking everyone, and then announced [in French]:
>
> "Ladies and gentlemen, tonight I will present a number to you that you will not see; you will not see it, but you will know it. Now I will begin. A young man loves a woman. He spends his entire fortune on her until it's gone. The woman at first pretends to love him for his money's sake. But then she also falls in love. And tonight she has said: 'I will work and will support you.' However, the young man, having lost his fortune, now does not want to lose his honor as well. The two lovers are making up their minds to die."
>
> Thomas stopped speaking and looked all around.

The initial response of Maxim's audience was confusion and consternation at this strange story. "What's it to us?" some wondered aloud. But then Frederick replied: "Just this much: in ten minutes, they will be dead. My regards to you, ladies and gentlemen!"

> Suddenly the entire nightclub was in an uproar. One could hear people crying: "No! It cannot be! We must not let them!" Thomas was surrounded on all sides. . . . A couple of people came up to Thomas, bowed respectfully, and said something to him.
>
> Thomas called a waiter, had him bring a tray, and using the same hand movements once again quieted the crowd. Then he said:

"We've decided to change the finale of the number that you will not see but will know. They will not die, they will get married. And now I will collect the money that you will give to save them."

He first took the tray to the people who had been speaking to him. One hundred pound, fifty pound, and smaller banknotes were piled onto it.

After that we returned to the manager's office. We had forgotten to knock before entering and as we went in we discovered the two lovers embracing. Placing the tray in front of them, we quickly withdrew.

What Adil witnessed was Frederick's singular mix of calculation and kindness, which he seasoned, on this occasion, with a generous dollop of melodrama. Frederick was probably genuinely touched, but he also enhanced his reputation without having to spend a pound, embellished a dramatic story by inventing the lovers' suicide pact, enthralled his audience with his own performance, and forged a bond with his clients that would keep them coming back for more.

Within a few months after opening Maxim, Frederick was able to tell Ravndal that business was "going very well," but then he added—"taking present conditions into consideration." His immediate concern was the economic crisis that was ravaging the city. But he also realized very clearly that he was in a tiny oasis surrounded by a swarm of threats and that his situation was still precarious from a variety of perspectives. Valli had not relented and continued to bombard the American and British diplomats with pleas that "you force my husband to show concern for his child and me," to which he responded by sending some money. Several merchants were still unhappy with how slowly he was paying his bills. The Allied warships filling the Bosporus were a constant reminder of the menace that hung over the city, as were the armed patrols by the Interallied Police on the city's streets. After his experience of revolution and civil war in Russia, Frederick took the danger of widespread upheaval seriously, to the extent of stipulating that his contract with the bandleader Carter would be "annulled in case of Marshal law being declared or Maxim being closed by the authorities."

Constantinople was also in a state of tumultuous change as its centuries-old social fabric unraveled under the occupation. The emasculation of the sultanate's civic institutions, the influx of hundreds of thousands of indigent foreign and Turkish refugees, the soaring living expenses, the thousands of bellicose young men on leave from their ships and barracks—all led to an upsurge in everyday crime and public violence. People who were out late at night, like Zia Bey and his wife, tried to rush through the streets of Pera and especially Galata because they were not safe. Pickpockets preyed on passersby during the day (even Ravndal lost a pocket watch this way) while "second story men" shinnied up and down rain gutters to plunder residences when their owners were out. Businesses had to hire armed watchmen who spent the night striking the pavement with sticks at regular intervals to scare off thieves. Greek, British, and other Allied soldiers got drunk and started fights in the streets, making some residents reluctant even to venture out after dark. In Maxim one night, an Italian count started "a fracas" with a Lieutenant "Bubbles" Fisher of the U. S. Navy and drew a pistol from under his coat, but the lieutenant deftly disarmed him. Prostitution was rife and many desperate Russian women became streetwalkers. Ten thousand cocaine addicts in the city were estimated to consume ten kilos of the drug a day.

However, of all the threats that hung over Frederick, the most serious was in distant Washington, D.C. The blow fell early in 1922. In January, the State Department completed its review of his passport application, and Ravndal received the response on February 21. His assistant, John Randolph, needed only one sentence to inform

Frederick: "With reference to your application for a Department passport I have to advise that the Department of State has disapproved same, and this office accordingly is not disposed to accord you further protection as an American citizen." Randolph also informed Berlin, which put an end to Valli's hopes for a passport or for help against Frederick.

The letter to Ravndal was signed by Wilbur J. Carr, the number six man in the State Department. This was a fairly high position, and his response carried the weight and authority of the American government. What he said was hardly surprising, given Frederick's comments on the application. Carr focused on Frederick's admission that he did not intend to return to the United States because of his business interests abroad. He also made special mention of Frederick's "living in a free-love relationship with the white woman whom he alleges to be his wife." Carr's final reason for "disapproving" Frederick's application, however, was that "even should he be in a position to submit evidence of his alleged American birth, favorable consideration could not be given . . . because it is apparent from the foregoing statement of the circumstances in his case that he has abandoned whatever ties he may have had with the United States."

For all of Frederick's knowledge of the ways of the world, it is odd that he did not appear fully to grasp this "disapproval" and believed that something other than his skin color and long life abroad was the problem. He talked about the matter frankly with the young naval intelligence officer Robert Dunn, explaining that he had been denied a passport because he could not prove his American birth. When Dunn objected that providing a birth certificate would surely solve the problem, Frederick replied with a "resigned and wistful" expression on his face as he "bore with the ignorant Yankee": "Say, Mista Dunn, you know jes' as well as Ah does dat us niggers down in Mississipp' ain't never got no birth co-tificates." Frederick was not above poking fun at himself with this kind of linguistic self-caricature (and Dunn was not above recording it), but the point remains that he believed all he needed was proof of his American birth.

In the meantime, the start of the summer season was approaching and there was an important new development in the life of the city that Frederick was eager to exploit—an influx of American tourists. In early spring of 1922, Constantinople began to reemerge as a popular destination for cruise ships plying the Mediterranean. In March alone nearly three thousand tourists came ashore for a day or two, the largest number since before the war. Their gaily illuminated ships enlivened the drab Galata quay and were a striking contrast to the hulking gray warships lining the Bosporus. As the prosperous-looking tourists trooped through the city, they were followed with a calculating gaze by restaurateurs, antiquarians, souvenir peddlers, and Russians who still had jewelry, furs, or other valuables to sell.

High on the list of tourist attractions—in addition to taking a quick look at the wonders of ancient Stambul and picking up some souvenirs—was having a drink at a stylish place with music and dancing, something that had been legally denied at home for two years, since the start of Prohibition. American tourists quickly spread the word that Maxim was the fanciest nightclub in town, and for the next few years many of Frederick's former countrymen made it an obligatory stop during their visits.

Most of the time Frederick limited himself to regaling the Americans with his trademark mix of personal attention, seductive atmosphere, haute cuisine, good liquor, excellent jazz, flashy acts, and a smooth dance floor. But on occasion he and his staff also put on a show that revealed his extravagant side, and played to the tourists' naïveté and their if-this-is-Constantinople-it-must-be-Tuesday itinerary. Negley Farson, an American businessman and writer who had known Frederick in Moscow during the war and ran into him again in Constantinople, describes what sometimes happened.

When a big White Star liner came into Constantinople with a shipload of suddenly-wealthy American tourists on a round-the-world trip, all of Thomas's Russian girl waitresses jumped into Turkish bloomers, and Thomas put on a fez, got out his prayer rug and prayed towards Mecca. . . .

We had watched the American tourists being rushed around Constantinople all day in charabancs. They entered Maxim's like a chorus themselves, rushed to the tables around the dancing floor and stared at the bloomered dancing girls.

"Very Turkish!" explained their guide-interpreter. "Just like a harem—what?"

Half an hour later he stood up and looked at his watch.

"Ladies and Gentlemen—this concludes our trip to Turkey. Ship sails in twenty minutes. Transportation is waiting for you outside the door. All aboard! All aboard for Jerusalem and the Holy Land—we will now follow the footsteps of the Master!" . . .

Thomas salaamed them out, bowing with pressed hands— "Good-bye, Effendi. Good-bye, Effendi!"—then he took off his fez and became a nice Mississippi Negro again.

Farson's concluding epithet may sound condescending, but he genuinely admired Frederick and saw him as "very sophisticated."

However, many of the American tourists differed from Farson because they brought with them the same attitudes Frederick had encountered when dealing with the diplomats in Constantinople and bureaucrats in Washington; the difference was that none of the tourists had any doubts about Frederick's origins and all were happy to buy his drinks. Southerners' reactions were invariably the most flagrant. Mrs. Lila Edwards Harper, a fifty-year-old matron from Montgomery, Alabama, spent a month in Constantinople and talked with Frederick at some length. Once she returned home, she could not wait to tell others what she saw and heard. "Everyone in Constantinople knows Fred Thomas," she gushed. "He is a good polite negro, rolling in wealth, and an admirable host. His career is an amazing story, worse than fiction." Mrs. Harper was struck primarily by two things: Frederick's rags-to-riches story, which he recounted to her in detail (including the fact that he encountered no "color line" in Russia); and that his waitresses were Russian noblewomen who had been his "most fashionable patrons" in Moscow. "Nobody avoids them on account of their misfortune," she commented, with what is actually rather mean-spirited surprise: "I've seen the English consul dance with the waitress who served his dinner. She was a countess in the old days."

Frederick treated Mrs. Harper the same way he did all his patrons. But because she viewed him through the lens of her white southern narcissism, she took his polish and charm as personal tributes: "Thomas is from Mississippi and was as hugely pleased at meeting a Southern woman from America as he could be. . . . Nobody objects to the fact that the manager of the restaurant is a negro." She added: "He's one of the dozen or so negroes in Constantinople. They are never presumptuous. I saw Thomas sitting at a table with one of his Russian lady dancers, but that was the only unusual sight I saw. The diners find him a likable, obliging negro." Mrs. Harper makes it sound as if dealing with people like her was what made Frederick know his natural place. In fact, knowing how to deal with her type is what helped him become rich again, and that was his best revenge.

Frederick was friendly by disposition and also charmed his customers for the simple reason that this was usually the easiest way to get what he wanted from them. But there were limits, and he was no Pollyanna. The numerous military men in Constantinople could be especially difficult to handle, owing to the way that alcohol and the proximity of attractive women fueled their aggressiveness. The English were the worst offenders—because of their numbers in Pera, because they were armed in contrast to the other Allies, and because of their arrogance. Captain Daniel Mannix, a seasoned American naval officer newly arrived in Constantinople, witnessed this unsavory concoction at Maxim one evening. He was curious about the place and its "American Negro" owner because he had heard that Frederick "had done a lot for other refugees and was generally liked and respected." A short while after settling in at a table with friends, Mannix noticed that two drunken Englishmen were abusing a Russian waiter for some reason. Suddenly, one of them leaned forward and hit the Russian in the face, but the waiter only stepped away. Then the Englishman reached out and hit him again, and this time the waiter responded with a blow of his own.

> Instantly both Englishmen went into a perfect spasm of fury, yelling and waving their fists in a frenzy of rage. By now Thomas had come up and he asked mildly what the trouble was. One of the men, shaking his fist in Thomas' face, screamed, "He struck an ENGLISHMAN!" Thomas replied grimly, "You shake your fist in my face again and I'll strike another." The Englishman recoiled in open-mouthed astonishment while his friend turned to stare at Thomas unbelievingly. A few seconds later both left the cafe, still seemingly in a daze.

Mannix saw the Englishmen's behavior as a shocking expression of their sense of national inviolability. But Frederick was neither impressed nor cowed, and in characteristic fashion came to his employee's defense. He also knew that this would not damage his relations with the British authorities, because of Maxim's popularity with the representatives of all the Allied powers.

Even Admiral Bristol, the most senior American in the city, patronized Maxim, especially for dancing. The music and entertainment there were always Western European and Russian. But on one memorable evening Bristol presided over a special party that included Turkish folk music and dancing that Frederick had arranged with the help of the young journalist Adil. The performer was known as "Champion Osman, the Tambura-Player"; he was a master of the "bağlama," a long-necked, traditional stringed instrument, and the "Zeybek," a martial folk dance peculiar to western Anatolia. When Adil brought him to Maxim, Frederick's initial reaction to the big, slow-moving old man, with his handlebar mustache, thick fingers, and eyeglasses, was skeptical. But after Osman changed into his costume, Adil was relieved to see that Frederick's face broke into a broad smile at the transformation that the diffident old man had undergone.

After a dramatic drumroll, Osman walked out onto Maxim's dance floor. The impression he produced was extraordinary because of his costume—a colorful head wrap, short baggy pants, a yataghan thrust through the sash around the waist of his embroidered jacket—and the contrast between his enormous body and the tiny bağlama. This was the first time that a Turkish folk artist had ever appeared in a Pera nightclub. When Osman began to play a virtuoso impro-visation called a "koşma," the audience listened entranced, scarcely breathing. When he had finished, the silence at first was so complete that "one could've heard the humming of a mosquito," as Adil re-called; then wild applause erupted. Osman replied with a calm and dignified bow, as if he had spent all his life performing for foreign dignitaries. Following a signal to the bandleader, who started up a Zeybek tune, Osman stretched out his arms and began the high-stepping dance, adding some remarkable moves that even Adil had never seen before. When it was over, the audience again exploded with applause. Admiral Bristol's wife came up to Osman and invited him to their table. Showing worldliness that few expected from him, the old man offered his arm to the lady and escorted her back, to the delight of Maxim's entire audience. When his hosts offered him champagne, he did not refuse it as a Muslim, but touched the glass to his lips and took two sips before putting it down. When offered a cigarette, he smoked it and, once he had finished, politely asked for permission to leave.

*   *   *

Elegant, pricey Maxim was at the upper end of popular tourist entertainments in Constantinople. But the city had many other levels, both native and foreign, and there was a lot to choose from if you had eclectic tastes or were not a prude. An American naval officer who went to a Russian restaurant where "the waitresses were all refugee Russian girls chosen obviously for their good looks" kept being urged, "You can be as wicked as you like" by the maître d'hôtel, a man "with a black beard who looked like Rasputin." Vertinsky's nightclub "La Rose Noire," in which his singing was the prime official attraction, was reputedly shut down when a police raid "unearthed quantities of cocaine and 100 per cent syphilis among the lady servants and entertainers." There were exotic "Oriental" entertainments that one could attend, like the "camel fights" between pairs of beasts that were held in the MacMahon Barracks Hippodrome in Taxim Square, not far from Maxim.

American tourists also treated as entertainments some Turkish cultural traditions and rituals of the Ottoman court that survived under the Allied occupation. The weekly ceremonial procession of the sultan to his mosque for worship attracted crowds of observers because of the magnificence of the scene: lined-up palace guards in bright scarlet; units of cavalrymen richly uniformed in red breeches, hussar jackets, and astrakhan hats, their lances tipped with red and green pennants; the sultans' horses caparisoned with tiger skins and silver mountings. Especially popular with tourists were the dervishes, Sufi Muslim ascetics who resembled Western monks in some ways. Their religious practices, which varied by sect, included the famous dance-like "whirling," as well as a form of collective prayer that supercilious foreigners called "howling." There were also lurid forms of self-mortification, with individuals searing their bodies with red-hot irons, striking themselves with swords or spiked iron balls, and even thrusting daggers through both cheeks.

But probably the oddest entertainment in Constantinople was the "cockroach races" that the Russians invented. In an attempt to control the spread of gambling in the city, in April 1921 the Allied authorities forbade the "lotto" games of chance that Russian refugees had introduced all over Pera. After casting about for some other source of income, several enterprising souls dreamed up the idea of staging races using the ubiquitous insects. They sought permission from the head of the British police, who, being a "true sportsman," enthusiastically granted it. A large, well-lit hall was found and a giant table was set up in the center, its surface covered with a series of tracks separated by low barriers. Announcements of a new "Cafarodrome" —after the French "cafard," "cockroach"—were posted throughout the district. The public poured in. Men with feverishly glistening eyes and women with flushed faces crowded around the table, transfixed by the sight of the enormous black cockroaches. Each had a name—"Michel," "Dream," "Trotsky," "Farewell," "Lyulyu." A ringing bell signaled the start of the race. Released from their cigar-box "stables," the cockroaches dashed forward, pulling tiny, two-wheeled sulkies fashioned out of wire; some, dumbfounded by the bright lights, froze, waving their feelers around uncertainly to the despair of their fans. Those that reached the end of their runs found stale cake crumbs as their reward. Pari-mutuel winnings could reach 100 Ltqs—the equivalent of several thousand dollars today. The success of the first Cafarodrome was so great that competing "racetracks" began to pop up all over Pera and Galata, with word spreading to Stambul and even Scutari. Some of the organizers quickly became rich and started to make plans to leave for a new life in Paris. If you had the money, you could buy a forged passport, and if your assets were portable and the Interallied Police did not know you, you could board a ship and escape.

9

SULTAN OF JAZZ

In late summer of 1922, just when Maxim was emerging as the pre-eminent nightclub in Constantinople and Frederick was finally beginning to enjoy genuine financial success, the historical ground under his feet began to shift. Once again, his life and the life of the country he had adopted began to diverge, just as they had when he reached the pinnacle of his financial and social success in Russia on the eve of the October Revolution. The Turkish Nationalist movement had started to liberate the country from foreign invaders. And central to Mustafa Kemal's aims was to put an end to the Allied occupation of Constantinople, which had created the artificial oasis where Maxim had thrived.

Following their victory at Sakarya, the Nationalists resumed their campaign against the invading Greek army in August 1922 and launched a major offensive in western Anatolia. The Greeks broke and fell back in disarray to Smyrna on the Aegean coast, where they had begun their invasion three years earlier, and which the Allies had promised Greece. On September 9, the Nationalists took Smyrna, thus completing their reconquest of Asian Turkey; several days later a vast fire, apparently started by the victorious Turks, burned much of the city, causing many deaths and much hardship among the Greek and Armenian populations. The only part of Turkey that remained in foreign hands now was on the European side of the Straits in the north, which included Constantinople. Kemal's forces continued their advance and two weeks later entered what the Allies considered a "neutral zone" near Chanak on the Asian side of the Dardanelles, precipitating a crisis that almost led to war with Great Britain. A diplomatic solution averted conflict at the last minute, but the relations between the occupying powers and a renascent Turkey had irrevocably changed.

In Constantinople, the news of the Nationalists' advance, two hundred miles away, greatly alarmed the Americans. On September 23, Admiral Bristol circulated a memorandum explaining that the United States would remain neutral should fighting break out between Turkish and Allied forces, but would still evacuate all American citizens living in and near the city. A detailed list of all 650 Americans (including a young journalist named Ernest Hemingway) was prepared but, needless to say, Frederick and his family were not on it.

The Nationalists now had the upper hand and nothing stood in the way of their goal to reclaim the rest of their country. On October 11, 1922, Britain, France, and Italy accepted Kemal's demands and signed the Armistice of Mudanya. They also agreed to a new peace conference to renegotiate the onerous Treaty of Sèvres, which had provided for the partition of the Ottoman Empire and the internationalization of Constantinople.

Kemal next shifted his attention to his internal enemy—the sultan. Mehmet VI, a bespectacled, studious-looking man who inherited the throne from his brother, had opposed the Nationalists from the start and blamed them for the disaster that had befallen the Ottoman Empire after the war. For a time, his government in Constantinople, whose powers had already been severely limited by the Allies, continued to function independently from the Nationalist government that had formed in Angora. The Nationalists also initially attempted to remain loyal to the sultan personally, but the final rupture between them became inevitable. On November 1, 1922,

Kemal and the Nationalists proclaimed the abolition of the sultanate. Two weeks later, Mehmet VI slipped out of the Dolmabahçe Palace, boarded a British warship, and fled to Malta and permanent exile on the Italian Riviera.

When the Lausanne peace treaty was signed on Tuesday, July 24, 1923, the news was as bad as the foreigners in Constantinople had feared. The Allies had been forced to give up all of their imperialistic plans for Turkey itself and would soon be evacuating the city. Frederick had been waiting for the news and understood its gravity. The very next day, Wednesday, July 25, he hurried to the American consulate general and, in effect, threw himself on the diplomats' mercy. Despite the rejection he had received earlier, getting American recognition was now the only hope he had left.

It is surprising that this time the American diplomats were more receptive to Frederick's appeal and agreed to try to help him. Why? As their later comments and actions suggest, their collective conscience was not entirely clear because of the role they had played in the State Department's rejection. They were also not indifferent to the pleasures that could be had at Maxim, which a number of them patronized. And they now began to sympathize with Frederick on a purely human level—with his hard-won success, his unusual vulnerability because of the drastic change in Turkey's political situation, and the urgency of his plight.

Immediately upon signing the Lausanne treaty, the Turkish authorities announced that all foreigners in Constantinople would have to register with the police by August 1. To comply, Frederick would need official identification as a foreign national; without it, he could be subject to deportation and the loss of his property. Because this deadline was only a week away, Ravndal agreed to expedite Frederick's appeal and to send a telegram to Washington, albeit at Frederick's expense and provided he brought the money in advance.

Ravndal telegraphed the State Department on Thursday, July 26, asking that Frederick's case "be reopened." As justification, he explained that creditors' claims against Frederick "have been practically all disposed of," and that Frederick promised to pay income tax for the past several years, if "he is recognized." Showing more than a perfunctory interest in helping Frederick, Ravndal even searched for a precedent in a vast diplomatic compendium that dealt with such matters (Moore's *Digest*) and invoked a case from 1880 that he thought was similar.

But Ravndal was also bound by State Department policies regarding repatriation, and the conditions he specified under which Frederick could be granted an "emergency certificate of registration" were heartless. The certificate would include Frederick's children but not his "wife" (the skeptical quotation marks were Ravndal's), and Frederick would have until May 1924 to return to the United States and place his children in school. In other words, Frederick's price for American protection would be to give up Elvira; to dispose of Maxim; to accept a permanent, inferior status as a black man in the United States; and to doom his sons to the same fate. Nevertheless, Frederick went along, although it is possible that he had other ideas about what he might do if he got his hands on a passport that would allow him to travel, or at least to escape from Constantinople. (As he surely knew by now from newspapers as well as from traveling entertainers who worked for him, Paris had become a haven for many black American musicians and entrepreneurs.) The day after Ravndal sent the telegram, Frederick signed a typed note, certifying that he was "always ready to fulfill all the obligations that an American citizen is bound to," and that he was "quite willing to pay my income tax for these past three years, amounting to about a thousand Dollars [equivalent to $40,000 today]; this, as soon as my new citizenship papers will be delivered to me."

The response from Washington arrived in less than a week and was as disheartening as it was brief: "You are informed that the Department is unable to reverse its decision as indicated in its mail instruction of 20 January, 1922. Collect $2.70."

But Frederick was still not prepared to give up. He had one very influential acquaintance left in the city—Admiral Mark Bristol. A stern-looking man with a firm gaze that fitted his high rank and position, Bristol was also very kind and, together with his wife, did much valuable charitable work in Constantinople, including helping Russian refugees and founding an American hospital. Bristol took a personal interest in Frederick's plight and asked Larry Rue, the correspondent of the *Chicago Daily Tribune* who also knew Frederick, to investigate. Rue canvassed other Americans in the city as well as Frederick's employees and wrote a strong letter to Bristol on August 24, 1923. He affirmed that Frederick was "obviously an American"; that after his initial stumbles he had achieved "enviable" success in his business; that he was widely admired for being a humane employer; and that the State Department had discriminated against Frederick when it denied him a passport on the basis of a "rule which is freely waived for others whose intentions, citizenship, business methods and Americanism are considerably more in doubt than his." Rue also reported that neither Allen nor Ravndal had objections to Frederick any longer, and that they would both "really like to help him out of this dilemma." Rue concluded that if the State Department did nothing to protect Frederick from the risk of having his property confiscated by the Turks, "There ain't no justice."

There are several inaccuracies in Rue's letter, which are presumably due to the efforts by all concerned to put the best possible face on their dealings with Frederick. Allen's claim that he would like to help Frederick is difficult to reconcile with his central role in sabotaging Frederick's earlier passport applications, although it is possible that Allen's attitude had evolved during the ensuing two years. Rue's report that Ravndal did not have any objections to Frederick was belied by the way Ravndal referred to Elvira in his telegram to Washington on July 26. Despite all these reservations, it is still remarkable that so many of the influential white Americans in the city would have rallied around Frederick in this way.

Bristol did not forget Frederick's case. In late December 1923, he asked Edgar Turlington, a solicitor in the State Department and his official legal adviser, to "have an extended conversation" with Frederick about his past in order to try to gather information that might persuade the State Department to reverse its decision. The resulting six-page autobiographical narrative that Turlington produced traces Frederick's life from his birth to his arrival in Constantinople and contains many details that are still readily verifiable. He also gives the names of several people who could vouch for Frederick's American origins. Turlington incorporated this narrative into a letter he addressed on February 8, 1924, to George L. Brist of the Division of Passport Control at the State Department. Turlington also added that although he himself was in no position to verify independently much of what Frederick said,

> I have no doubt, from his manner and general appearance, that he was born and largely brought up in the southern part of the United States. Among the Americans in Constantinople there is, so far as I could discover, no doubt whatever of Thomas' being an American, and the reasons for the denial of an American passport to Thomas are far from clear.

However, once again all the efforts came to nothing. Brist did ask a colleague to check the Passport Division's records, but the clerks again failed to find or, if they found them, to produce any of Frederick's applications. Even more egregious is that Turlington gave Brist the name of a naval officer who was living in Washington at the time, who had been to Maxim, and who knew the Cheairs family—the onetime owners of Frederick's parents. But Brist and his colleagues either did not pursue this easy lead, were not persuaded by it, or chose to let it get lost in the great State Department paper shuffle. In the end, it proved impossible for Bristol, Rue, or anyone else to undo the damage that had been done to Frederick's case earlier by the diplomats in Constantinople and the officials in Washington.

In the meantime, things in Constantinople were not going as badly as had been feared. The August 1 deadline had come and gone, but Frederick had not been deported and Maxim had not been seized. Because Turkey was an overwhelmingly Muslim country, there was much talk initially about prohibition, which would have been ruinous for Maxim and other establishments like it. In October 1923, for example, dire rumors had spread that all drinking establishments would be closed, and stores of liquor would be dramatically thrown into the sea. But although some closings did follow, pressure to reverse this policy began immediately. Many Turks were now accustomed to Western-style nightlife and wanted it to continue. Soon, a few private clubs were authorized to provide drinks to members. Maxim, which had become an important part of the city's increasingly secularized popular culture, was prominent among them. By the spring of 1924, clubs, gardens, hotels, restaurants, and casinos were allowed to serve liquor, provided they had government permits (the Gazi, Mustafa Kemal, himself was reputedly a tippler).

Following the Treaty of Lausanne, the changes in the country's government and in Constantinople's administration were rapid, dramatic, and epochal in historical terms. But initially at least they did not affect Frederick's life and affairs in any very striking ways. The Allied forces began the evacuation of the city on August 29, 1923, only five days after the treaty was signed. It was completed on Tuesday, October 2, at 11:30 in the morning, when the British, French, and Italian commanding generals and their remaining troops carried out a brief but impressive ceremony in the open square by the Dolmabahçe Palace. With Allied and Turkish units drawn up on the sides of the square, and under the eyes of dignitaries including foreign ambassadors and the high commissioners, the generals inspected the troops; then the Allied and Turkish colors were presented, and the Allied forces marched off. "In a twinkling of an eye," a great, jubilant Turkish throng flooded the square, according to an American who was present. The Allied fleets left the same afternoon and, in contrast to their imperious arrival five years earlier, now seemed to be "slinking out of port." "Had these vessels had tails," the American commented, "I can imagine that they would surely have been securely curled behind their hind legs." Three days later, on October 5, the Nationalist army reached the Asian side of Constantinople; the following day it crossed the Bosporus and landed in Stambul near Topkapi Palace. On October 13, the capital was officially moved to Angora. The final step in the country's transformation came on October 29, 1923, with the proclamation of the Turkish Republic and Mustafa Kemal's election as its first president. In 1935 the grateful nation that he created would give him the honorary name Atatürk, "Father of the Turks."

After the Allies left, the first thing that changed in Constantinople was the appearance of the crowds on the city's streets. The British, French, Italian, and American naval uniforms that had filled Pera and Galata were replaced by those of the Turkish army and navy. The number of prostitutes working the streets also dropped because the authorities closed many of the city's "resorts of ill fame." Shop signs and advertising banners in the European districts began to change in accordance with the new government's decree that everything would now have to be in Turkish, with foreign lettering allowed only if it was smaller.

The fall of 1923 after the Allies' departure is probably when Frederick sent his oldest son, Mikhail, to study in Prague. Because all hope of getting American recognition now seemed to be lost, it made sense to get him out of (potential) harm's way by taking advantage of the Czech government's very generous offer to provide young Russian émigrés with a free higher education. By 1922, some two thousand had arrived in Prague from all points in the Russian diaspora, including Constantinople. Because Mikhail had been born in Moscow and spoke Russian fluently, he was eligible. (It is also likely that he was motivated to leave because there were still unresolved tensions between him and Elvira.) Father and son would never see each other again.

Despite the tectonic political and cultural shifts in the city, Maxim remained popular with both residents and tourists and continued to do very good business for a number of years longer. This appears to have given Frederick a heady sense of liberation and achievement, and unleashed an extravagant streak in him. He liked to tell visiting Americans about his remarkable life in Russia; about how in Constantinople he surmounted "difficulties that would stagger the ordinary man"; and how he had "once more mounted the pinnacle of success as the owner and proprietor of the most noted and most popular amusement palace in the Near East." Before long, he started boasting to visitors that he was "conservatively rated to be worth at least $250,000," which would amount to $10 million today. Even if this was a two-, three-, or fourfold exaggeration, it still suggests the impressive scale of his success.

For many of Frederick's clients, his appeal as a host was the infectious, personal pleasure he took in the gaiety that he orchestrated in his nightclub. Sergey Krotkov, a Russian émigré musician who worked for him for several years, recalled how Frederick would suddenly decide that it was time for an elaborate spree. He would put on the top hat that had become his signature and would lead a procession of all of Maxim's employees—waiters, dishwashers, musicians, cooks, performers—from Taxim Square down one of Pera's main streets, to the accompaniment of the band's drums and the clash and clatter of its cymbals. They would stop at every bar they encountered and Frederick would buy everyone a round of drinks.

Even when he was working in his office at Maxim, he kept a bottle of champagne chilling in an ice bucket on his desk so that he could offer a glass to anyone who came to see him. It was this kind of behavior that led émigrés to see in him the same "broad" Russian nature they valued in themselves.

The other side of Frederick's expansive generosity was his continued insistence on personal loyalty from everyone he included in his circle. The bond this allowed him to forge with his employees was another reason for his success, and Krotkov experienced this as well. Krotkov was a master of the Hawaiian ukulele, an instrument that was sweeping the world in the early 1920s, and was very popular at Maxim. One evening he had been invited to a private event elsewhere before having to perform at Maxim for another boatload of American tourists. Krotkov arrived very late for his turn onstage, to find Frederick waiting for him in a rage at the entrance: "Tvoya svoloch!" ("Yours a bastard!"), he yelled in his expressive but grammatically flawed Russian. "My your mug will smash! The Americanas came, and yours not played—your run and play!" "Fyodor Fyodorovich," Krotkov pleaded, "I know I'm late. Please forgive me, I took a taxi." He then dashed to the stage. When Krotkov had completed his set, a waiter asked him to come to the bar. Frederick was standing there, his face beaming: "Yours played well. The Americanas listened and clapped." There were two tumblers of vodka before him. "Yours drink good yet?" he asked.

Frederick's penchant for spontaneous expressions of good feeling prompted him to host a Fourth of July celebration at Maxim in 1924. The nightclub was filled with American businessmen, merchant sailors, mining engineers, and, as an observer put it, other "American adventurers" from every corner of the Near East. Feelings ran especially high and "the jovial American Negro proprietor" was generously "setting up drinks on the house time and again." Completing the festive setting were a jazz band playing "Last Night on the Back Porch (I Loved Her Best of All)" and a bevy of Greek and Levantine dancing girls.

* * *

With Maxim a success, and facing what seemed like a cloudless future despite the revolutionary transformation of Turkey that was under way, Frederick's thoughts once again turned to growth.

During Constantinople's summers, temperatures can climb to oppressive heights for weeks, driving many residents to seek cooler locations somewhere on the water. In early summer of 1924, Frederick decided to open a new place in Bebek, a quiet suburb overlooking a pretty cove on the European shore of the Bosporus, some five miles north of Galata. Together with a senior employee from Maxim, "Mr. Berthet," he took over a Russian restaurant called "Le Moscovite" that had a terrace by the water. Frederick renamed the place "La Potinière" ("The Gossip") and began to entice customers with what had been his foolproof formula—dinner and dancing under the open sky, a bar with special cocktails, and his own celebrated self as the host.

However, Constantinople's weather can be erratic, and that summer, shortly after La Potinière opened, it turned disastrous. Torrential rains at the end of June flooded parts of the city, transforming the main streets into rivers, damaging houses, breaking windows, and knocking out electricity. There was serious destruction outside the city as well, with bridges in villages washed out and fruit and nut orchards badly damaged. On the heights of Pera, Maxim was not affected too much, and its open terrace remained popular. But the rainstorms apparently damaged La Potinière, and customers stayed away from the place, because after the summer season ended Frederick decided not to reopen it. He had lost some money on his investment, and such a stumble was unusual for him. It must have rankled him that two competitors in Bebek had succeeded where he had not. La Rose Noire, which changed hands several times after Vertinsky first opened it several years earlier, had also moved to Bebek that summer and appeared to be thriving. And the following year a resurrected Le Moscovite, which now advertised itself as the "ex-Potinière," had a good season as well.

More—and far more serious—competition was to come. Tourism was still on the rise in Constantinople. A noticeable jump occurred in early spring of 1925, when hundreds of American and British tourists started arriving every week. During the first half of 1926, the number swelled to twenty-one thousand, which was nearly double the tally for the same period the previous year. Although most tourists spent only a day or two rushing past the famous sights before heading off to the Mediterranean, it did not take long for other entrepreneurs to see the potential that Constantinople had and to start dreaming up ways to capitalize on it.

The most audacious plan was to create a rival Monte Carlo on the banks of the Bosporus. In late summer and fall of 1925, word spread through Constantinople that a syndicate headed by Mario Serra, an aggressive young businessman from Milan, had rented for a period of thirty years the Yildiz Palace complex on the northeastern edge of the city as well as the Çiragan Palace on the shore of the Bosporus just below it. This arrangement had been approved at the highest levels of the Turkish government, by the Council of Ministers and President Kemal himself. The jewel of the Yildiz complex was the Şale Kiosk, a palace that had been the sultans' residence in the late nineteenth century. Its appearance was highly incongruous for Constantinople because on the outside it resembled an enormous Swiss chalet (whence the first part of its Turkish name), whereas inside it was elaborately decorated with carved marble, mother-of-pearl inlaid wood, frescoes, and gilded plaster. Serra intended to transform the palace's magnificent throne room into a gambling casino and to use the other halls for bars, restaurants, and dancing. In the huge park outside there would be sporting facilities, a roller coaster, and possibly a golf course, while other amusements would be set up by the large lake and in the smaller buildings on the grounds. Plans for the Çiragan Palace involved rebuilding the white marble structure, which had been badly damaged by fire (it had formerly been the sultan's harem), and turning the entire place into a luxury hotel (which it is today). For all this Serra agreed to pay the Turkish government 30,000 Ltqs a year in rent—that would come to around $1 million now—plus an annual tax of 15 percent on his profits. Because the government of the Turkish Republic was hardly sentimental about the Ottoman past, it was also willing to let him buy some of the luxurious furnishings that remained in the palace, including massive pieces of furniture, handmade rugs hundreds of square yards in size, and mirrors covering double-height walls. The Yildiz project was on a scale that would eclipse not only every other attraction that the city might offer to a rich tourist, but also potentially any other comparable destination in Europe. Indeed, there was talk that it might lead to the birth of a new Turkish Riviera.

Frederick understood what this grandiose plan could mean for him and that he needed to do something about it. He reportedly initially discussed with representatives of the Standard Oil Company of America, which had major long-standing financial interests in the region, the possibility of transforming Hagia Sophia into a casino or a "temple of jazz." As absurd and blasphemous as this idea may sound—this was, after all, one of the most famous ancient religious buildings in the world—it was picked up by American newspapers at the end of 1926 and the beginning of 1927. One newspaper reported that "a group of business men" in Constantinople had concluded that "the edifice is unsuitable for religious services." Word spread, and companies eager to take part started to write to the American consulate general in Constantinople. The "American Association of Jazz Bands," for example, asked "for full acoustic details" of the vast edifice (whose central cupola is taller than a fifteen-story building), and with a "can do" aplomb that was undaunted by any cultural or practical concerns promised "to provide the largest jazz band in the world with the largest number of most powerful saxophones." However, the Turkish authorities never seriously considered this appalling project, and it came to nothing. Frederick decided that he would have to expand on his own, and on as big a scale as he could manage. This seemed not only possible but plausible because Maxim continued to pull in crowds with its time-tested entertainments, which now regularly included black jazz bands.

But history was not standing still in the Turkish Republic. In its on-going process of secularization, it abolished the caliphate (formerly, Ottoman sultans had also been Muslim caliphs, but the republic's experiment with separating the two ended in less than a year). The last representative of the Ottoman dynasty, Caliph Abdülmecid II, left Constantinople for Switzerland by train on March 3, 1924; a week later, he was followed by the few princes and princesses who had lingered behind. The fez was officially abandoned in favor of Western hats for men. On April 17, 1924, the Russian imperial embassy on the Grande rue de Pera was transferred to the Soviet government, marking Turkey's friendly relations with the Soviet Union (and symbolically confirming Frederick's now complete statelessness).

There were new laws as well that targeted establishments like Frederick's and that reflected the Turkish Republic's attempt to find a path between Muslim traditions and secular Western culture (and to raise revenues). Taxes were introduced on the consumption of alcoholic beverages and on dancing in public: a "First Class" place like Maxim had to pay the equivalent of around $1,500 a month for the latter. Restrictions were also placed on the hours when "dancings" could operate, on the events they could organize without special au-thorization, and on the age of young women who could be admitted. Shop signs that were in Turkish and a foreign language were taxed, with the amount depending on the size of the foreign lettering. Dur-ing the period 1924–1926, operating an establishment like Maxim became progressively more expensive.

It was also becoming more difficult for foreigners to live and work in Constantinople. Xenophobia increased as the Turkish Republic dismantled the old privileges that had been granted to Europeans. In 1924 an unsuccessful attempt was made in Constantinople to force employers to replace their Christian employees with Muslims. Two years later a new law required that Turkish workers replace all foreigners, including dames serveuses, waiters, headwaiters, cooks—in short, the core group of Frederick's employees at Maxim. He may have needed to hide behind Turkish partners himself. To verify compliance, officials began to check identification papers throughout the city. Early in 1926 a law was introduced mandating the use of Turkish in bars, in restaurants, and on bills; any establishment that persisted in using French would be punished.

All these changes caused great anxiety and hardship for Constantinople's many foreigners, including the several thousand Russian refugees who had stayed behind after nearly two hundred thousand others left. Some of the remaining Russians sought Turkish citizenship, as did Frederick. After vacillating for a while, the new republic decided not to grant it to large numbers of stateless foreigners, and this decision forced many more to leave the country. Even though the Russians' identity papers had lost their meaning when their homeland ceased to exist, they were able to travel on the strength of the "Nansen passports" that the League of Nations started to issue in 1921. Had Frederick not claimed all along that he was an American, he might have been able to get one of these too. Fridtjof Nansen and Frederick actually met on June 9, 1925, when Nansen, the Norwegian Nobel Peace Prize laureate, went to Maxim during a visit to Constantinople. However, by then it was too late for Frederick to tell the truth, and Maxim was still doing too well for him to want to leave.

By early spring of 1926 Frederick had found the property that would be his answer to Serra's Yıldız casino. About a dozen miles up the

Bosporus from Constantinople on the European side is a picturesque cove with a town called Therapia (now Tarabya) that was
popular with wealthy natives and foreigners as an escape from the
city's crowds and summer heat. The rich built luxurious villas; the
foreign diplomats built "summer embassies." There were several
good hotels and restaurants right on the water that caught the
cooling breezes.

Frederick opened his "Villa Tom" there in early June and continued to operate Maxim during that summer as well. He spent lavishly
to create a new destination that would give the members of Constantinople's fashionable set everything they could possibly want: sophisticated dinners, dancing on a terrace by the water under a moonlit
sky, a "Negro Jazz" band, a magnificently illuminated garden filled
with flowers, and constantly varying entertainments—a "Venetian
evening," a "Neapolitan program," an "aristocratic Charleston competition," a "Monster Matinee." And when the night's performance
drew to a close, there were spectacular fireworks overhead.

At first, Villa Tom looked like a success—the city's night owls
came, enjoyed themselves, and lingered until dawn. But the place had
cost a lot to open and was expensive to run. A problem also emerged
regarding its location: Therapia was twice as far from the city as
Bebek, where Frederick had tried opening La Potinière two years
earlier, and the distance seems to have put many people off. Frederick realized that he would have to take on the additional expense
of providing transportation from Constantinople if he was going to
induce clients to make the trip. A few weeks after the opening, he
hired and advertised a "luxury boat," promising to return revelers to
the city at 2 a.m. But this did not turn attendance around. Frederick's
income that spring and summer started to falter. He had to cut back
on paying bills and other expenses, just as he had several years earlier.

This time, one of his first victims was his own daughter Olga.
A year earlier, in July 1925, together with her Russian husband, she
had managed to get from Romania to Paris, where she enrolled as a

student. For the previous three years Frederick had been supporting her with a sizable monthly allowance, but when his expenses began to mount prior to opening Villa Tom he stopped sending money to her and, inexplicably, broke off all communication. Olga waited anxiously for several months, until July 1926, at which point she went to the American consul general in Paris, Robert Skinner, for help in finding out what had happened to her father. Skinner, in turn, contacted Allen in Constantinople, reporting that Olga was "very worried" and "absolutely penniless." Allen's response was as brief as protocol required: he confirmed Frederick's address at Maxim and explained that because Frederick had been denied American protection, "this office is . . . not able to exert any influence on him or otherwise interest itself in him." Following this exchange in late July 1926, nothing is known about any further communication between Olga and her father.

Although the government of the United States had washed its hands of Frederick, many of the people with whom he did business in Constantinople continued to think of him as an American. Consequently, when he stopped paying his bills on time, some of his smaller and less savvy creditors began once again to bring their complaints to the officials in the consulate general. A Russian waiter at Maxim, who had managed to circumvent employment regulations pertaining to foreigners, sent a pathetic complaint to Admiral Bristol about how Frederick had stopped paying him his full wages in June, around the time that Villa Tom had opened, and had not paid him for months despite repeated pleas. A merchant who supplied flowers to Villa Tom described how he had waited at Frederick's office as late as "3 o'clock in the morning" in an attempt to collect the remaining half of the sum owed him, the equivalent of some $2,000 today. The Americans must have been dismayed to see such familiar complaints after their intercessions on Frederick's behalf. They gave everyone the same response: "This office is unable to offer you any assistance towards collection of the sum which Mr. Thomas is alleged to owe you."

However, there was a new, ominous development as well: Frederick's bigger and better-connected creditors did not bother to contact the consulate general. Because foreigners like Frederick no longer had extraterritorial protection, there was no reason to involve the American diplomats; Turkish laws were now sufficient to cover any eventuality.

That fall and winter Frederick's problems got worse. After closing Villa Tom for the season, he began to try to salvage his financial situation by refocusing exclusively on Maxim. But on September 26, 1926, the "Yildiz Municipal Casino," as it was now officially called, opened for business. It did so not only with the fanfare befitting its size and splendor but also with official support from the city government, which made it into an even more significant event in the city's nightlife. Invitations had gone out in the name of the prefect of Constantinople, and his assistant joined Serra in welcoming the six hundred guests at the palace doors and in cutting the ribbon to the gambling salon. Practically the entire diplomatic corps came, as did the city's military and civilian authorities, the leading members of society, and representatives from the Grand National Assembly, the country's parliament in Angora. Despite the large turnout, the palace was so vast that it did not feel crowded. The casino was an instant success: men and women flocked to the six baccarat tables and four roulette tables in what a journalist characterized as "probably the most luxurious gaming room in the world."

Gambling made the Yildiz Municipal Casino a unique destination in the city, but the place also had everything else for which Maxim was famous, and more of it—fine restaurants, bars, tearooms, black jazz bands, dances in the afternoon, dinner dances in the evening, variety entertainment, and an enormous, beautifully illuminated park overlooking the Bosporus where one could stroll, ride, shoot, and play tennis. Yildiz also stayed open every day from 4:30 p.m. until 2 a.m., or later; it staged lavish special events regularly; and it provided fifteen automobiles to ferry guests back and forth from their homes and the city center.

The money poured in. During its first year of operation, the Casino is estimated to have paid the city government 130,000 Ltqs, which would be around $3 million today; this means that Serra's syndicate grossed $20 million. Yildiz had completely eclipsed Maxim, and Frederick's clients began to abandon him at the worst possible time. He tried to continue, but nothing he attempted worked, not even the special evenings that had been exceptionally profitable in the past and that now proved very difficult to organize. He announced a "first grand gala" of the season with a "ball of parasols" only on December 18, 1926; the next such event, featuring a masked ball, was not until two months later, on February 17.

Apart from the debts weighing him down, Frederick was also beset by new and continually shifting legal restrictions, taxes, and penalties. An Englishman who visited Constantinople in 1927 underscored this: "Obstacles are placed in the way of all foreigners now doing business in Turkey. Fines are imposed upon the flimsiest pretext and there is no redress without endless litigation in Turkish courts." As for the legal system itself, "Laws and regulations are being passed at such a rate that none can keep pace with them." In fact, early that year, a wave of stringent restrictions swept through Constantinople that were aimed at enterprises like Maxim. The governor of the province announced labyrinthine regulations about who could, and who could not, attend public dances, dance together, and receive dance instruction. A week later, several hundred cabarets were closed because they had all somehow transgressed aspects of the existing regulations.

The last glimpse of Frederick and Maxim that we have is a sad one, but it elucidates what went wrong. Carl Greer, a middle-aged businessman from Ohio on a grand tour of the eastern Mediterranean, visited three nightspots in Constantinople at the end of April 1927 and compared them. The first was a place near the consulate general called the "Garden Bar" that he described as "the only prosperous cabaret" in the city. Greer concluded that it was successful because it had "no such thing as a cover charge" and welcomed a range of clients, from big spenders prepared to pay several hundred dollars for a bottle of French champagne to penny-pinchers who nursed a glass of lemonade throughout an entire evening's show. The second place was Maxim, which Greer characterized as "a much more ornate establishment than the successful Garden Bar." But despite its swanky appearance he found it a "disheartening" sight because "the dance floor stood empty and the number of diners was never as great as the personnel of the orchestra that entertained them." What had happened was obvious to Greer: after making "a great deal of money during the occupation," Frederick could no longer attract his former clientele and was "now engaged in the painful process of losing all his profits." The third place Greer visited was where Constantinople's smart set had moved—the Yildiz Casino, and it elicited all his superlatives: "the show place among the resorts of the East, if not of the entire world . . . magnificence truly oriental . . . the gaming room causes any casino in the French Riviera to appear by comparison commonplace." He also noted the crucial detail that there were "three hundred players" gathered around the Yildiz Casino's tables. In short, the niche that Frederick had inhabited in the city's nightlife was now gone, and he was trapped, unable to adapt. Maxim could not compete with Yildiz's splendor and attractions, but neither could Frederick afford to make Maxim more broadly accessible, because of the size of his debt.

In the end, he tried to escape. Around the beginning of May 1927, just a few days after Greer had glimpsed Maxim's last breaths, and with creditors on the verge of having him arrested, Frederick fled to Angora in the hope that he would be out of their reach. The distance from Constantinople was approximately three hundred miles, and the train crept along for the better part of an entire day, with long stops at stations. It was like a grotesque parody of his escape from Odessa eight years before. Frederick's best hope was a long shot, as he surely realized. But he had escaped disaster before and was prepared to try once again. He was now fifty-four, and it could not have been easy.

The new Turkish capital was being created out of an ancient but obscure town in arid, hilly central Anatolia, with a population of only seventy-four thousand in 1927. However, it was growing rapidly as the republic expanded its bureaucratic institutions and offered a boom town's opportunities for entrepreneurs. Frederick found a prominent resident, Mustafa Fehmi Bey, who owned property on the Yeni Çehir hills by the Çankaya Road with a splendid view of the entire city. Their plan was—predictably—to transform this site into a "marvelous summer garden," a fully "modern establishment" with a "restaurant of great luxury" that would be called "Villa Djan." The summer season was about to begin and they would have to hurry. Because of his renown and expertise, Frederick would naturally be in charge of the construction, organization, and future direction of the new garden.

Frederick and his new partner got only as far as hiring some of the staff before the money, or the promise of money, gave out. There was also stiff competition from existing establishments run by Russian émigrés. Soon the familiar problems began—debts, broken agreements, and angry diplomats. In June, the French consul general in Angora, who did not know that Frederick had been disowned by the United States, but was aware of his "deplorable" past in Constantinople, as he put it, complained to his American counterpart. A certain Mr. Galanga, a chef Frederick hired and then had to dismiss, was stuck in the city because he did not have the money to pay his hotel bill, something that Frederick was contractually obligated to do.

Meanwhile, the expected disaster struck in Constantinople and Frederick's creditors seized Maxim. In late May, they allowed the editors of a magazine called *Radio* to put on a concert of classical music in the former nightclub, although they made a pointed announcement that no food or drinks would be served. A month later, Frederick's former place in Therapia reopened under new ownership. It was now identified as "ex-Villa Tom" and, in what may have been a vindictive gesture by someone who knew of Frederick's past in Moscow, had been renamed "Aquarium."

Following the collapse of his plans for the Villa Djan, Frederick got a job for a short period as an assistant waiter in a restaurant in Angora. It was his bad luck that a former Constantinople customer happened to be in town and stopped by the restaurant. He saw Frederick in his new role and was surprised that the "likable negro" and "ex-proprietor of Maxim" was actually still alive. Frederick put on his bravest face and insisted that he was "flourishing," but in fact he was earning only 30 Ltqs a month, comparable to $700 today. This was barely a living wage, especially if he was trying to send money to Elvira and his two sons. Frederick was also cocky, perhaps too much so for his own good: he asked the visitor to give word to his creditors in Constantinople that he was quite prepared to pay them, but "on the condition that they come to Angora."

Whether the taunt provoked them, or they tracked him down on their own, Frederick's creditors did catch up with him around mid-October of 1927. This time, there were no more discussions or negotiations: he was arrested and imprisoned in Angora. His total debt was a crushing 9,000 Ltqs, equivalent to about $250,000 today. Not only could he not pay any part of it, he did not even have the money to buy additional food to supplement the prison's meager rations. Frederick's friends and former employees in Constantinople took up a collection and sent him money so that he would not go hungry. Elvira and the boys survived largely on their charity as well. But life soon became so difficult for them that she made a desperate gamble and, leaving her sons behind in the care of friends, went to Europe to find some way to rectify their situation.

* * *

It is highly ironic that Frederick's end coincided with the demise of the Yildiz Casino, whose success had sealed Maxim's failure. In the spring of 1927, the Turkish government decided to impose new taxes on Serra, which he refused to pay, claiming that his annual levy already covered them. The disagreements continued until, on September 12, 1927, at 10:30 in the evening when Yildiz was in full swing, the general procurator of the Turkish Republic unexpectedly appeared with several assistants and ordered the casino closed. His official pretext was that Turkish citizens, including women, had been gambling there; Yildiz—like the casino in Monte Carlo, which Monegasques could not enter—was supposed to be open only to foreigners. The matter went to trial and rumors quickly proliferated, including that the Gazi himself wanted Yildiz shut down because it was earning too much money for foreigners. Whatever the backstage plots, the Yildiz Casino never reopened, and the palace eventually became a museum. One cannot help wondering whether Maxim might have survived if the Casino had been closed earlier in 1927. But perhaps it would have made no difference: the lesson an American diplomat drew from the Yildiz affair is that it illustrated once again "the difficulties which foreign concessionaires have in their dealings with the Turkish authorities."

Details about Frederick's last months are scanty. By Christmas of 1927 he was in prison in Constantinople, where he appears to have been transferred because that is where he had incurred his debts. It was a bitter coincidence that the new owners reopened his former nightclub as "Yeni Maxim"—"New Maxim"—on December 22. They enticed patrons with the same mix of ingredients that Frederick had perfected: dinner, dancing, jazz, an American bar. They would continue to do this for decades to come.

Conditions in Turkish prisons were harsh no matter where a prison was located. Most of the buildings were very old—the central prison in Stambul, which was directly opposite the famous Sultan Ahmed Mosque, had been built in the fourteenth century. Typically, many inmates were housed together in large cells and without regard to the nature of their crimes; someone sentenced to fifteen days for a misdemeanor could be locked up with a hardened criminal who had been given fifteen years. Prisoners were also left largely to their own devices. Bedding, sanitation, and health care were primitive. The quality and quantity of food varied. The ability to buy extra food was always essential.

In late May of 1928, Frederick fell ill with what was described in an official American consular report as "bronchitis"; it was more likely a recurrence of the pneumonia that had nearly killed him twice before. His condition was sufficiently serious for him to be taken to the French Hospital Pasteur in Pera, which was on the Grande rue de Pera, just off Taxim Square and a five-minute walk from Yeni Maxim. The nuns who ran the hospital accepted him as a charity case.

Frederick died there on Tuesday, June 12, 1928, at the age of fifty-five. Because Elvira was out of the country, all funeral arrangements were made by his friends. One of these was Isaiah Thorne, a black man from North Carolina who had worked for him at Maxim and who became his token executor. Another was Mr. Berthet, who had collaborated with Frederick during the ill-fated venture in Bebek and was also one of the boys' guardians. Frederick left no possessions to speak of.

The following day at 2:30 p.m. Frederick's body was taken to the St. Esprit Roman Catholic Cathedral in nearby Harbiye for a funeral service. Later that afternoon he was buried in the "Catholic Latin" Cemetery in the Feriköy district north of Taxim, not far from where he had first opened Stella. His sons and some sixty other people attended. There was no money for a permanent headstone, and the exact location of Frederick Bruce Thomas's grave in the cemetery, which still exists, is unknown. In one of the few American newspaper articles to note his death, he was referred to as Constantinople's late "Sultan of Jazz."

EPILOGUE

Death and Life

Life was very hard for Frederick's family after his imprisonment. Elvira learned of his death in Czechoslovakia, where she had gone in a desperate attempt to regain her German citizenship. (Germany would not let her in without a passport, and the closest she could get was Czechoslovakia, which shared a long border with Germany and continued to be exceptionally hospitable to Russian émigrés.) Elvira could not have stayed in Constantinople any longer because of restrictions on employment for foreigners. Her plight was even worse because she was a semi-invalid, and her condition prevented her from doing manual labor. She believed that if she could get her German citizenship back, she would have a firmer legal standing in Turkey and would be able to help her sons.

But to her shock, Elvira found that she had fallen into a new legal hell by leaving Turkey. "If you could have seen the tragedies that has been my life on account of all this difficulties," she wrote in English to an American official, "you would shudder, at the thought, what a cruel thing law and its application is in cases like mine." From the German government's perspective, she had forfeited her citizenship by marrying a foreigner, and there was nothing she could do to get it back while he was alive. Elvira also discovered that she was trapped in Czechoslovakia because the Turkish authorities refused to let her return to Constantinople. Only the painful news of Frederick's death freed her. In a remarkable act of courage and endurance, she crossed the border into Germany illegally, on foot and without any identification so that she would not be sent back if caught, and turned herself in to the authorities. Now that she was a widow, she could petition the German government to have her citizenship restored. It would take five years, and she would not be able to return to her sons in Turkey until 1933.

In the meantime, Bruce and Frederick Jr., or "Fred" as he was called in English, had known real hardship. They had to drop out of school when their father's financial difficulties began. Isaiah Thorne effectively adopted them when Elvira was away, and the only jobs they could find were marginal, with "very low" wages, as Fred described it. They worked mostly as waiters in restaurants in Angora and Constantinople, including Yeni Maxim. Both also occasionally found work as "jazz singers" in nightclubs.

And then, suddenly, in a way no one could have predicted, the American government changed its mind. On November 25, 1930, at Thorne's instigation, Fred and Bruce went to the American consulate general in Constantinople to apply for a passport. Thorne put them up to it because he wanted to help them escape the hardships of their lives in Turkey by taking them with him to North Carolina, where he had family.

The consulate had become a different place. New people worked there, and some of those who had known Frederick in the past had had a change of heart. The recently arrived vice-consul Burton Y. Berry interviewed the brothers, filled out the necessary forms very carefully, and wrote a remarkably detailed statement in support of their application. He implied that Frederick's request for a passport in 1921 had been denied because of racism; he defended Frederick for wanting to stay close to Russia because of the valuable property he had in Moscow; and he explained with great sympathy and historical understanding why a black man from the South should not have been expected to have documentary evidence of his birth. In very measured language, Berry then suggested the obvious—that a search of the State Department's archives would undoubtedly yield Frederick's previous passport applications, and that these would support his sons' petition to be recognized as American citizens on the strength of their father's origin.

By now, people and attitudes had also changed in the State Department. This time the clerks in the Division of Passport Control found the numerous applications that Frederick had filed between 1896 and 1914, and that had been there all along. On January 17, 1931, they wrote back: "The Department has carefully considered the case of Mr. Thomas and from evidence in its files in the case of his father, Frederick Bruce Thomas, is satisfied of his American citizenship, and the application under acknowledgment is accordingly approved." It no longer made any difference that Frederick had spent most of his life abroad, or that his sons had never set foot in the United States. The secret of his Russian citizenship also remained hidden in Russian archives. Charles Allen, who had effectively sabotaged Frederick's applications a decade earlier, was now "consul in charge" in Istanbul and issued the boys their passport on March 17, 1931.

But all of Thorne's and Elvira's plans still came to nothing. Thorne did not succeed in taking the boys to the United States because he could not raise the money, and Elvira was neither able to find work nor able to help her sons after she returned to Constantinople. In fact, because of her poor health, they had to take care of her.

By 1935, Elvira and her sons were at their wits' end. Her last resort was an appeal to the American consulate for money so that the young men could travel to the United States. But the diplomats did not have allocations for this purpose, and all they could suggest was that the brothers try to find jobs on an American ship that was returning home.

Despite worsening xenophobia in Turkey, Fred and Bruce managed to scrape out an existence for themselves and their mother for several more years, somehow circumventing the laws that restricted most work to Turkish nationals. Fred finally found a way out in March 1938. The SS *Excello*, an American merchant ship, had docked in Istanbul and was short one crew member. A sailor had jumped ship in Greece and Fred signed on in his place as a "messman." The ship sailed on March 18 and arrived in New York City on April 26, 1938, forty-four years after Frederick Bruce Thomas had left.

Little is known of either brother's subsequent fate. Shortly after arriving in New York, Fred found a job in Manhattan. Later, he may have continued to work in the American merchant marine. For Bruce, things had begun to look up briefly after Fred left Istanbul because he managed to get a contract to sing in Paris, where he hoped to earn enough money to travel to the United States. However, the beginning of World War II in September 1939 thwarted his plans and he remained in Turkey, continuing to lead a precarious existence performing in nightclubs and working in restaurants. In 1943 he came to the consulate in Istanbul, saying that he wanted to enlist in the American army, but his offer was refused.

It was not until the war was over that Fred reestablished contact with Bruce and their mother in Turkey. In February 1948, a decade after he had left on the *Excello*, two African-American newspapers— one in New York City and one in Chicago—published a letter from a black American friend of Elvira's in Istanbul asking anyone who knew the whereabouts of Frederick Thomas Jr. to pass on to him that his mother "is an invalid and needs his support, [and] is very anxious to hear from him." The message apparently reached Fred, because the following year he tried to enlist the State Department's help in finding out about Bruce's "welfare," and in 1950 he applied (unsuccessfully) to the department to help pay for Bruce's passage to the United States from Turkey.

Nevertheless, Bruce managed to get to the United States on his own the same year. He traveled via Western Europe, and during the summer of 1950 he stopped in Paris, where he had a brief and unhappy meeting with Mikhail, his half brother, that centered on money; they had not seen each other in a quarter of a century. Bruce then took a ship from Rotterdam that arrived in New York City on September 9, 1950, fifty-six years after his father had left.

Nothing is known about the relations between the brothers in the United States. Bruce died on April 13, 1960, at the age of forty-five, in Los Angeles, where he worked as a cook and had lived for the previous two years. Fred outlived his brother by a decade and died in Rochester, New York, on February 12, 1970, at the age of fifty-five.

Elvira's fate is unknown but she probably died in Istanbul in the late 1940s or 1950s. Olga's traces also disappear after she lost contact with Frederick in 1926, when she was living and studying in Paris.

Irma's fate was tragic. After initially living with Valli following their escape to Berlin in 1921, Irma came under the care of a local Lutheran pastor for several years. In 1925, when she was sixteen, she asked the American consulate in Berlin for help in locating her father because she had not heard from him "for some years." Berlin contacted Ravndal, who responded promptly with Frederick's address at Maxim. Whether or not Frederick ever helped Irma when she was in Berlin and he still had money is not known. Irma never entirely got over the unhappiness of her childhood or her troubled relations with her father, and some years later, after having married and moved to Luxembourg, she committed suicide.

Frederick's oldest son, Mikhail, was alone among the five children in escaping extreme hardship or tragedy. He studied agronomy in Prague, where he was also an enthusiastic boxer, becoming the city's Russian student boxing champion. After graduating from the university, he lived in Belgium and then Colombia before settling in France. During the war he worked for the Resistance. Afterward, he made a living by playing numerous small roles in French television series and in French and international films, at times with major stars like Audrey Hepburn, Cary Grant, William Holden, and Yul Brynner. He also sang at the famous Russian émigré nightclub "Scheherazade" in Paris—popular old Russian and Gypsy songs and African-American spirituals. His cultural orientation, despite his cosmopolitan past, was largely Russian. He died in Paris in 1987.

Frederick's descendants live in France to this day. Mikhail had two children, and his son, Bruce, was married to a prominent French designer known for her upscale and playfully sensual lingerie—Chantal Thomass. She adopted and then kept his—and Frederick's—surname, albeit modified for French pronunciation. It now survives in the name of her flagship store on the rue Saint-Honoré, one of the most famous shopping streets in Paris, as well as her boutiques in many other fashionable locations and cities around the world.

Frederick Bruce Thomas would have been pleased and amused.

ACKNOWLEDGMENTS

It is a pleasure to express my heartfelt thanks to a number of people who helped me greatly while I worked on this book: Eugene A. Alexandrov for his remarkable recall of myriad details from the distant past and for deciphering pages of old German handwriting; David Bethea, Paul Bushkovitch, and Glenda Gilmore for taking time from their busy schedules to answer my questions, to read drafts, and to give me their expert advice; Judith Flowers and Flo Larson for their hospitality and their crucial help with research in Coahoma County, Mississippi; Tatjana Lorkovic for securing microfiche collections of old Russian journals for Yale's Sterling Memorial Library that proved essential for my work; Vera Prasolova and Leonid Vaintraub for important assistance in Russian archives that yeilded remarkable documents; Bruce Thomass, Frederick Bruce Thomas's grandson, for his hospitality, for sharing his family's history with me, and for his generosity in allowing me to include a handsome photograph of his grandfather in this book. I owe a unique debt of gratitude to András J. Riedlmayer for suggesting sources, for helping me search collections in the Fine Arts Library at Harvard University, for fielding questions and reading a draft, for identifying several vivid Turkish recollections of Frederick Thomas, and especially for his great kindness in translating them for me.

I am also very grateful for advice and suggestions about a wide range of subjects that I received from Allison Blakely, Lenny Borger, James C. Cobb, Allegra di Bonaventura, Edward Kasinec, Konstantin

Kazansky, Philip Mansel, Christine Philliou, Norman Saul, Boris Savchenko, David Schimmelpenninck van der Oye, Mary Schwartz, Vadim Staklo, and Elena Uvarova. Many people assisted me with research in locations both near and far, and I owe debts to them all: Aylin Besiryan, Vincent L. Clark, Andrei Dubinsky, Padre Felice, Katherine Foshko, Edip Golbasi, Camille Jove, Diana Lachatanere, Angela Locatelli, Soeur Maria, Shannon M. Martinez, Kevin Pacelli, Andrew Ross, Charles Nicholas Saenz, and William and Alicia Van Altena.

My search for information about Frederick Thomas took me to numerous archives, libraries, and other repositories, and the staffs of the following were especially helpful (even when what seemed like promising leads turned out to be dead ends, as happened more than once): Bakhmeteff Archive (Columbia University); Bibliothèque de Documentation Internationale et Contemporaine (Nanterre, France); Coahoma County Courthouse (Clarksdale, MS); Centre des Archives Diplomatiques de Nantes (France); the Filson Historical Society (Louisville, KY); Fundación IWO (Buenos Aires, Argentina); Gemeentearchief Rotterdam (the Netherlands); Gosudarstvennyi Arkhiv Rossiiskoi Federatsii (Moscow); Hoover Institution Library (Stanford University); Immigration History Research Center (University of Minnesota); Imperial War Museum (London); Mandeville Special Collections Library (University of California, San Diego); Massachusetts Historical Society (Boston); Moorland-Spingarn Research Center (Howard University); Seeley G. Mudd Manuscript Library (Princeton University); National Archives (England); National Archives and Records Administration II (College Park, MD); Rauner Special Collections Library (Dartmouth College); Saint-Esprit Cathedral (Istanbul); Shelby County Archives (Memphis, TN); Schomburg Center for Research in Black Culture (New York); Sterling Memorial Library (Yale University).

For believing in this book, for sage advice on how to present it, and for skillfully guiding it to a hospitable port, I would like to thank my literary agent, Michael V. Carlisle of InkWell Management, and his able assistant, Lauren Smythe. I am deeply grateful to Joan Bingham, my editor at Grove/Atlantic, for her enthusiastic embrace of *The Black Russian* and for her wisdom and skill in shaping its final version.

Finally, thanks to my wife, Sybil, my children, Nicholas and Sophia, my father, Eugene A. Alexandrov, and my late mother, Natalia Alexandrov, for their support and their patience during the years that I worked on "FT."

SOURCES

ARCHIVES AND UNPUBLISHED MATERIALS

CADN   Centre des Archives Diplomatiques de Nantes, France.

CC   Coahoma County Courthouse, Chancery Court Records, Clarksdale, MS.
CCD   Chancery Dockets Books (plus volume).
CCI   Index Land Deeds Books (plus volume).
CCM   Chancery Court Minutes Books (plus volume).
CCR   Deed Record Books (plus volume).

Cemetery "Cherry Hill Cemetery, Coahoma County, MS," and "Cheairs Cemetery," typed registers of burials compiled by Judy Flowers and Graydon Flowers, Dublin, MS.

CP   Consular Post Records (plus city and box or volume number), Department of State, Record Group 84, NARA II.

CPI   Consular Post Records Istanbul (plus volume number), Turkey, Department of State, Record Group 84, NARA II.

DF   Frederick Thomas Dossier, Passport Correspondence (Cutter File), 1910–1925, box 322, file 130 T 3675, RG 59.

DP   Diplomatic Post Records (plus country or city and volume number), Department of State, Record Group 84, NARA II.

DPT   Diplomatic Post Records Turkey (plus volume number), Department of State, Record Group 84, NARA II.

DV   Valentine Thomas Dossier, Passport Correspondence (Cutter File), 1910–1925, box 321, file 130 T 3671, RG 59.

FC   Farikeuy Catholic Cemetery, Record Books, Istanbul.

FO   Foreign Office Records, National Archives, Kew, Richmond, Surrey, England.

GARF   Gosudarstvennyi Arkhiv Rossiiskoi Federatsii, Moscow.

Hoover   Hoover Institution Library, Stanford University, Palo Alto, California. Fisher: Edgar J. Fisher Papers.

Interviews   Bruce Thomass, November 8, 2006; June 16, 18, 2009; November 15, 2010; Paris.

LC   Library of Congress, Washington, DC.

Mabry   Mabry Malcolm, editor, "Hopson Bayou Neighborhood," 1996. Compilation of articles by Olive Edwards from *Here's Clarksdale*, 1980–1983, and others; plus additional materials. North Delta Museum, Friars Point, MS.

MLB   Mark Lambert Bristol Papers, War Diary, Library of Congress, Washington, DC.

NARA   National Archives and Records Administration, Washington, DC.

NARA II   National Archives and Records Administration II, College Park, MD.

North   North Delta Museum, Friars Point, MS.

Pence   Harry Pence Papers, Mandeville Special Collections Library, University of California, San Diego.

RG 59   Record Group 59, Department of State, NARA II.

RG 84   Record Group 84, Department of State, NARA II.

RGIA   Rossiiskii Gosudarstvennyi Istoricheskii Arkhiv, St. Petersburg.

SE   Saint Esprit Catholic Cathedral, Record Books, Istanbul.

Serpoletti   A. Z. Serpoletti, "Moskovskie uveselitel'nye sady. Ocherk, 1928, okt. 4." F. 533. Sobranie vospominanii i dnevnikov. Gosudarstvennyi tsentral'nyi teatral'nyi muzei imeni A. A. Bakhrushina, Moscow.

TsANTDM   Tsentral'nyi Arkhiv Nauchno-Tekhnicheskoi Dokumentatsii Moskvy, Moscow.

TsIAM   Tsentral'nyi Istoricheskii Arkhiv Moskvy, Moscow F. 1476: Records of the Saints Peter and Paul Lutheran Evangelical Church, Moscow.

TT   Edgar Turlington's transcript of Frederick Bruce Thomas's autobiographical statement; in Turlington to George L. Brist, 8 February 1924, 7 pages, Passport Correspondence (Cutter File), box 322, 130 T 3675, DF, RG 59.

Bibliography

Abbott, Mary. *A Woman's Paris. A Handbook of Every-Day Living in the French Capital*. Boston, MA, 1900.

Adil, Fikret. *Gardenbar Geceleri*. Istanbul, 1990.

Ahmad, Feroz. *The Making of Modern Turkey*. London, 1993.

Aiken, Charles S. *The Cotton Plantation South Since the Civil War*. Baltimore, MD, 1998.

Alekseev, A. G. *Ser'eznoe i smeshnoe. Shest'desiat piat' let v teatre i na estrade*. Moscow, 1984.

Al'perov, Dmitrii. *Na stsene starogo tsirka. Zapiski klouna*. Moscow, 1936.

The American Slave: A Composite Autobiography. Series One, Vol. 7: *Oklahoma and Mississippi Narratives*. General Editor George P. Rawick. 1941. Rpt. Westport, CT, 1972.

Andreev, Vadim L. *Istoriia odnogo puteshestviia. Povesti.* Moscow, 1974.

Andreyev, Catherine, and Ivan Savický. *Russia Abroad: Prague and the Russian Diaspora, 1918–1938.* New Haven, CT, 2004.

Anisimov, Aleksandr V. *Teatry Moskvy. Vremia i arkhitektura.* Moscow, 1984.

Annals of Our Colonial Ancestors and Their Descendants; or, Our Quaker Forefathers and Their Posterity. Compiled by Ambrose M. Shotwell. Lansing, MI, 1895.

Argus [Mikhail Zheleznov]. "Slukhi i fakty." *Novoe russkoe slovo.* October 19, 1965, 2.

Armstrong, Harold. *Turkey in Travail. The Birth of a New Nation.* London, 1925.

Ascher, Abraham. *The Revolution of 1905.* Vol. 1. Stanford, CA, 1988.

Auditorium. Chicago, 1890.

Baedeker, Karl. *Belgium and Holland, Including the Grand-Duchy of Luxembourg. Handbook for Travelers.* Leipzic, 1901.

———. *London and Its Environs. Handbook for Travelers.* Leipzic, 1898.

———. *London and Its Environs. Handbook for Travelers.* Leipzig, 1908.

———. *Paris and Environs, with Routes from London to Paris. Handbook for Travelers.* Leipzig, 1904.

———. *Russia with Teheran, Port Arthur, and Peking. Handbook for Travelers.* Leipzig, 1914.

———. *South-Eastern France, Including Corsica. Handbook for Travelers.* Leipzic, 1898.

Baker, James. *Turkey.* New York, 1877.

Bareilles, Bertrand. *Constantinople. Ses cités franques et levantines.* Paris, 1918.

Beatty, Bessie. "The Bogy-Man of the Bosporus." *The Century Magazine,* Vol. 104, No. 5 (September 1922), 705–15.

Bercaw, Nancy. *Gendered Freedoms. Race, Rights, and the Politics of Household in the Delta, 1861–1875.* Gainesville, FL, 2003.

Biographical and Historical Memoirs of Mississippi. Vol. 1. Chicago, IL, 1891.

Biographical Directory of the United States Congress, 1774–Present, http://bioguide.congress.gov/scripts/biodisplay.pl?index=b000968.

Blakely, Allison. *Russia and the Negro: Blacks in Russian History and Thought.* Washington, DC, 1986.

"Blanche Kelso Bruce." *Black Americans in Congress,* Senator, 1875–1881,

Republican from Mississippi, http://baic.house.gov/member-profiles/ profile.html?intID=127.

Bogart, Ernest Ludlow, and John Mabry Mathews. *The Centennial History of Illinois. Vol. 5: The Modern Commonwealth, 1893–1918.* Springfield, IL, 1920.

Bohon, John W. "Brusilov Offensive (4 June to 20 September 1916)." *The European Powers in the First World War: An Encyclopedia.* Edited by Spencer C. Tucker et al. New York, 1996, 145–47.

Bond, Beverly G., and Janann Sherman. *Memphis: In Black and White.* Charleston, SC, 2003.

Bonner, Jimmy A. *Propping on a Gooseneck. Boyhood Wanderings of the Last of the White Mississippi Delta Sharecroppers. Coahoma County, Mississippi.* Starkville, MS, 2005.

Borovsky, Victor. *Chaliapin: A Critical Biography.* New York, 1988.

Brieger, James F. *Hometown, Mississippi.* Jackson, MS, 1997.

Brooklyn Daily Eagle Almanac, 1894. Brooklyn, NY, 1894.

Brooklyn Daily Eagle Almanac, 1901. Brooklyn, NY: n. p., 1901.

"Bruce, Blanche Kelso." *Biographical Directory of the United States Congress, 1774–Present,* http://bioguide.congress.gov/scripts/biodisplay. pl?index=b000968.

Brygin, Nikita. "Tainy, legendy, zhizn'. Fakel voobrazheniia." *Gde obryvaetsia Rossiia.* Editors A. A. Taubenshlak and E. L. Iavorskaia. Odessa, 2003, 410–88.

Burdzhalov, Eduard N. *Russia's Second Revolution: The February 1917 Uprising in Petrograd.* Translated and Edited by Donald J. Raleigh. Bloomington, IN, 1987.

Campbell, James. *Talking at the Gates: A Life of James Baldwin.* Berkeley, CA, 1991.

Caron's Directory of the City of Louisville for 1893. Louisville, KY, 1893 [and subsequent yearly editions for 1894, 1895, 1896].

Cheairs, Calvin, et al. v. Lucius Smith et al. *Reports of Cases Argued and Determined in the High Court of Errors and Appeals, for the State of Mississippi.* Vol. 37. Edited by James Z. George. Vol. 8, Parts of Terms of April 1859, October 1859. Philadelphia, PA, 1860, 646–68.

Cheairs', Calvin, Executors v. Samuel D. Cheairs' Administrators. *Report of*

Cases Decided by the Supreme Court of Mississippi at the October Term 1902. Vol. 81. Reported by T. A. McWillie. Nashville, TN, 1903, 662–75.

Chicago by Day and Night. The Pleasure Seeker's Guide to the Paris of America. Chicago, IL, 1892.

Cleveland, William L., and Martin Bunton. *A History of the Modern Middle East.* Boulder, CO, 2009.

Cobb, James C. *The Most Southern Place on Earth: The Mississippi Delta and the Roots of Regional Identity.* Oxford, 1992.

Cockfield, Jamie H. "Philip Jordan and the October Revolution, 1917." *History Today.* Vol. 28, No. 4 (April 1978), 220–27.

Cohn, David L. *The Mississippi Delta and the World. The Memoirs of David L. Cohn.* Edited by James C. Cobb. Baton Rouge, LA, 1995.

———. *Where I Was Born and Raised.* Boston, MA, 1948.

Constantinople To-Day, or The Pathfinder Survey of Constantinople. A Study in Oriental Social Life. Directed by Clarence Richard Johnson. New York, 1922.

Criss, Nur Bilge. *Istanbul Under Allied Occupation, 1918–1923.* Leiden, 1999.

Dadamian, Gennadii G. *Teatr v kul'turnoi zhizni Rossii (1914–1917).* Moscow, 2000.

Daniels, Roger. *Guarding the Golden Door: American Immigration Policy and Immigrants Since 1882.* New York, 2004.

deCoy, Robert H. *Jack Johnson. The Big Black Fire.* Los Angeles, 1969.

Deleon, Jak. *The White Russians in Istanbul.* Istanbul, 1995.

The Department of State Personnel and Organization. December 31, 1921. Washington, DC, 1922.

Despatches from United States Ministers to Russia, 1808–1906. Record Group 59. Microfilm M-35. Washington, DC: National Archives and Records Service. 1953.

De Windt, Harry. *Russia as I Know It.* London, 1917.

Dickerson, Susan, et al. v. W. N. Brown (October 1873). *Reports of Cases Decided by the Supreme Court of Mississippi.* Vol. 49, *October Term, 1873, April Term, 1874.* Vol. 1. Jackson, MS, 1874, 357–76.

Dickerson, W. H., v. Lewis T. Thomas (April 1890). *Reports of Cases Decided by the Supreme Court of Mississippi.* Vol. 67, *October Term, 1889, April Term, 1890.* Philadelphia, PA, 1890, 777–89.

———. (October 1890). *Reports of Cases Decided by the Supreme Court of Mississippi.* Vol. 68. *October Term, 1890, April Term, 1891.* Philadelphia, PA, 1891, 156–58.

Dmitriev, Iu. A. "Akvarium." *Estrada Rossii. Dvadtsatyi vek. Leksikon.* Editors E. D. Uvarova et al. Moscow, 2000, 20–21.

Dolgorukov, Kniaz' Pavel Dmitievich. *Velikaia Razrukha.* Madrid, 1964.

Dos Passos, John. *Orient Express.* New York, 1927.

Dowling, Timothy C. *The Brusilov Offensive.* Bloomington, IN, 2008.

Dow's Memphis Directory, 1885. Memphis, 1885 [and subsequent yearly editions for 1886, 1887, 1888, 1889, 1890, 1891, 1892].

Drake, St. Clair, and Horace R. Clayton. *Black Metropolis. A Study of Negro Life in a Northern City.* Revised and enlarged edition. Vol. I. New York, 1970.

Drape, Joe. *Black Maestro: The Epic Life of an American Legend.* New York, 2006.

Duke, Vernon. *Passport to Paris.* Boston, MA, 1955.

Dunn, Robert. *World Alive: A Personal Story.* New York, 1956.

Dwight, H. G. *Constantinople Old and New.* 1915. Rpt. New York, 2002.

Dzhunkovskii, Vladimir F. *Vospominaniia.* 2 Vols. Editor A. L. Panina. Moscow, 1997.

Edwards, Olive. "The Hopson Bayou Neighborhood." *Here's Clarksdale,* Vol. 14, No. 5. (September–October 1980), 6–8.

———. "The Hopson Bayou Neighborhood." *Here's Clarksdale,* Vol. 15, No. 5 (September–October 1981), 6–8.

Elson, Louis Charles. *European Reminiscences, Musical and Otherwise.* Philadelphia, PA, 1896.

Engel, Barbara Alpern. *Between the Fields and the City. Women, Work, and Family in Russia, 1861–1914.* Cambridge, 1994.

Engelstein, Laura. *Moscow, 1905: Working-Class Organization and Political Conflict.* Stanford, CA, 1982.

"Episkop-Negr." *Niva. Illiustrirovannyi zhurnal literatury, politiki i sovremennoi zhizni,* No. 44 (October 30, 1904), 880.

"The Fall of Kerensky. Circumstantial Narrative of Capture of the Winter Palace and Kerensky's Escape—The Women Defenders." *The New York Times Current History. The European War.* Vol. XIV. *January–March 1918.* New York, 1918, 302–7.

Farson, Negley. *The Way of a Transgressor.* New York, 1936.

Fitzpatrick, Sheila. *The Russian Revolution.* 3rd ed. New York, 2008.

"Freedmen's Bureau." (2008). In *Encyclopædia Britannica.* Retrieved Aug. 13, 2008, from Encyclopædia Britannica Online: http://www. search.eb.com/eb/article-9035296; http://en.citizendium.org/wiki/ Freedmen's_Bureau#_ref-8.

Fussell, Paul. *Uniforms. Why We Are What We Wear.* Boston, MA, 2002.

Gaisberg, F. W. *Music on Record.* London, 1946.

Garrigues, Henry J. *A Text-Book of the Science and Art of Obstetrics.* 2nd ed. Philadelphia, PA, 1907.

Gde obryvaetsia Rossiia. Editors A. A. Taubenshlak and E. L. Iavorskaia. Odessa, 2003.

Gilbert, Morris. "Alors, Pourquoi?" *The Smart Set.* Vol. LXXII, No. 3 (November 1923), 47–48.

Greer, Carl Richard. *The Glories of Greece.* Philadelphia, PA, 1936.

Griffiths, William R. *The Great War.* The West Point Military History Series. Garden City Park, NY, 2003.

Gurko, Vladimir I. "Sobytiia v Odesse." *Gde obryvaetsia Rossiia.* Editors A. A. Taubenshlak and E. L. Iavorskaia. 1924. Rpt. Odessa, 2003, 129–54.

Hamilton, G. P. *The Bright Side of Memphis. A Compendium of Information Concerning the Colored People of Memphis, Tennessee, Showing Their Achievements in Business, Industrial and Professional Life and Including Articles of General Interest on the Race.* Memphis, TN, 1908.

Hanioğlu, M. Şükrü. *Atatürk: An Intellectual Biography.* Princeton, NJ, 2011.

Harris, Leslie M. *In the Shadow of Slavery: African Americans in New York City, 1626–1863.* Chicago, IL, 2003.

Herlihy, Patricia. *The Alcoholic Empire. Vodka and Politics in Late Imperial Russia.* Oxford, 2002.

Herring, George C. *From Colony to Superpower. U.S. Foreign Relations Since 1776.* New York, 2008.

Heyking, Baron A. *Practical Guide for Russian Consular Officers and Private Persons Having Relations with Russia.* London, 1904.

Hildebrand, Arthur Sturges. *Blue Water.* New York, 1923.

Holmes, Burton. *Travelogues. With Illustrations from Photographs by the Author.* Vol. 8. *St. Petersburg. Moscow. The Trans-Siberian Railway.* New York, 1910.

Holquist, Peter. *Making War, Forging Revolution: Russia's Continuum of Crisis, 1914–1921*. Cambridge, MA, 2002.

Hotaling, Ed. *Wink. The Incredible Life and Epic Journey of Jimmy Winkfield*. New York, 2005.

Houghteling, James L., Jr. *A Diary of the Russian Revolution*. New York, 1918.

Il'in, Pavel. "Glava IV. Geografiia kul'tury Moskvy v kontse XIX—nachale XX veka." *Moskva rubezha XIX i XX stoletii. Vzgliad v proshloe izdaleka*. Editors Pavel Il'in and Blair A. Rubl. Moscow, 2004, 131–94.

Il'in, Pavel, and Mikaella Kagan. "Glava I. Moskva na perelome stoletii." *Moskva rubezha XIX i XX stoletii. Vzgliad v proshloe izdaleka*. Editors Pavel Il'in and Blair A. Rubl. Moscow, 2004, 18–63.

Insurance Maps of Memphis, Tennessee. New York: Sanborn Map and Publishing Company, 1888.

Insurance Maps of Memphis, Tennessee. Vol. 2. New York: Sanborn-Perris Map Company, 1897.

Ippolitov, Sergey, et al. *Tri stolitsy izgnaniia. Konstantinopol', Berlin, Parizh*. Moscow, 1999.

Jahn, Hubertus F. *Patriotic Culture in Russia During World War I*. Ithaca, NY, 1995.

Johnson, Jack [John Arthur]. *Jack Johnson in the Ring and Out*. Chicago, IL, 1927.

Johnson, William E. *The Liquor Problem in Russia*. Westerville, OH, 1915.

Jukes, Geoffrey. *The First World War: The Eastern Front, 1914–1918*. Oxford, 2002.

Kantorovich, V. "Frantsuzy v Odesse." *Gde obryvaetsia Rossiia*. Editors A. A. Taubenshlak and E. L. Iavorskaia. Rpt. Odessa, 2003, 248–65.

Karay, Refik Halid. "Caz Faslı" [1922]. Rpt. in *Guguklu Saat*. Istanbul, 1940, 102–5.

Kazansky, Konstantin. *Cabaret russe*. Paris, 1978.

Keeny, S. M. "Relief Work in Poland and Russia." *American Oxonian*. Vol. 9, No. 1 (January 1922), 102–7.

Kelly, Catriona. *Children's World. Growing Up in Russia, 1890–1991*. New Haven, CT, 2007.

Kenez, Peter. *Civil War in South Russia, 1918: The First Year of the Volunteer Army*. Berkeley, CA, 1971.

————. *Civil War in South Russia, 1919–1920: The Defeat of the Whites.* Berkeley, CA, 1977.

————. *A History of the Soviet Union from the Beginning to the End.* 2nd ed. Cambridge, 2006.

Kettle, Michael. *Churchill and the Archangel Fiasco. November 1918–July 1919.* New York, 1992.

Kitchen, Karl K. *The Night Side of Europe, as Seen by a Broadwayite Abroad.* Cleveland, OH, 1914.

Klement'ev, Vasilii F. *V bol'shevitskoi Moskve (1918–1920).* Moscow, 1998.

Kostrova, Varvara. *Litsa skvoz' gody. Sobytiia. Vstrechi. Dumy.* St. Petersburg, 2006.

Kriger, Vladimir A. *Akterskaia gromada. Russkaia teatral'naia provintsiia, 1890–1902.* Moscow, 1976.

Kurukin, Igor', and Elena Nikulina. *"Gosudarevo kabakskoe delo." Ocherki piteinoi politiki i traditsii v Rossii.* Moscow, 2005.

Kuznetsov, Evgenii. *Iz proshlogo russkoi estrady. Istoricheskie ocherki.* Moscow, 1958.

Labor Contracts of Freedmen, Records of the Assistant Commissioner for the State of Mississippi, Bureau of Refugees, Freedmen, and Abandoned Lands, 1865–1869. Record Group 105. Microfilm M826, Rolls 43-50. Washington, DC: National Archives Microfilm Publications, 1971.

The Lakeside Annual Directory of the City of Chicago, 1889. Reuben H. Donnelley, Compiler. Chicago, IL, 1889 [and subsequent yearly editions for 1890, 1891, 1892, 1893].

Langum, David J. *Crossing Over the Line: Legislating Morality and the Mann Act.* Chicago, IL, 1994.

Lawford, Stephen. *Youth Uncharted.* New York, 1935.

LeMoyne Normal Institute, Memphis, Tennessee. 1883–1884. Memphis, 1884. Online at http://www.archive.org/stream/lemoynenormalins001emo.

Letopis' rossiiskogo kino, 1863–1929. Edited by A. S. Deriabin et al. Moscow, 2004.

Lewis, Bernard. *The Emergence of Modern Turkey.* 3rd ed. New York, 2002.

Life and Labour of the People of London. Vol. 9. Edited by Charles Booth. London, 1897.

Lloyd, Craig. *Eugene Bullard. Black Expatriate in Jazz-Age Paris.* Athens, GA, 2000.

Lobanov-Rostovsky, Prince Andrey. *The Grinding Mill. Reminiscences of War and Revolution in Russia, 1913–1920*. New York, 1936.

Lockhart, R. H. Bruce. *British Agent*. New York, 1932.

Lomax, Alan. *The Land Where the Blues Began*. New York, 1993.

Lotz, Rainer E. *Black People: Entertainers of African Descent in Europe and Germany*. Bonn, 1997.

Mackenzie, Compton. *First Athenian Memories*. London, 1931.

———. *My Life and Times. Octave Five, 1915–1923*. London, 1966.

Maksimov, Valery, and Andrey Kokorev. *Chelovek iz "Yara."* Moscow, 2001.

Mannix, Daniel P., 3rd. *The Old Navy*. Editor Daniel P. Mannix 4th. New York, 1983.

Mansel, Philip. *Constantinople: City of the World's Desire, 1453–1924*. London, 1995.

Marcosson, Isaac F. "When Constantinople Went Dry." *Saturday Evening Post*. Vol. 196, No. 36 (March 8, 1924), 40–48.

Margo, Robert A. *Race and Schooling in the South, 1880–1950. An Economic History*. Chicago, IL, 1990.

Margulies, M. S. *Letopis' revoliutsii*. Berlin, 1923.

The Marriage Laws of Soviet Russia. New York: Russian Soviet Government Bureau, 1921.

McKay, Claude. "Soviet Russia and the Negro." *Crisis* (December 1923), 61–65.

———. "Soviet Russia and the Negro (Concluded)." *Crisis* (January 1924), 114–18.

McMeekin, Sean. *History's Greatest Heist: The Looting of Russia by the Bolsheviks*. New Haven, CT, 2009.

Merriman, John. *A History of Modern Europe. From the French Revolution to the Present*. Vol. 2. 2nd ed. New York, 2004.

Monakhov, Nikolai F. *Povest' o zhizni*. Leningrad, 1936.

Monkhouse, Allan. *Moscow, 1911–1933*. Boston, MA, 1934.

Moore, Jerrold Northrop. *Sound Revolutions. A Biography of Fred Gaisberg, Founding Father of Commercial Sound Recording*. London, 1999.

Moore, John Bassett. *A Digest of International Law*. 8 Vols. Vol. III. Washington, DC, 1906.

Morfessi, Yurii. *Zhizn', Liubov', Stsena. Vospominaniia russkogo baiana*. Paris, 1931.

Munholland, J. Kim. "The French Army and Intervention in Southern Russia." *Cahiers du Monde Russe et Soviétique*. Vol. 22, No. 1 (January–March 1981), 43–66.

Murat, Princess Lucien. "A French Princess Savours Turkish Delights." *Vogue* (April 1922), 70, 76.

Nansen, Dr. Fridtjof. *Armenia and the Near East*. London, 1928.

Nordhoff, Charles. *The Cotton States in the Spring and Summer of 1875*. New York, 1876. Rpt. New York, n. d.

Oats, Willie Lee, Jr. *Delta Blues. The History of My Family and Life on the Plantation*. St. Louis, MO: Willie Lee Oats, Jr., 1980.

Okunev, Nikita P. *Dnevnik moskvicha*. Paris, 1990.

Palmer, Scott W. *Dictatorship of the Air. Aviation Culture and the Fate of Modern Russia*. Cambridge, 2006.

Papers Relating to the Foreign Relations of the United States, 1918, Russia. Vol. 2. Washington, DC, 1932.

Papers Relating to the Foreign Relations of the United States, 1919, Russia. Washington, DC, 1937.

Peffer, Nathaniel. *The White Man's Dilemma. Climax of the Age of Imperialism*. New York, 1927.

Peimani, Hooman. *Conflict and Security in Central Asia and the Caucasus*. Santa Barbara, CA, 2009.

Penn, Jefferson. *My Black Mammy. A True Story of the Southland*. [Privately printed, United States, no place: no publisher], 1942.

"The People's Commissariat of Finance, Its Financial Policy and the Results of Its Activities for 1917–1919." *Soviet Russia*, Vol. 2, No. 9 (February 28, 1920), 218–22.

Pervititch, Jacques. *Plan Cadastral d'Assurances*. Constantinople: S. P. I. Fratelli Haim, July 1923.

Petrosian, Yury A. *Russkie na beregakh Bosfora (Istoricheskie ocherki)*. St. Petersburg, 1998.

Pisar'kova, L. F. "Moskovskaia duma v period revoliutsii (1905–1917)." *Moskovskii arkhiv. Vtoraia polovina XIX—nachalo XX v.* Edited by E. G. Boldina and M. M. Gorinov. Moscow, 2000, 574–91.

Pitcher, Harvey. *Witnesses of the Russian Revolution*. London, 1994.

Polk, R. L., and Company's Memphis Directory, 1892. Vol. II. Memphis, TN, 1892.

Ponafidine, Emma Cochran. *Russia—My Home. An Intimate Record of Personal Experiences Before, During and After the Bolshevist Revolution*. Indianapolis, IN, 1931.

Priest, Lyman W. "The French Intervention in South Russia, 1918–1919." MA dissertation, Stanford University, 1947.

Puckett, Newbell Niles. *Black Names in America: Origins and Usage*. Editor Murray Heller. Boston, MA, 1975.

Putevoditel' po Moskve 1913. Editor I. P. Mashkov. Rpt. Moscow, 1998.

Radunskii, Ivan S. *Zapiski starogo klouna*. Editor Iu. A. Dmitriev. Moscow, 1954.

Radzinskii, Edvard. *Rasputin: Zhizn' i smert'*. Moscow, 2001.

Raffalovich, Arthur. *Russia: Its Trade and Commerce*. London, 1918.

Redhouse, Sir James William. *An English and Turkish Dictionary in Two Parts. Part the First, English and Turkish*. London, 1856.

Reed, Christopher Robert. *Black Chicago's First Century*. Vol. 1. *1833–1900*. Columbia, MO, 2005.

Register of the Department of State. May 1, 1922. Washington, DC, 1922.

Register of the Department of State. July 1, 1933. Washington, DC, 1933.

Reshid, Mehmed. *Tourist's Practical Guide to Constantinople and Environs*. Pera [Constantinople]: Anglo-American Book and Newsagency, 1928.

Reynolds, Clark G. *On the Warpath in the Pacific. Admiral Jocko Clark and the Fast Carriers*. Annapolis, MD, 2005.

Riasanovsky, Nicholas V. *A History of Russia*. 3rd ed. New York, 1977.

Rieber, Alfred J. *Merchants and Entrepreneurs in Imperial Russia*. Chapel Hill, NC, 1982.

Rostovtsev, Mikhail A. *Stranitsy zhizni*. Leningrad, 1939.

Rowan, Arthur. *I Live Again. Travel, Secret Service and Soldiering in India and the Near East*. London, 1938.

Ruga, Vladimir, and Andrei Kokorev. *Moskva povsednevnaia: Ocherki gorodskoi zhizni nachala XX veka*. Moscow, 2006.

Russkaia armiia na chuzhbine. Gallipoliiskaia epopeia. Editor S. V. Volkov. Moscow, 2003.

Sack, A. J. *The Birth of the Russian Democracy.* New York, 1918.

Sackett, Fred J. Letter to the *Boston Daily Globe,* quoted in "Negro Lost Fortune in Russia, Got Another in Constantinople." *Boston Daily Globe* (May 14, 1926), 7.

Sacks, Marcy S. *Before Harlem. The Black Experience in New York City Before World War I.* Philadelphia, PA, 2006.

Saul, Norman E. *Conflict and Concord. The United States and Russia, 1867–1914.* Lawrence, KS, 1996.

———. *Distant Friends. The United States and Russia, 1763–1867.* Lawrence, KS, 1991.

———. *War and Revolution. The United States and Russia, 1914–1921.* Lawrence, KS, 2001.

Savchenko, Boris A. *Estrada retro. Yury Morfessi, Aleksandr Vertinsky, Iza Kremer, Petr Leshchenko, Vadim Kozin, Izabella Iur'eva.* Moscow, 1996.

Schimmelpenninck van der Oye, David. *Russian Orientalism: Asia in the Russian Mind from Peter the Great to the Emigration.* New Haven, CT, 2010.

Shaw, Stanford J. *From Empire to Republic. The Turkish War of National Liberation 1918–1923, A Documentary Study.* Vol. I. *The Rise and the Fall of the Ottoman Empire, 1300–1918.* Ankara, 2000.

———. *From Empire to Republic. The Turkish War of National Liberation 1918–1923, A Documentary Study.* Vol. II. *Turkish Resistance to Allied Occupation, 1318–1920.* Ankara, 2000.

———. *From Empire to Republic. The Turkish War of National Liberation 1918–1923, A Documentary Study.* Vol. IV. *Final Victory: Emergence of the Turkish Republic, 1922–1923.* Ankara, 2000.

Sheremet'evskaia, Natal'ia E. *Tanets na estrade.* Moscow, 1985.

Shneider, Il'ia. *Zapiski starogo moskvicha.* Moscow, 1970.

Silverlight, John. *The Victor's Dilemma. Allied Intervention in the Russian Civil War.* London, 1970.

Slide, Anthony. *The Encyclopedia of Vaudeville.* Westport, CT, 1994.

Slobodskoi, A. "Sredi Emigratsii." *Beloe delo. Konstantinopol'-Gallipoli.* Editor S. V. Karpenko. Moscow, 2003, 5–102.

Spear, Allan H. *Black Chicago: The Making of a Negro Ghetto, 1890–1920.* Chicago, IL, 1967.

Sperco, Willy. *Turcs d'hier et d'aujourd'hui (D'Abdul-Hamid à nos jours).* Paris, 1961.

Spravochnaia kniga o litsakh, poluchivshikh na 1913 god kupecheskie i promyslovye svidetel'stva po g. Moskve. St. Petersburg, 1913.

"Staryi Moskvich." "Moskva v kontse veka. Iz vospominanii starogo Moskvicha. 4. Sharl' Omon." *Russkaia mysl'* [*La Pensée russe*, Paris], No. 2648 (August 17, 1967), 4; No. 2650 (August 31, 1967), 4.

Sydnor, Charles Sackett. *Slavery in Mississippi.* Gloucester, MA, 1965.

Talmadge, I. D. W. "Mother Emma." *Opportunity. Journal of Negro Life* (August 1933), 245–47.

Teffi, N[adezhda]. "Constantinople—The Rusty Door to the East." *Living Age,* Vol. 312, No. 4053 (March 11, 1922), 565–69.

Thurston, Robert W. *Liberal City, Conservative State: Moscow and Russia's Urban Crisis, 1906–1914.* New York, 1987.

Tolstoy, Leo. *War and Peace.* Trans. Richard Pevear and Larissa Volokhonsky. New York, 2007.

Trow's New York City Directory. Vol. CVII. *For the Year Ending July 1, 1894.* New York, 1894.

Troyat, Henri. *Daily Life in Russia Under the Last Tsar.* Trans. Malcolm Barnes. New York, 1962.

Trukhanova, Natal'ia Ignat'eva. *Na stsene i za kulisami. Vospominaniia.* Moscow, 2003.

Tumanov, Kniaz' Iazon K. "Odessa v 1918–19 g.g." *Morskie zapiski. The Naval Records.* Vol. 22, No. 1, Issue 59 (1965), 65–90.

Tuminez, Astrid S. *Russian Nationalism Since 1856. Ideology and the Making of Foreign Policy.* Lanham, MD, 2000.

Ul'ianova, G. N., and M. K. Shatsillo. Introduction. P. A. Buryshkin. *Moskva kupecheskaia.* 1954. Rpt. Moscow, 1991, 5–36.

United States Bureau of Refugees, Freedmen, and Abandoned Lands. *Records of the Assistant Commissioner for the State of Mississippi, 1865–1872.* Microfilm, 50 Rolls. Washington, DC: National Archives and Records Service, 1971.

Utesov, Leonid. *S pesnei po zhizni.* Editor Iu. Dmitriev. Moscow, 1961.

Uvarova, Elena D. "Ermitazh." *Estrada Rossii XX Vek. Entsyklopediia.* Editors E. D. Uvarova et al. Moscow, 2004, 764–66.

———. "Var'ete." *Estrada Rossii XX Vek. Entsyklopediia.* Editors E. D. Uvarova et al. Moscow, 2004, 105–7.

———. "Yar." *Estrada Rossii XX Vek. Entsyklopediia.* Editors E. D. Uvarova et al. Moscow, 2004, 788–89.

Van Riper, Benjamin W. "City Life Under the Bolsheviks." *Atlantic Monthly* (February 1919), 176–85.

Varlamov, Aleksei. *Grigorii Rasputin-Novyi.* Moscow, 2007.

Vecchi, Joseph. *"The Tavern Is My Drum." My Autobiography.* London, 1948.

Vertinsky, Aleksandr. *Pesni i stikhi.* Washington, DC, 1962.

Vsia Moskva. Moscow, 1901, 1911, 1913, 1916, 1917.

Waldron, Peter. "Late Imperial Constitutionalism." *Late Imperial Russia: Problems and Prospects.* Edited by Ian D. Thatcher. Manchester, UK, 2005, 28–43.

Wallenstein, Peter. *Tell the Court I Love My Wife: Race, Marriage, and Law— An American History.* Gordonsville, VA, 2004.

Weeks, Linton. *Clarksdale and Coahoma County.* Clarksdale, MS, 1982.

Wharton, Vernon Lane. *The Negro in Mississippi 1865–1890.* The James Sprunt Studies in History and Political Science, Vol. 28. Chapel Hill, NC, 1947.

White, T. W. *Guests of the Unspeakable. The Odyssey of an Australian Airman —Being a Record of Captivity and Escape in Turkey.* London, 1928.

Wilder, Craig Steven. *A Covenant with Color. Race and Social Power in Brooklyn.* New York, 2000.

Williams, Edward V. *The Bells of Russia. History and Technology.* Princeton, NJ, 1985.

Williamson, Joel. *A Rage for Order. Black/White Relations in the American South Since Emancipation.* New York, 1986.

Willis, John C. *Forgotten Time: The Yazoo-Mississippi Delta After the Civil War.* Charlottesville, VA, 2000.

Wood, Ruth Kedzie. *The Tourist's Russia.* New York, 1912.

Xydias, Jean. *L'Intervention française en Russie. 1918–1919. Souvenirs d'un témoin.* Paris, 1927.

Yildiz, the Municipal Casino of Constantinople: The Historical Past of the Palace and Park of Yildiz. Constantinople: A. Ihsan, 1926.

Zia Bey, Mufty-Zade K. *Speaking of the Turks.* New York, 1922.

Zorkaia, Neia M. *Na rubezhe stoletii. U istokov massovogo iskusstva v Rossii 1900–1910 godov.* Moscow, 1976.

Zürcher, Erik J. *Turkey. A Modern History.* London, 1993.

NOTES

Abbreviations

Individuals

Frederick	Frederick Bruce Thomas
Hedwig	Hedwig Thomas
Valli	Valentina "Valli" Thomas
Elvira	Elvira Jungmann; after 1918, Mrs. Elvira Thomas

BHC	British High Commissioner, Constantinople
USHC	United States High Commissioner, Constantinople
BSS	British Secretary of State
USSS	United States Secretary of State

Titles

AC	*Atlanta Constitution*
Am	*Artisticheskii mir*
As	*Artist i stsena*
Az	*Artist i zritel'*
B	*Le Bosphore*
BDG	*Boston Daily Globe*
BG	*Boston Globe*
CD	*Chicago Daily*
CDe	*Chicago Defender*
CDE	*Columbus Daily Enquirer*
CDM	*Charleston Daily Mail*

CDT	Chicago Daily Tribune
CM	Constantinople-Matin
CT	Chicago Tribune
DNT	Duluth News-Tribune
EN	Evening News
ES	Eastern Spectator/Le Spectateur d'Orient
HC	Hartford Courant
ICC	Iowa City Citizen
JO	Le Journal d'Orient
LAT	Los Angeles Times
MG	Manchester Guardian
Mv	Moskovskie vedomosti
Nrs	Novoe russkoe slovo
NYT	New York Times
NYTr	New York Tribune
ON	Orient News
P	Programma
Rezh	Restorannaia zhizn'
Rzh	Rampa i zhizn'
S	Stamboul
Sa	Stsena i arena
SFN	San Francisco Chronicle
Tg	Teatral'naia gazeta
Ti	Teatr i iskusstvo
Tk	Teatr i kino
VM	Vsia Moskva
Vp	Vecherniaia pressa
Vt	Var'ete i tsirk
WP	Washington Post

Prologue

xi–xiii   **Jenkins:** Jenkins to USSS, April 6, 22, 1919; Burri on Odessa, CP Odessa, box 1, RG 84. **conditions in Odessa:** *Papers Relating 1919*, 751, 753;

Munholland, 49–50, 53; Brygin, 478; Xydias, 302. **d'Anselme:** Munholland, 56–58; see also Margulies, 307; Kantorovich, 261; Kettle, 249–53; Priest, 90. **Bagge:** BHC to BSS, April 26, 1919; Bagge's interview with d'Espèrey, April 20, 1919, FO 371/3964, 362–65, NA.

xiii–xiv   **Frederick's stolen passport:** Frederick to Ravndal, May 10, 1921, CPI 337. **Russian citizenship:** petition to Imperial Ministry of Internal Affairs, Aug. 2, 1914: RGIA f. 1284, op. 247, d. 26. 1914–1915 g.g. (5 pp.); **application presented to Nicholas II and his approval:** RGIA f. 1276 (Sovet ministrov), op. 17, d. 345, ll. 134–35 ob.

xv–xvii   **evacuation:** Jenkins's reports to USSS, CP Odessa, box 1, RG84. **Olga:** BHC to USHC, Feb. 26, 1920, DPT 411. **Frederick's loss of fortune, Odessa's banks:** Sackett; Gurko, 147; Kettle, 253. Jenkins's reports to USSS, ibid. Bagge interview with d'Espèrey, April 20, 1919, and Bagge to Graham, May 8, 10, 12, 1919, Letter and memoranda on evacuation of Odessa, FO 371/3964, 362–97, NA.

xvii–xix   *Imperator Nikolay*'s delays, d'Anselme's announcement, London Hotel: Lobanov-Rostovsky, 332–33; Kettle, 253; Kantorovich, 263. **confusion indescribable:** Jenkins's reports to USSS, CP Odessa, box 1, RG84; Silverlight, 207. **Cooke:** BHC to BSS, April 25, 1919; Cooke on evacuation of Odessa, FO 371/3964, 337–61, NA; Kettle, 254, 255–57. MLB, April 10, 1919, Special Report on Odessa Evacuation. *Imperator Nikolay*'s departure, Bolsheviks arrive, Odessa's appearance: Jenkins's reports to USSS, ibid. Lobanov-Rostovsky, 338; Kantorovich, 264; Tumanov, 85; Kettle, 256.

xx–xxi   *Imperator Nikolay* and conditions: Lobanov-Rostovsky, 338; Kettle, 256. Bagge to Graham on evacuation of Odessa, FO 371/3964, 366–97, NA. *Imperator Nikolay*'s voyage: Chevilly to Haut Commissaire, April 7, 1919; Bigaut to Vincent, April 21, 1919; d'Espèrey to Haut Commissaire, April 6, 7, 16, 1919; Vincent to Poulon, April 22, 1919, Ankara (ambassade), lot no. 2, Haut-Commissariat français à Constantinople, année 1919, boxes 2, 38, CADN.

xxi–xxii   **"delousing":** it was similar throughout the Constantinople area: Tumanov, 87; N. Kormilev, "Proshchai, Odessa! 2," *Nrs*, May 8, 1975, 3; I. Gardner, "Bredovyi khorovod," *Nrs*, July 15, 1977, 2.

xxii–xxiii   **d'Espèrey and French arrangements:** d'Espèrey to Haut Commissaire,

April 6, 16, 1919; Vincent to Poulon, April 22, 1919, Ankara (ambassade), lot no. 2, Haut-Commissariat français à Constantinople, année 1919, boxes 2, 38, CADN. Vincent to British Naval Attaché, April 14, 1919, FO 371/3964, 415–18. **Bolsheviks in Odessa:** *Papers Relating 1919*, 768; *Gde obryvaetsia Rossiia*, "Oblozhenie burzhuazii," 272. **Thomases arrive in Constantinople:** DF. **"nervous collapse":** Jenkins to USSS, "Urgent" telegram, May 29, 1919, Department of State, Decimal File, box 1460 (123J 411/65), RG 59.

xxiii–xxiv **Constantinople and Bosporus:** "City of Minarets and Mud," *NYT*, Nov. 5, 1922, 4, 13; "Constantinople, Where East Met West," *AC*, Aug. 5, 1923, 21; Marcosson; Armstrong, 71–72.

Chapter One

1 **"The Most Southern Place on Earth":** Cobb. **Hannah and Lewis, November 4, 1872:** information about Frederick's parents and his date of birth is compiled from various sources: TT, CC, U.S. Census data for 1870 (the Thomas family was counted twice by mistake) and 1880, and his passport applications. **they had been slaves:** TT; Sackett. **blacks outnumbered whites, most blacks owned nothing:** 1870 U.S. Census, Schedule 1: Population, and Schedule 3: Productions of Agriculture, Coahoma and Tallahatchie Counties, Mississippi; Cobb, 30; Weeks, 34; Aiken, 9–10, 17.

1–2 **1869 auction:** CCR S, 19. Lewis was credited with having produced 48 bales of cotton by June 1, 1870 (U.S. Census, Schedule 3, Productions of Agriculture, District No. 5, Tallahatchie County, Mississippi), which means that he took possession of the land before the spring of 1869. **Cheairs brothers:** TT; Edwards, 1981, 6–7; Edwards, in Mabry, 1, 59. Cheairs family members were still active in the area in the 1880s and 1890s: Calvin Cheairs' Executors v. Samuel D. Cheairs' Administrators, 671; 1880 U.S. Census, Special Schedules of Manufactures, Nos. 7 and 8, District No. 110, Tallahatchie County, Mississippi. **depression, land prices:** Cobb, 54–55, 74; Willis, 45–46. **Thomases' first season:** 1870 U.S. Census, Schedule 3, Tallahatchie, ibid.

NOTES 271

2–4   Coahoma County's appearance, character, settlement: Cobb, vii, 5, 8,
        10, 14, 30, 43, 78; Weeks, 3, 9, 34; Bonner, 31–32; Edwards, 1980, 7. **lives
        of the rich:** Cobb, 16. **lives of slaves, mosquitoes, black children's
        mortality:** Cobb, 20–22; 13, 45; Weeks, 7; Williamson, 47. **slaves kept
        illiterate:** Margo, 7–8.

4–5   **freedmen, sharecropping, whites thwart land rental:** Cobb, 51, 55,
        60, 71; Aiken, 17; Williamson, 46.

  5   **Frederick's siblings, parents:** U.S. Censuses, 1870, 1880. In court
        documents filed in 1890 and 1891, India mentioned only Frederick and
        her daughter, his half sister, Ophelia.

6–7   **Lewis's character:** see below, Memphis newspaper stories for October
        1890; Dickerson v. Thomas (April 1890), 781. **parents' literacy:** India
        was literate: CC, 1880 U.S. Federal Census for Coahoma County, MS.
        Lewis was illiterate: 1870 U.S. Federal Census, Tallahatchie County,
        MS. In all CC documents he "makes his mark." **names:** Puckett; I am
        also grateful to Professor Glenda Gilmore for additional information.
        Bruce: *Biographical Directory*; "Blanche Kelso Bruce."

7–9   **Frederick's childhood, hunting, fishing, wildlife:** Cobb, 15, 44; Weeks,
        7; Bonner, 32, 59, 2; Cohn, 1948, 26. **smells and sounds:** Bonner, 56–61,
        128, 127; Oats, 2; Cohn, 1995, 2.

9–10 **1870 census data:** Schedule 3, Productions of Agriculture in District No.
        5, Tallahatchie County. **48 bales:** estimate based on data from 1870 census.
        hired hands: 1880 U.S. Census, Schedule 2, Productions of Agriculture in
        District 101, Coahoma County, shows "Key" and "Ralph Florida" in the
        Thomas household.

10–11 **land transactions:** CCR: I, 295–96; L, 229–30; Q, 69–70, 615–617; R,
        269–270; S, 19–20, 306–307; V, 412–16; W, 258–59; CCR CC, 155–58.
        CCD 1: case 655, 317; case 900, 446. CCM 3: 113, 211, 249, 300, 365–66,
        368, 378–80, 492–93, 510–11, 543–44, 582–83, 595–97, 628–29. CCM 4,
        1893–1905: 33, 218, 221–23, 231–32. CCD [no number], Probate Side:
        230, 510. CCI E: 282–85. **white English partner:** CCR L: 229–30;
        George Rudman: Ancestry.com, Incoming U.S. Passenger Lists, and
        1880 U.S. Census.

11–13 **Thomases donate land:** CCR S: 306–7. **blacks and churches:** Aiken,
        21; Lomax, 70; Wharton, 256–57, 262; Williamson, 47, 172–73. **church**

a log cabin: Sydnor, 41. A.M.E. Church in Friars Point: Willie Oats Jr. to Florence Larson, Aug. 12, 1996, North. Cherry Hill church: Edwards, 1980; Edwards, in Mabry, 22; Nicholas, in Mabry, 33, 34; Brieger, 167. Cheairs brothers: Samuel and other family members are buried in the Cherry Hill Cemetery: Cemetery. churches in Mississippi: Williamson, 53; Aiken, 26; Wharton, 248; Weeks, 143. On white schools in Coahoma County in 1870, and the first white school in Clarksdale in 1884, see Weeks, 142. Bureau of Refugees: "Freedmen's Bureau." Black education: Wharton, 249; Margo, 6.

13–17 second major turning point: Dickerson v. Thomas (April 1890) and Dickerson v. Thomas (October 1890). Quoted phrases and specific details are drawn from the published reports. There are discrepancies between the state supreme court's summary and the much more detailed account in CC; I have used both sets of documents. Dickerson's wealth: *Biographical and Historical Memoirs*, 647–68. "it weren't no use in climbin": quoted by Sacks, 13.

17–19 Maynard and the Cutrer brothers: CCD 1: case 655, 317; Weeks, 92, 165–66. Cutrer's crime was reported widely: "Slandered Once Too Often," *BDG*, July 31, 1890, 4; "The Shooting of Editor F. F. Chew," *CDT*, Aug. 1, 1890, 5; "An Editor Fatally Shot," July 31, 1890, *NYT*, 5. Dickerson family's roots: Weeks, vii, 73; U.S. Census Slave Schedule, 1860; U.S. Censuses, 1870, 1880. first scandal: Dickerson et al. v. Brown; Wallenstein, 82–84; Bercaw, 158–61. Before the Civil War, it was illegal in Mississippi to emancipate a child born to a female slave. Cheairs et al. v. Smith et al. refused to confirm a will in which a white planter attempted to free two mulatto children. $115,000: U.S. Census, 1870.

19–21 newspaper in Jackson: quoted in Bercaw, 160. Dickerson clan: U.S. Censuses 1880, 1900. Lewis's case against Dickerson: CCD 1: case 655, 317; CCM 3: 113, 211, 249, 300, 365–66, 368, 378–80, 492–93; case also summarized: Dickerson v. Thomas (April 1890). boardinghouse: TT. court's decision on April 19, 1889: CCM 3: 378–80. "misrepresentations": Dickerson v. Thomas (April 1890), 783. courthouse location: Weeks, 175. Clarksdale's founder: "John Clark," in *Biographical and Historical Memoirs*, 553–54. Daniel Scott, warring factions: "A Mob in Mississippi," *BDG*, July 8, 1887, 1. Dickerson and train station: Weeks, 73.

21–22   court's "Opinion": Dickerson v. Thomas (April 1890), 784, 781. "writ
of assistance": CCM 3: 492–93.

22–23   Thomases deed half their farm: CCR CC: 155-58. "lynchingest"
state: Cobb, 91. Thomases move to Memphis in summer of 1890:
this can be deduced from TT; *Dow's Memphis*, 1891, 120–21; in Coahoma
County, the verdict's aftershocks lasted from April 1889 until October
1890, with a peak in June 1890. A Shelby County death record indicates
that Lewis had been a Memphis resident since 1887; this seems to be
an error, although it is possible that he visited the city more than once.

23–24   sixty thousand, largest cotton market, 1866 race riot, lynchings increase. *Dow's Memphis*, 1889, 47; Bond and Sherman, 46, 70–71. rented
a house: *Memphis Avalanche*, Oct. 29, 1890, 1. *Dow's Memphis*, 1891,
920–921. house and its location: *Insurance Maps of Memphis*, 1888 and
1897. Lewis's work: *Dow's Memphis*, 1891, 920–21, and advertisement
following 968; TT; Memphis newspaper articles (see below).

24–25   Frederick's job: TT. Weir's market: *Dow's Memphis*, 1891, 968. Howe
Institute: TT, in which he refers to the school as "Howe's University"; Bond and Sherman, 94; *Annals*, 162. Eastbrook was principal c.
1888–1892. Howe curriculum: Bond and Sherman, 42, 71, 94; *LeMoyne
Normal Institute*, 1883–1884, which probably resembled Howe's a half
dozen years later.

25–28   boarders at Lewis and India's house, events that followed: local
newspapers provided extensive and often lurid coverage: *Memphis Appeal*,
Oct. 29, 1890, 4; Oct. 31, 1890, 5; *Memphis Avalanche*, Oct. 29, 1890, 1;
Oct. 31, 1890, 1; Nov. 2, 1890, 11; *Memphis Public Ledger*, Oct. 28, 1890,
1; Oct. 29, 1890, 2; Nov. 1, 1890, 5; *Memphis Daily Commercial*, Oct.
29, 1890, 5; Oct. 31, 1890, 5. There are some discrepancies among the
accounts. In a number of instances, I quote or repeat the exact wording
of the newspaper stories.

28–29   supreme court's explanation: Dickerson v. Thomas (October 1890),
158. India's petition: CCM: 510–11; CCD Probate Side: case 431,230.
her revival of lawsuit: CCM 3: 543-44. case's convolutions: CCM
3: 595–97, 628–29; there is some confusion in the court documents
regarding the size and location of the property. In 1891, India revived
a second lawsuit that Lewis had begun against James A. Peace: CCR Q:

69–70; CCM 3: case 900, 582–83; Weeks, 32, 61, 63, 83. **Dickerson's death**: CCM 4: case 655, 218; U.S. Census 1880. **Coahoma County Chancery Court's decision:** CCM 4: 221–23, 231–32; CCI E: 282–85. **India in Memphis:** presumably with Ophelia, she moved to a smaller house at 417 Clay Street: *Polk's Memphis Directory for 1892*, 963, 1108, 1148; *Insurance Maps of Memphis, 1897.* **India moved to Louisville:** she worked for the family of William C. Kendrick: *Caron's Directory 1893*, 616, 1092; *1894*, 616, 1089; *1895*, 604, 1078; *1896*, 646, 1154 (her name is given erroneously as "Indiana"). **Frederick's "desire to travel":** TT.

Chapter Two

30–34 **Frederick left the South:** in those years, young black men from the country who left home usually sought work in southern cities; Williamson, 59. **Arkansas character:** Nordhoff, 37. **"drifted," St. Louis, 1890:** TT. **St. Louis:** http://stlouis.missouri.org/heritage/History69/#golden. **Chicago's history, character:** Spear, 1–4, 140–41. **blacks in Chicago:** Reed, *Black Chicago's First Century*, 65, 230, 241, 249, 359. **Gallagher:** TT; *Chicago by Day and Night*, 208; *The Lakeside Annual Directory, 1889*, 655; *1890*, 2573; *1891*, 843; *1893*, 1947. **Auditorium Hotel:** TT; "Two Jolts for Jack Johnson," *CDT*, Nov. 2, 1912, 8; *Auditorium*, 11ff., 77, 86.

34–35 **Columbian Exposition, Panic of 1893:** Bogart and Mathews, 394–401, 398–99. **Frederick in New York:** TT. **New York:** Wilder, 116–19, 269 n. 29; Sacks, 3–5, 22–23, 26, 32–36, 42–43, 45–46. **blacks and Brooklyn:** Harris, 279–288.

35–36 **Clarendon Hotel:** TT; *Brooklyn Daily, 1894*, 105. **Williams:** TT; Slide, 559; *Trow's New York City Directory, 1894*, 1506. **Herman:** TT. **Frederick's singing:** Penn, 24–28.

37 **ships, travel abroad:** TT; "Marine Intelligence," *NYT*, for Sept. and later months, 1894; Baedeker, *London*, 1898, 2. **Frederick's departure, arrival in England:** passport applications; *UK Incoming Passenger Lists*, Oct. 16, 1894, Ancestry.com; Baedeker, *London*, 2–3.

37–39 **The English and racial prejudice:** "The Negro Abroad," *BDG*, Feb. 2, 1902, 44; "Victoria's Black Knight," *NYTr*, July 30, 1893, 18. **preju-**

diced American: "The Negro's Paradise," *CDT*, Sept. 26, 1891, 10. Drysdale: "London Overrun with Dark-Skinned Colonials," *NYT*, June 20, 1897, 20.

39–40 **"Conservatory of Music":** TT. Frederick may have been referring to the "West London Conservatoire of Music," which did provide training in voice as well as instrumental music: *The Musical Times and Singing Class Circular*, Aug. 1, 1896, 508. **boardinghouse, restaurant:** TT. **India's mortgage:** CCR E: 282–85.

40–41 **Paris:** TT. **letter of introduction:** Eustis to Police Prefect, July 12, 1895, DP France 588, RG 84. **ferries:** Baedeker, *London*, 1898, 5. **learning French:** Baedeker, *Paris*, xi. **Frederick confident and extroverted:** see Lloyd, 47, who makes this point about another black man learning French well. **Frederick's addresses:** Frederick's 1896 passport application, Eustis to Police Prefect, ibid.

41–42 **Johnson:** quoted in Lloyd, 38–39. **French less class-conscious:** Abbott, 27, 8; *Life and Labour*, 149–50; Elson, 279. **romantic possibilities:** "Negroes Have a Chance," *EN*, Dec. 28, 1898, 7.

43–45 **passport, ambassador and son are southerners:** March 17, 1896, Emergency Passport Applications, 1877–1907, NARA microfilm publication M1834, roll 11. "Death of James B. Eustis," *NYT*, Sept. 10, 1899, 11. **Brussels, Ostend, Cannes, Restaurant Cuba, Germany:** TT; Baedeker, *Belgium*, 193; Baedeker, *South-Eastern France*, 257–58. **German discipline:** Vecchi, 20–23, 24.

45–51 **Drysdale in Monaco:** his first article that mentions Frederick: "A Glimpse of Monte Carlo," March 6, 1898 [dated Feb. 10], 16; I repeat some of Drysdale's turns of phrase verbatim. **Drysdale born in Pennsylvania:** "William Drysdale Dead," *NYT*, Sept. 21, 1901, 7. **romanticized South:** Sacks, 43–45. **Frederick's real name:** evidence that "George" is actually Frederick is compiled from various sources: Penn, 28–30; TT; Frederick's passport applications and early photographs; Drysdale, "Gambling at High Noon," *NYT*, March 20, 1898, 17. **Pullman porters:** Reed, *Black Chicago's First Century*, 194–95. **Frederick's French:** Drysdale, "Monaco a Venerable City," *NYT*, April 3, 1898, 16. **language study:** Abbott, 37–38. **Frederick about locals' abilities:** Drysdale, "Monte Carlo and Monaco," *NYT*, March 13, 1898, 16.

51–52   **Frederick left for Italy:** TT; "Monaco a Venerable City," *NYT,* April 3, 1898 [dated March 7], 16. **grand duke:** Penn, 29–30. **authoritarian Russian Empire:** Heyking, 51–55. **Frederick's passport:** May 13, 1899, Emergency Passport Applications, 1877–1907, NARA microfilm publication M1834, roll 14, Vol. 22, NARA.

53   **Dreyfus:** Merriman, 810–12. **Russian peasants:** Riasanovsky, 409–15.

Chapter Three

54–56   **Arrival formalities, customs, surveillance, uniforms, train to Moscow:** Baedeker, *Russia,* xviii–xxi; Troyat, 13–17; De Windt, 2–3; Holmes, 7–11; Fussell, 16–17.

56–58   **first year in Russia:** TT; B.P.S., "Moskovskii obzor var'ete i tsirka," *Vt,* Oct. 1, 1912, 5. **St. Petersburg, Odessa, Moscow:** Baedeker, *Russia,* 99, 89, xvi, 395, 277. **Moscow's churches:** *Putevoditel' po Moskve,* 323. **Bonaparte:** Tolstoy, 871, gives a historically accurate description. **Kremlin, "nothing above Moscow":** Baedeker, *Russia,* 278.

58–59   **"soundscape":** Williams, xv–xvi; Shneider, 79. **electric tramway, horsepower:** Il'in and Kagan, 40. **Muscovites' appearance:** Baedeker, *Russia,* 277; De Windt, 26–27; Shneider, 81; Wood, 111. **Russians' Asiatic streak:** Schimmelpenninck, 3–4. **black people in Russia:** see Blakely's indispensable study.

60   **McKay:** McKay, 1924, 114, 115; McKay, 1923, 65. **Harris:** Talmadge, 247. See also "Episkop-negr"; Drape, 114; Hotaling, 91. For black performers in Russia, see Lotz. **"Southern woman":** "Constantinople Cafe Owned by Southern Negro," *CDE,* Oct. 7, 1922, 7.

61–62   **Frederick's addresses, Triumphal Square:** Il'in and Kagan, 42; Il'in, 134, 141-42; Frederick's passport application, June 29, 1907, CPM 534. **valet:** Marcosson, 44; "Russian Nobility Now Work for Ex-Servant in Turkey," *CDe,* April 12, 1924, A1; Kitchen, 88. **Hedwig, marriage, children:** Frederick's wedding: TsIAM, f. 1476, op. 2, d. 14, l. 311 ob.; Hedwig's passport application, Dec. 17, 1909, CPM 534. **Chukhinsky Lane:** *VM 1901,* 453, 272, 393, 1112. **provincial feel:** Il'in and Kagan, 49–50.

63–64   **Aquarium:** "Staryi Moskvich"; Dmitriev, 20; Radunskii, 49; Monakhov,

36–38; Kriger, 168; Anisimov, 84–88. **Aumont:** Uvarova, "Var'ete," 106; Ruga and Kokorev, 426.

64–66   **Trukhanova:** Trukhanova, 23, 48–49, 52, 53, 57, 58–59.

66–67   **Russo-Japanese War, American historian:** Riasanovsky, 445–47. **Russo-American relations:** Saul, 1991, 339–96; 1996, 484–85, 509–11. **anti-Chinese racism:** Daniels, 3, 12–26. **"unbecoming for Americans to criticize":** Herring, 352; Saul, 1996, 476–77, 523–27.

68–70   **1905 Revolution:** Riasanovsky, 450–51; Merriman, 789–91. **siege of the Aquarium, Moscow:** Engelstein, 49, 197–98, 220; Ascher, 315–22. **ambassador's telegram:** *Despatches from United States,* reel 65, Dec. 11, 1905. **killings and executions:** Riasanovsky, 458; Fitzpatrick, 35.

70–71   **numbers of Americans:** *Despatches from United States,* reel 65, Dec. 26, 1905. **Frederick's explanation a dozen years later:** DF. **more detailed variant:** "Many Ugly Women Still Retain the Veil," *CDM,* Aug. 13, 1926, 2. **Berlin ties:** American Consulate, Danzig, to American Embassy, Berlin: Sept. 13, 1909, CP Danzig 17, p. 25, RG 84. Frederick's Sept. 14, 1909, passport application has a note explaining his reasons for going to Germany (Emergency Passport Applications, 1907–1910, Vol. 1, Germany, RG 59). **Frederick may have had a restaurant in Berlin:** "Two Jolts for Jack Johnson," *CDT,* Nov. 2, 1912, 8.

71–74   **Aumont's problems:** Uvarova, "Var'ete," 106; Dmitriev, 20; Kriger, 173–74. **Yar, Sudakov:** Uvarova, "Yar"; Maksimov and Kokorev, 91–92, 125, 127, 195, 196, 200, 209, 211, 213. **Frederick moved family:** *VM 1911,* 571; *VM 1901,* 89; *VM 1917,* 101. **racetrack:** Maksimov and Kokorev, 131. **airplanes:** Palmer, 18. **Natruskin:** Maksimov and Kokorev, 91–92; *Rzh,* Nov. 1, 1913, 6; Nov. 15, 1913, 7–9; Dec. 1, 1913, 6–7. Ruga and Kokorev, 414. **tribute to Sudakov, celebration:** Maksimov and Kokorev, 194–202.

74–76   **Gaisberg:** Gaisberg, 34; Moore, 161; Borovsky, 546–48. Gaisberg makes some mistakes about Frederick. **extravagant sprees:** Maksimov and Kokorev, 223–24. **Norton:** Roy Norton, "Spendthrifts," *NYTr,* July 6, 1913, SM 3–4, 19; quotation from p. 4. Norton makes some mistakes about Frederick.

76–77   **Irma:** TsIAM, f. 1476, op. 2, d. 24, ll. 5 ob.–6; Translation, Pastoral Certificate, Sts. Peter and Paul Lutheran Church, Moscow, CPI 337

(Corresp. 1921). **Hedwig's death:** Report, American Consular Service, Moscow, Feb. 10, 1910, Numerical and Minor Files of the Department of State, 1906–1910, NARA Microfilm Publication M 862, roll 1152, RG 59; Interview, June 18, 2009; Frederick's descendants did not know the real name of his first wife. Garrigues, "Abnormal Labor," 376 ff; Wilcox, 197–206.

77–78   **Valli:** TsIAM, f. 1476, op. 2, d. 22, ll. 255 ob.–256; her relations with Frederick are documented extensively in DV. The spelling of her first name varies in the documents, depending on transliteration. **terrorism and violence:** Tuminez, 140–41.

Chapter Four

79–81   **Aquarium's reopening:** *As*, Nov.–Dec. 1911, 5; Serpoletti, 54/56; *P*, July 1912, 10–12; *As*, May 1 [?], 1911, 11–12; *As*, Sept.–Oct. 1910, 18; Dmitriev. **Aumont's curse:** *As*, June [?] 1911, no. 5, 14. *As* appeared irregularly; when the month is uncertain, I give it with a question mark. **Martynov's first name and patronymic:** *VM 1901*, 273; *VM 1917*, 319. **Tsarev was maître d'hôtel:** *As*, July–Aug. [?] 1911, no. 15, 7. **Frederick's trip:** *Am*, Feb. 1912, 1, 2; *Am*, March 1912, 2; Frederick's passport application, 7 March 1912, DP Berlin 352, RG 84. His trip very likely resembled that of Yakov Shchukin (owner of the Hermitage Garden in Moscow, and Aquarium's only real competitor [Uvarova, "Ermitazh," 764–65]), described by Monakhov, 117–21. **Frederick paid too much:** Gamma, "Akvarium," *P*, July 1912, 11–12. **Duncan and Brooks:** *CDe*, Feb. 3, 1923, 13.

81–83   **Aquarium's first season:** *Am*, May 1912, 3, 17. **journalists covering Moscow theatrical life:** *Am*, June 1912, 2, 3; Gamma, "Akvarium," *P*, July 1912, 10–12; *Vt*, Oct. 1, 1912, 4. **other entertainment venues in Moscow:** Baedeker, *Russia*, 273–74.

83–84   **frequent visitor:** *Rezh*, May 15, 1913, 4.

84–87   **Lockhart:** Lockhart, 70–72; he mistakenly refers to Frederick as "British."

87–88   **Frederick rich:** *Am*, Sept. 1912, 5. **Gamma on Frederick's race:** "Akvarium," *P,* July 1912, 10–12. **Chicagoans:** "Two Jolts for Jack Johnson," *CDT,* Nov. 2, 1912, 8.

88–90   **September 1912:** *Am,* Sept. 1912, 5. **"Skating-Palace":** advertisement, *P,* Oct. 1912, 24. **"Chanticleer" and Adel:** Serpoletti, 57/59; *P,* July 1912, 15; *Am,* Sept. 1912, 12; *Tg,* Feb. 9, 1914, 12; *Vt,* Feb. 28, 1914, 8–9. **Muscovites cheered:** *Am,* Sept. 1912, 12; *As,* May [?] 1912, No. 10, 16; *Vt:* Oct. 1, 1912, 6; Oct. 27, 1912, 5; Nov. 10, 1912, 6. **"Maxim," renovations:** *Am,* Oct. 1912, 2; "Ob otsenke vladeniia, prinadlezhashchego sukonnoi i kozhevennoi fabriki 'Alekseia Bakhrushina Synov'ia,'" TsIAM, f. 179, op. 62, d. 16118, l. 10; "Maksim," 1912, TsIAM, f. 179, op. 63, d. 16142, ll. 1, 3; **by mid-October interior ready:** *Vt,* Oct. 14, 1912, 6. **Duncan and Brooks:** *CDe,* Feb. 3, 1923, 13. **October 20 opening:** *Vt,* Oct. 20, 1912, 5; *Am,* Oct. 1912, 2. The original Russian jingle reads "Poidu k Maksimu ia, / Tam zhdut menia druz'ia."

90–91   **complication:** *Vt,* Oct. 14, 1912, 6. **churches:** 1902 and 1914 maps of Moscow. **church hierarchs:** e.g., *Vt,* April 6, 1914, 12. **Moscow's secular authorities:** *Mv,* Sept. 11, 1913, 2. **Adel's difficulties:** *Rezh,* Sept. 13, 1913, 7; *Rzh,* June 13, 1910, 395. **Adrianov:** Dzhunkovskii, II, 65. **"someone" not named:** *Rezh,* Sept. 13, 1913, 7; Kitchen, 89–90, reports that Frederick told him of friendly relations with several grand dukes. **Maxim's opening:** *Rzh,* Nov. 11, 1912, 9; *Am,* Nov. 1912, 7. **"first-class variety theater":** *Am,* Nov. 1912, inside front cover.

92–93   **Frederick's ads:** e.g., *Rzh,* Nov. 25, 1912, 3. **"Salon Café Harem":** Shneider, 85; *Rezh,* Sept. 13, 1913, 7; *Tg,* Sept. 29, 1913, 2. **one commentator:** *Rezh,* Sept. 13, 1913, 7; April 1, 1913, 8.

93–94   **pneumonia:** *P,* June 1912, 14. **Frederick's relations with Valli:** Interviews, Nov. 8, 2006, and June 16, 18, 2009. The Thomass family's oral history differs significantly from what can be reconstructed about Frederick's life on the basis of published and unpublished documents. **wedding:** there are somewhat different dates, and Moscow is the location, in different sources: Jan. 5, 1913, TsIAM, f. 1476, op. 2, d. 22, ll. 255 ob.–256; Jan. 22, 1913, DV. **photograph:** Valli to Ravndal, Feb. 13, 1922, CPI 352.

94–95   **moved family:** the addresses were 39 Bolshoy Kozikhinsky Street: *VM 1913,* 575; and a building belonging to the Saint Ermolay Church,

Sadovaya-Kudrinskaya Street: *Spravochnaia kniga o litsakh*, 273. **eight-room apartment:** *Sa*, Feb. 15, 1915, 15; Dunn, 421; *VM 1916*, 361; *VM 1917*, 491. **education in Russia:** Thurston, 158, 160. **foreign languages, servant beating:** Interview, Nov. 8, 2006; the Thomass family history has the servant die as a result, with Frederick covering it up, which seems implausible.

95–96   **Elvira:** Valli to Ravndal, Feb. 13, 1922, CPI 352; Elvira to Allen, March 8, 1933, CPI 443; TT; Reynolds, 52; "In the Days of the High Commissioners," *Asia*, Dec. 1923, 952; "Turkish Delight," *Outlook*, Oct. 25, 1922, 329; Argus. **dancer and singer:** "Negro Lost Fortune in Russia," *BDG*, May 14, 1926, 7; "Russian Princesses and Duchesses Earn a Living in Constantinople," *Syracuse Herald*, Oct. 7, 1922, 3. **Gerlach:** http://www.tpa-project.info/body_index.html. **American cowgirl:** *Vt*, Dec. 25, 1913, 10. **Elvira's languages:** Elvira to Allen, March 8, 1933, see above, and July 22, 1935, DPT 629; *ON*, June 16, 25, 1920, 4; "Spectacles et Concerts," *S*, June 17, June 20, July 8, 1920, 3; Elvira's announcement of Frederick's death, *S*, June 13, 1928, 3. **Frederick and Elvira's affair:** the birth of their first son in September 1914 indicates that the affair began no later than Jan. 1914: Frederick's Passport Application, Sept. 15, 1921, DF. **Frederick Jr.'s birth date:** ibid.; and Dept. of State to American Consul, Istanbul, Jan. 17, 1931, DPT 430. **Bruce's birth date:** given as April 12, 1915, in Frederick's Passport Application, Sept. 15, 1921, DF, and in Dept. of State to American Consul, Istanbul, Jan. 17, 1931, above. But this must be a mistake if Frederick Jr.'s birth date is correct, because there is less than nine months' time between them.

97   **businesses with Tsarev:** *Rezh*, May 15, 1913, 3, and June 10, 1913, 6; *Tg*, Sept. 29, 1913, 2. **Martynov:** *Vt*, July 1, 1913, 3; *Am*, Sept. 1913, 4. **Theatrical Stock Company:** *Rezh*, June 10, 1913, 6; Jan. 15, 1914, 7-8; *Tg*, June 1, 1914, 6–7; "Svedeniia," RGIA, f. 1276, op. 17, d. 345, l. 135 ob.

98–100   **Kitchen:** Kitchen, 87–90.

100–103 **music agreement, Konsky:** Konsky's pursuit of Frederick is detailed in letters that he wrote to his employer during the period 1913–1917: CADN, Fonds Saint-Pétersbourg, Série cartons et registres, Numéro d'article 538, pp. 204–7, 212, 213, 244–47, 249, 251, 279–85, 287, 302, 303, 347, 372, 378, 401, 402, 406, 407, 458.

104–106   **"the most famous," Jack Johnson:** Ken Burns in his documentary film *Unforgivable Blackness: The Rise and Fall of Jack Johnson* (2005), quoted in http://en.wikipedia.org/wiki/Jack_Johnson_(boxer). **Johnson and the Mann Act:** Langum, 179–86. **Frederick's offer:** "Moscow, Russia, Offers Jack Johnson His Only Chance to Fight Again," *SFN*, Oct. 30, 1912, 13; "Jack Johnson Wants to Leave City of Chicago," *DNT*, Nov. 1, 1912, 1; "This Is Tough on Chicago," *Kansas City Star*, Nov. 1, 1912, 5B; "Johnson Will Go to Russia," *Grand Forks* (North Dakota) *Daily Herald*, Nov. 2, 1912, 2; "Two Jolts for Jack Johnson," *CDT*, Nov. 2, 1912, 8; "Johnson's Saloon Closed," *NYT*, Nov. 2, 1912, 1; "Jack Johnson Signs for Fight in Russia," *EN* (San Jose, California), Nov. 1, 1912, 5. **Klegin, "in the hands of":** "Johnson Would Go to Russia," *LAT*, Oct. 25, 1912, III3 (dispatch dated Oct. 23). **picked up by the foreign press:** e.g., "Jack Johnson Charged with Abduction," *MG*, Oct. 19, 1912, 18; "Attempt to Lynch Jack Johnson," *Observer* (England), Oct. 20, 1912, 9; untitled note, *Le Figaro* (France), Oct. 19, 1912, 1. **"negro named Thomas":** "Two Jolts for Jack Johnson," ibid.

106–108   **Johnson in Russia:** Johnson, 92; *Mv*, July 12/25, 1914, 4. It is possible that Frederick met Johnson earlier in Western Europe: *Tg*, March 23, 1914, 12. Johnson mistakenly refers to "George" rather than "Frederick." In addition to Johnson's own mistakes and exaggerations about Frederick, even more egregious ones are reported by deCoy, 180–83.

Chapter Five

109–110   **aftermath of 1905 war:** Riasanovsky, 472–74, 479–82; McMeekin, xvi–xviii. **Sarajevo, war:** Merriman, 964 ff; Riasanovsky, 464. **"blood and faith":** *Mv*, July 16/29, 1914, 3.

110–113   **Frederick's petition:** RGIA, f. 1284, op. 247, d. 26. 1914–1915. **Adrianov's note:** RGIA, Departament obshchikh del (1811–1917 gg.), f. 1284, op. 247, d. 26. 1914–1915. **form at heart of petition:** RGIA, Sovet ministrov (1905–1917 gg.), f. 1276, op. 17, d. 345, l. 135 ob. **Nicholas's approval:** RGIA, f. 1276 (Sovet ministrov), op. 17, d. 345, ll. 45, 46, 47, 50, 134, 135 ob.

113–115 **Frederick's passport renewal:** June 24, 1914, Emergency Passport Applications Filed at Diplomatic Posts Abroad, RG59. **Thomas family history:** Interviews. **youngest sons recognized:** State Department to Consul General, Istanbul, Sept. 17, 1935, Decimal File, 367.1115–Thomas, Bruce and Frederick/2, RG 59. **Valli's 1916 application:** July 27/Aug. 9, 1916, DV.

115–116 **Moscow demonstrations:** *Mv,* July 16/29, 1914, 3. **German economic ties:** Raffalovich, 311. **benefit evening:** *Rzh,* Aug. 16/29, 1914, 1, 4; *Tg,* Aug. 17/30, 1914, 2.

116–117 **Germans outside Paris:** Merriman, 975–77, 986–88; Riasanovsky, 464. **trainloads of prisoners:** "Austria's Heavy Losses," *Scotsman,* Sept. 9, 1914, 6.

117–118 **prohibition, U.S. Senate request:** Kurukin and Nikulina, 224–30; Herlihy, 64–65; Johnson, *Liquor,* 194–95, 202–4. **observers concluded that Russians embraced sobriety:** "One Man's Work Sobers Russia," *NYTr,* Nov. 19, 1914, 3; "Exit Vodka," *Mg,* Dec. 7, 1914, 5; "Russia Without Vodka," *Mg,* March 10, 1915, 12; "Russians Sell Last Belongings for Liquor," *HC,* Nov. 15, 1914, 3. **Muscovites' legal method:** "The Truth About Vodka," *Bonfort's Wine and Spirit Circular,* March 25, 1915, 391. **illegal stills:** "Russia Without Vodka," *Mg,* ibid.; "Russia Totally 'Dry,'" *WP,* Jan. 2, 1915, 3.

119–120 **bribing, bootlegging, drinking:** Al'perov, 381–82; Maksimov and Kokorev, 237–39. **Zhichkovsky:** Kurukin and Nikulina, 228–30; name and patronymic are from *VM 1917,* 181. **French champagne:** Alekseev, 89. **Frederick's success:** *Am,* Aug. 1915, 2; *Ti,* June 28, 1915, 463.

120–122 **January 1915, Przemyśl:** Griffiths, 54. **Ottoman Empire, Constantinople:** Riasanovsky, 464–66. **"For the Russian Army":** *Rzh,* Jan. 18, 1915, 8; Feb. 1, 8, 1915, 3; *Tg,* Feb. 8, 1915, 5. **Maxim shut:** *Am,* April 1915, 4. Maxim had also been briefly shut down in the fall of 1914, but by January 1915, it was back in business and reported doing very well: *Am,* Jan. 1915, 5. **Frederick continued to "prepare energetically":** *Am,* April 1915, 4. **Bruce's birth:** Frederick's Passport Application, 15 Sept. 1921, DF.

122–123   Serpoletti: *Am*, April 1915, 7–8. **Serpoletti's story:** I. Yadov [the surname derives from "poisonous"], " 'Evropeets.' Direktor iz Petrograda," *Am*, April 1916, 8.

123–125   **German advance, "mad bacchanalia":** Merriman, 988; **"Tobacco for the Soldier":** *Rzh*, May 19, 1915, 10; *Mv*, May 20, 1915, 3; May 21, 1915, 3 (Frederick's surname mistakenly given as "Tomson"); *Sa*, June 2, 1915, 9, 12. **merchants' philanthropy:** Ul'ianova and Shatsillo, 22.

125–126   **rampaging mobs, political cost:** *Mv*, May 31, 1915, 4; Dzhunkovskii, II, 59–61, 563–66. **English eyewitness:** Houghteling, 48. **Zimmermann's store:** Al'perov, 369; Dzhunkovskii, II, 562–63. **damage estimate:** "Blames Germans for Riots in Russia," *NYT*, Oct. 19, 1915, 3.

126–127   **war's first anniversary, grand duke's dismissal, Gallipoli:** Merriman, 990; Riasanovsky, 466–67. **Ciniselli Circus:** *Tg*, June 7, 1915, 8. **oldest building of its kind in Russia:** "Sankt-Peterburg Entsiklopediia," http://www.encspb.ru/article.php?kod=2804016386; http://petersburgcity.com/family/theatres/circus/; http://www.ruscircus.ru/glav21. **auction:** *Tg*, June 7, 1915, 8; *Ti*, Dec. 15, 1915, 945–46; *Am*, Dec. 1915, 3; March 1916, 3; *Sa*, Dec. 26, 1915, 19–20.

127–128   **Odessa:** Baedeker, *Russia*, 386, 395–96. **Frederick's trips:** *Tk*, Feb. 6, 1916, 5–6; April 2, 1916, 7; July 16, 1916, 9; July 30, 1916, 9. **villa:** *Am*, March 1917, 5.

128–129   **war's second year:** *Ti*, Sept. 6, 1915, 661; *Ti*, Sept. 13, 1915, 694; *Ti*, Sept. 20, 1915, 705; *Am*, Oct., 1915, 5; *Sa*, Oct. 5, 1915, 13; *Sa*, Dec. 25, 1915, 16; *Sa*, May 14, 1916, 16; *Am*, Oct. 1916, 2; Maksimov and Kokorev, 246–47. **wartime impositions:** *Ti*, Nov. 1, 1915, 307–8; *Ti*, Nov. 8, 1915, 838; *Ti*, Dec. 6, 1915, 919; *Vt*, Dec. 25, 1916, 7; *Ti*, Jan. 31, 1916, 95; *Ti*, Feb. 14, 1916, 134. **Tsaritsa Alexandra:** Riasanovsky, 466–67; **"ministerial leapfrog":** Waldron, 34.

129–131   **tango craze:** *Vt*, Dec. 25, 1913, 10; *Tg*, Jan. 12, 1914, 12; *Vt*, Jan. 15, 1914, 4; *Rzh*, Feb. 23, 1914, 3; *Am*, March 1914, 13; *Rzh*, March 23, 1914, inside front cover. **"kingdom of the tango":** *Vt*, Dec. 25, 1913, 10. **"Tango of Death":** Sheremet'evskaia, 24–25; **"Wilhelm's Bloody Tango":** Jahn, 103. **"Cocainomaniacs":** *Vt*, Dec. 25, 1915, 6. **Vertinsky:** *Tg*, Jan. 3, 1916, 7–8; *Vt*, Jan. 1917, 6. **"Kokainetka":** Vertinsky, 78. **"Hashish Tango":** *Tg*, March 3, 1918, 6.

131–133   military losses, striking workers: Merriman, 1019, 1021–22; Burdzhalov, 29; Peimani, 194; Monkhouse, 51. Rasputin: Dzhunkovskii, II, 555,
563; Varlamov, 457–70; Radzinskii, 330–34. Frederick and Rasputin:
deCoy, 180–83.

133–134   "Brusilov Offensive": Dowling, xv; Bohon, 147; Jukes, 45. shortages:
Ti, Oct. 9, 1916, 829, 820. theaters packed: Sa, Jan. 10, 1916, 15.
Frederick leases theaters: Ti, Jan. 10, 1916, 32; Rzh, Jan. 31, 1916, 9;
Tg, April 3, 1916, 5; Rzh, April 10, 1916, 13; Tg, Jan. 1, 1917, 6; Tg, Feb.
5, 1917, 3. Frederick rewards employees: Am, Jan. 1917, 7; Ti, Jan. 1,
1917, 6; Sa, Jan. 17, 1917, 6.

134–135   buildings purchased, previous owners: Am, March 1917, 5. "Ob
otsenke vladeniia, prinadlezhashchego Brus-Tomas Fedoru Fridrikhovi-
chu, byvshemu grazhdaninu Severo-Amerikanskikh shtatov, Sretenskoi
chasti 1 uchastka No. 216/204 po Karetnomu riadu, Srednemu i Malomu
Spasskim pereulkam, d. 2, 1, 2": TsIAM, "Fond Moskovskikh gorodskikh
dumy i upravy," f. 179, op. 63, d. 12896, l. 1–4; TsANTDM, Plan vladenii
kniazei Kantakuzinykh, grafov Speranskikh, f. 1, op. 13, ed. kh. 109, d.
19, l. 5 ob. "Miss Julia Grant Married," NYT, Sept. 25, 1899, 7. 425,000
rubles: by Feb. 12, 1917, the exchange rate had dropped from 2 to 3.3
rubles to the dollar: Houghteling, 25.

Chapter Six

136–137   February Revolution, "hardly a whimper": Merriman, 1022–30; Riasanovsky, 505–8.

137–139   Moscow demonstrations: Sack, 235–36; Pisar'kova, 583. "Liberty
Parade," men of property endangered: Houghteling, 174–78; Rieber,
405; Okunev, 19. "Order Number One": Kenez, History, 18–19; Merriman, 1026–27.

139–140   Moscow theatrical life: Dadamian, 161; Tg, March 12, 1917, 6, 9.
Merchant of the First Guild: TsIAM, Fond moskovskoi kupecheskoi
upravy, "O prichislenii v kupechestvo byvshego severo-amerikanskogo
poddanogo Fedora-Fridrikha Tomasa s docher'iu Ol'goiu" (1917 god),

f. 3, op. 4, d. 4678, ll. 1–3. **Frederick's designation:** Rieber, 13, 36, 87, 124; Ul'ianova and Shatsillo, 20.

140–142   **calamitous historical events:** Merriman, 1030–33; Riasanovsky, 508–11. **Frederick and Moscow Soviet:** *Tg,* Sept. 17, 1917, 5; *Az,* Oct. 1, 1917, 12; *Rzh,* Oct. 8, 1917, 9; *Tg,* Oct. 17, 1917, 10. **Frederick first to align himself:** *Tg,* Oct. 25, 1917, 10. **Maxim leased:** *Tg,* Sept. 24, Oct. 17, 1917, 1; *Rzh,* Oct. 1, 22, 1917, inside front cover.

142–143   **Bolsheviks strike:** Riasanovsky, 511–12, 528; Merriman, 1033–37; "The Fall of Kerensky," 305; Pitcher, 238-39. **Englishman:** Monkhouse, 61.

143–144   **November 10 and 20, horrified city dweller:** Okunev, 99–100, 104, 106; Van Riper, 176–78. **Kremlin damaged:** *Rzh,* Nov. 19, 1917, 7; Okunev, 106. **American described:** Van Riper, 183. **anxious time:** Monkhouse, 62. **Maxim's old repertory:** *Rzh,* Oct. 8, 22, Nov. 19, Dec. 3, 16, 1917, inside front cover; Jan. 1918, 1. **Aquarium's high-minded fare:** *Tg,* Nov. 21, 1917, 6.

145–146   **Bolshevik cease-fire, Brest-Litovsk:** Riasanovsky, 528–29; Merriman, 1037. **American visitor, Bolsheviks hated Americans:** Van Riper, 177, 182.

146–149   **Valli's lover:** Frederick to Ravndal, American Consul General, Constantinople, 10 May 1921, CPI 337. **Germans in Odessa:** *Papers Relating, 1918,* 676. **Frederick's application denied, permission for Elvira:** Sackett. **Frederick's acquaintance:** Dunn, 421. **Frederick's near-murder:** Frederick to Ravndal, 10 May 1921, ibid. (Frederick's spelling preserved). **revision of family laws:** *The Marriage Laws,* 5, 42, 36, 55. **Frederick divorces, remarries:** TT, Frederick to Ravndal, 10 May 1921, ibid.

149–150   **Whites:** Riasanovsky, 532. **anarchist groups:** Okunev, 168. **Russians hoped Germans would occupy:** "Making Allies Out of Enemies," *Independent,* May 31, 1919, 312; Kenez, *Civil War 1918,* 162. **Frederick's maneuvers:** *Rzh,* Feb. 19/6, 1918, 6–7, 1, 10; *Tg,* March 3, 1918, 3. **Frederick's new lease, Evelinov:** *Ti,* Jan. 14, 1918, 24; *Sa,* Jan. 23, 1918, 2; *Tg,* Jan. 28, 1918, 3; *Rzh,* Feb. 1918, 1; *Ti,* Feb. 17, 1918, 50; April 21/8, 1918, 129. **Frederick's hopes unrealized:** *Rzh,* Feb. 1918, 1; *Tg,* March 3, 1918, 3; *Rzh,* March 30/17, 1918, 2, 11; Kazansky, 110.

Aquarium situation ends badly: *Sa*, Feb. 15, 1918, 4, 12; *Ti*, Feb. 17, 1918, 50; *Rzh*, Feb. 21/6, 1918, 9; *Ti*, May 5/22, 1918, 148–49. prohibition against "bourgeois" farces: *Ti*, May 5/22, 1918, 148–49, 150. classical ballet: *Rzh*, June 2/May 20, 1918, 8.

150–152 Bolsheviks' changes: McMeekin, 35–38; Riasanovsky, 529–30; "The People's Commissariat of Finance," 219. property expropriated: Okunev, 160.

152–154 robberies: Okunev, 138, 164. police ineffective: Klement'ev, 5. Sukhodolsky: *Tg*, March 3, 1918, 6; about the Sukhodolsky brothers' business dealings with Aquarium, see *Rzh*, May 4, 1914, 10. bank seizures, $100 billion to $150 billion: McMeekin, 17, 19, 20–21, 50. Tsarev in Kiev: *Rzh*, June 29/16, 1918, 8. June announcement of ban on theater middlemen: *Tg*, June 9, 1918, 6; Kazansky, 120. cholera: Okunev, 202. Socialist Revolutionaries: Holquist, 168–69. Nicholas II murdered: Okunev, 202. Frederick's remaining livelihood: Sackett. "sackers" ("meshochniki"): Ponafidine, 101; Okunev, 150; Dolgorukov, 103–4.

154–155 Frederick's escape: Valli to State Department, Jan. 16, 1921, DV; Sackett. cost of a passport, German behavior at border: Dolgorukov, 113–16. trains blocked: Klement'ev, 6. conditions on trains, pillaged stations, young women in danger: Kostrova, 20–26.

155–158 American entering German territory: by analogy with an Englishman, see White, 298. Austrian and German occupation, Bolshevik guerrilla warfare: White, 300; Bagge to Clark, February 4, 1919, FO 371/3963. Bolsheviks throw open prisons: Tumanov, 69. prominent lawyer: Margulies, 159. Frederick in newspapers: Savchenko, 196, and e-mail from Boris A. Savchenko, May 2, 2010. feast in time of plague: Tumanov, 68–70; Lobanov-Rostovsky, 330. Moscow entrepreneurs, performers: Savchenko, 195–96; Utesov, 78–79. private banks: Xydias, 301–2; Gurko, 147; Jenkins to USSS, 22 April 1919, CP Odessa, box 1, RG 84.

159–160 excited crowds: White, 309. magnificently equipped army, exotic appearance of soldiers: Kantorovich, 254–55, 259, 261–62; Brygin, 432; Xydias, 186; Silverlight, 107; Munholland, 55. Estimates of the number of troops vary from thirty thousand to eighty thousand. Allied troops around Odessa: Lobanov-Rostovsky, 329; Kantorovich, 258–59.

French occupation invigorated Odessa: Tumanov, 78–79. speculators busy, situation deteriorates: *Papers Relating, 1919,* 751–54; Munholland, 49–50, 53; Xydias, 261–62.

Chapter Seven

161–163   **Galata quay, Pera Palace Hotel, Frederick and Codolban:** Bareilles, 4; http://www.perapalace.com/en-EN/history/64.aspx; Kazansky, 120–22.

163–166   **Pera's mixed population:** *Constantinople To-Day,* 18; Criss, 21. **Frederick saw similarities:** Kazansky, 122. **soundscape, "Allahu Akbar":** http://islam.about.com/cs/prayer/f/adhan_english.htm. **city's noise and appearance:** Armstrong, 72–73; Frank G. Carpenter, "Colorful Life Along the Bosporus," *LAT,* April 13, 1924, J11, J22. **Armstrong:** Armstrong, 73–74. **Galata Bridge, Stambul:** "Turk Capital Inert Under Enemy Rule," *NYT,* June 26, 1922, 18; "City of Minarets and Mud," *NYT,* Nov. 5, 1922, 4, 13; "Constantinople, Where East Met West," *AC,* Aug. 5, 1923, 21; Carpenter, above; Reshid, 75, 86–87; Dwight, 4–10, 14, 16–17; Andreev, 192.

166–167   **Allied occupation:** Shaw, I, 144–45. **dismember Ottoman Empire:** Criss, 1, 8–9, 14; Zürcher, 138–39, 145–46, 149–53. **foreigners in Pera:** "British Constantinople," *NYT,* June 19, 1921, 35.

167   **Turks on race:** For this information I am indebted to Dr. András J. Riedlmayer, Documentation Center of the Aga Khan Program at the Fine Arts Library, Harvard University, e-mail Aug. 6, 2010. **no special word for "Negro":** Redhouse, 217. **Baldwin:** Campbell, 210.

167–170   **little Western entertainment:** Teffi, 566; Editorial, *ON,* Aug. 14, 1919, 1. **a few European-style establishments:** e.g., advertisements: *CM,* Nov. 10, 1918, 2; Dec. 18, 1918, 335; March 22, 1919, 340; April 6, 1919, 341; *S,* Nov. 22, Dec. 13, 1918, 4; *ES,* March 22, May 2, 1919, 2; **Galata port area, traditional Turkish habits:** *Constantinople To-Day,* 356–57, 261–63; Armstrong, 74; Teffi, 567. **moneylenders, usurious interest:** Rue to Bristol, Aug. 24, 1923, DPT 470. **Reyser and Proctor:** Note by Burri, Nov. 26, 1920, CPI 327. **3,000 Turkish pounds:** the sum paid by a new partner for Reyser and Proctor's half share (Note by Burri, above).

The exchange rate from 1920 to 1922 was approximately seventy American cents to one Turkish pound: *ON*, Dec. 1, 1920, 3; March 11, 1921, 3; Feb. 7, 1922, 3. **Ltqs:** common abbreviation for "livres turques," French for "Turkish pounds." **Proctor, "top limey spy," "political whispering gallery":** Gilbert, 47–48; Mackenzie, *First Athenian*, 331–33; Mackenzie, *My Life*,119–20; Rowan, 147; Dunn, 282–83, 288, 299, 420; Lawford, 130; White, 317.

170–171 **"Anglo-American Garden Villa," "Stella Club":** *ES*, June 14, 1919. **empty lot, Chichli:** Pervititch map. **old shade trees:** "Spectacles et Concerts," *S*, June 17, 1920, 3. **mini Aquarium:** Zia Bey, 158. Morfessi, 150, describes the rival garden that he opened in 1920; it probably shared generic features. **"Stella Club" on second floor:** *ES*, June 14, 1919, 2. **opening on June 24, 1919:** advertisement, *ON*, 4. **"Friends of the Salonica Army," "Moscow Maitre d'hôtel":** *ON*, July 20, 27, 1919, 4. **weather problems:** *ON*, Sept. 19, 1919, 3. **unique combination:** advertisements, *ON*, July 20, Aug. 12, 1919, 4; Sept. 7, 1919, 3.

172 **first jazz:** *ON*, Aug. 31, 1919, 3; *ON*, Sept. 23, 1919, 4. **Villa a success:** *ON*, Sept. 27, 1919, 1; *ON*, Oct. 31, 1919, 3; Nov. 13, 1919, 3.

173–174 **passport, Allen a Kentuckian:** *Register*, 1922, 86; "The Political Graveyard: Index to Politicians: Allen, C to D," http://politicalgraveyard.com /bio/allen2.html#0XZ1CO0HD. **Frederick's forms and what happened to them:** DF. **Frederick's invented sister:** Frederick never mentioned her again to American authorities. **Paris hospitable:** Lloyd, 75–76, 87ff. **Constantinople newspapers on American racial policies:** *ON*, June 19, 1920, 2; March 30, 1921, 3; "La question nègre aux États-Unis," *B*, Oct. 20, 1921, 1. **Frederick and Philippines:** "Many Ugly Women Still Retain Veil," *CDM*, Aug. 13, 1926, 2.

175–176 **high prices:** "Turk Capital Inert Under Enemy Rule," *NYT*, June 26, 1922, 18. **Capitulations:** *Constantinople To-Day*, 95–96, 329–30. **Matakias:** DPT 403. **Ravndal's past:** *Register*, 1922, 170. **Mendelino, Bulgarian (Bochkarov), baker:** CPI 320, DPT 412. **another man:** CPI 327. **French firm (Huisman):** CPI 327. **Ravndal's admonishment:** to Frederick, Dec. 19, 1919, CPI 320.

177–179 **search for Olga:** DPT 411. **Royal Dancing Club:** *ON*, Jan. 20, 24, 25, 29, 30, Feb. 6, 11, 20, March 6, 1920, 3. **baccarat; Bertha's Bar:** Gilbert, 47–48.

179–181   Frederick's relations with Bertha and Reyser: *ON*, May 13, 1919, 3, lists Bertha's Bar; the following day it is gone: *B*, May 14, 1920, 4; notes and correspondence: CPI 327. **Frederick to Ravndal; Elvira's help:** ibid.

181–183   **martial law:** Criss, 2, 16, 65, 71; Shaw, II, 808, 829–31; Zürcher, 142. **Wrangel:** Kenez, *Civil War South*, 1977, 261, 265–67; *S*, April 7, 1920, 2. **Pera's Russian restaurants:** *ON*, April 2, 1920, 4; April 30, 1920, 2; March 6, 1920, 4. **Strelna:** Morfessi, 66, 147–52.

183–185   **"dame serveuse":** Mannix, 27. **Caucasian jackets, "agents of vice," British ambassador's letter, cartoon:** Mansel, 398–99. **Baudelaire:** *ON*, Oct. 21, 1920, 2. **soubrettes:** Murat, 70. **tourist from Duluth:** *DNT*, Oct. 22, 1922, 12. **Russian officer kissing waitress's hand:** *S*, June 10, 1920, 2. **Murat:** Murat, 76.

185–186   **Zia Bey:** Zia Bey, 154–60.

186–187   **insinuations about Frederick:** Rue to Bristol, Aug. 24, 1923, DPT 470. **gala evenings for waitresses:** *ON*, April 4, 1922, 3. **charity festival:** *S*, July 20, 1920, 4; *ON*, July 23, 28, 1920, 2.

187–189   **new creditors, Allen's and Ravndal's tone, Zavadsky:** CPI 327, DPT 412. **Valli resurfaces:** Wheeler to USSS, July 18, 1920, Central Decimal File, 361.11/3465, RG 59. **Valli in Berlin:** CPI 326, 337, 352. **Valli's application for passport, related correspondence, Berlin consul, no record of Valli's application:** DV. **life in Berlin:** "Exchange Decline Depresses Berlin." *NYT*, Sept. 17, 1920, 26. **Valli's letters to American consulate general and British embassy:** CPI, 326, 337; FO 782/15, Correspondence Register, British Embassy, Constantinople, Nov. 16, 1921; Jan. 9, 23, 1922; Feb. 20, 1922. **"I request you to indicate":** CPI 326.

Chapter Eight

190–193   **Wrangel's evacuation, refugees:** Petrosian, 162–72; *Russkaia armiia*, 7–9; Ippolitov, 6–26; Andreev, 191–228. **makeshift housing, employment, money changers:** Slobodskoi, 80–90; Andreev, 173, 175, 187, 193–96. **officers sell medals:** *ON*, July 24, 1921, 2. **Dos Passos:** Dos

Passos, 13. **high culture:** Deleon, 66–67. **Alhambra Theater:** *S,* Nov. 20, 22, 26, 27, Dec. 2, 1920, 3. **Frederick's meals:** Argus.

193–195 **pneumonia:** *ON,* Dec. 14, 1920, 2. **passport application, Allen's statement:** DF. **diplomats documented past:** CPI 327. **Quinlan to Easley, Carr's response:** DF; *Department of State Personnel,* 30, 31, 25.

196–197 **Valli's documents:** DV. **Ravndal and "your husband," "your wife in Germany," Frederick's letter:** CPI 337; I preserve his spelling. **"free-love companion":** DF.

197–198 **Olga:** CPI 337; CP Paris 837; Paris Police Prefecture Archives, telephone inquiry, Dec. 16, 2007. **Elvira's outfits:** CPI 338. **American tourist:** Sackett. **English-language schools:** British school, *ON,* Aug. 24, 1920, 3; Bowen School for Boys, *ON,* April 1, 1921, 4; American School for Boys, *B,* Aug. 21, 1921, 3. **Mikhail in Prague:** Interview, Nov. 8, 2006.

198–200 **victories at Sakarya, Kemal as field marshal, "Gazi":** Cleveland, 177–78; Hanioğlu, 127; Lewis, 253–54. **Frederick's situation improves:** CPI 339, 354. **new passport application, Burri's assessment:** DF; there are mistakes on the form. **Burri a New Yorker:** http://political graveyard.com/bio/burrage-burrowes.html.

201–202 **Vertinsky:** *ON,* Oct. 2, 1921, 3. **New venture, Maxim:** *B,* Nov. 21, 1921, 2; Karay, 104–5; Hildebrand, 280; Argus. **"very special amusement":** *ON,* Oct. 8, 1921, 2; *JO,* Dec. 18, 1921, 3. **Carter:** CPI 344. **"greatest artistic event":** *B,* Nov. 21, 1921, 2.

202–205 **"Thomas, the founder," "heart of gold":** Sperco, 144. **less worldly Turk:** Karay, 104–5. **Adil:** Adil, 8–10. I am indebted to Dr. András J. Riedlmayer, of the Documentation Center of the Aga Khan Program at the Fine Arts Library, Harvard University, for calling Karay's and Adil's recollections of Maxim to my attention, and especially for his kindness in translating them into English (I have rephrased his translations).

205–206 **"going very well":** CPI 354. **Valli bombards diplomats:** CPI 352; Valli about Frederick to British embassy, Constantinople, Feb. 14, 1922, FO 782/15. **merchants' complaints:** CPI 338, 354. **provision in Carter contract:** CPI 344. **crime:** Zia Bey, 159; "Turk Capital Inert Under Enemy Rule," *NYT,* June 26, 1922, 18; "Constantinople Crime City," *WP,* Oct. 24, 1920, 66. **Ravndal's watch:** CPI 320. **Italian count:** Reynolds, 52. **cocaine addicts:** *B,* Aug. 26, 1921, 2.

206–208 State Department's review of passport application, Randolph's letter, Randolph informs Berlin, Carr: CPI 348. *Department of State Personnel*, 25. **Dunn:** Dunn 420–21; "He Knew the Country," *Kingston* (New York) *Daily Freeman*, Oct. 24, 1922, 3.

208–210 **American tourists:** *ON*, March 2, 3, 8, April 2, 1922, 2; Beatty, 705–6. **Farson:** Farson, 442–43. **Mrs. Lila Edwards Harper:** "Constantinople Cafe Owned by Southern Negro," *Columbus* (Georgia) *Daily Enquirer*, Oct. 7, 1922, 7; spelling normalized.

210–211 **Mannix:** Mannix, 275.

211–212 **Adil, "Champion Osman":** Adil, 37–38. I am indebted to Dr. András J. Riedlmayer, of the Documentation Center of the Aga Khan Program at the Fine Arts Library, Harvard University, for calling my attention to this source, and especially for his kindness in translating it into English (I have rephrased his translation).

213–214 **"as wicked as you like":** Mannix, 270; **Vertinsky's "La Rose Noire":** Duke, 77. **camel fights:** *ON*, March 4, 1922, 3. **procession of sultan, dervishes:** Dwight, 304–7; Sperco, 87, 113; Mannix 271–73. **cockroach races:** "Tarakan'i bega," *Zarnitsy*, May 8–15, 1921, 28–29.

Chapter Nine

215–217 **Turkish offensive:** Lewis, 253–54. **Bristol's memorandum:** Sept. 23, 1922: Hoover, Frank Golden Papers, box 36, file 15, Turkey/Americans in Constantinople; CPI 472. **650 Americans:** "List of Americans in Constantinople," Nov. 15, 1922, Pence, MSS 144, box 7, folder 7. **Mehmet VI:** Zürcher, 142; Lewis, 251–53, 257–59.

217–218 **Frederick's rush to consulate, diplomats' reaction:** DF; CPI 151, 363; Moore, *Digest*, 927, 936. **Paris as haven:** Lloyd, 74–75, 91, 95–96, 101–2, ff. **Frederick's note, Washington's response:** CPI 363.

219–221 **Bristol's involvement:** March 4, Nov. 13, 1923, MLB. **Rue to Bristol:** DPT 470 (typos corrected). **Turlington:** http://www.scribd.com/doc/45752619/Rhodes-Scholars-Roster [1911]; TT. **Brist asked colleague:** DF.

221–223 **vacillation on prohibition:** *Vp*, Oct. 8, 9, 10, 16, 17, 24, 25, 1923, 3;

Hoover, Fisher, Oct. 30, 1923, 3-4; Ravndal to World League Against Alcoholism, Dec. 1, 1923, CPI 370; *S*, March 19, 1924, 1; May 25, 1925, 2; March 6, 1926, 2; Jan. 11, 1927, 2. **epochal historical changes:** Shaw, IV, 1963–1964; Lewis, 261–62; **American present:** Hoover, Fisher, Oct. 7, 1923, 3–4. **crowds on streets:** Hoover, Fisher, Oct. 30, 1923, 4. **shop signs:** *Vp*, Oct. 9, 1923, 3. **Mikhail leaves for Prague:** Interview, Nov. 8, 2006; Andreyev and Savický, 41, 53, 65; Keeny.

223–224 **Frederick's boasting:** Sackett. **Krotkov, Frederick's "broad" Russian nature:** Argus (a band's percussion instruments are more likely than Krotkov's "pots and pans"). **Fourth of July:** "Gallant Yanks Organize a Klan to Rescue Pearl," *CDT*, July 27, 1924, 16.

225–226 **Bebek, downpours and destruction:** *S*, June 14, 15, 22, 24, 26–28, 1924; Jan. 20, 1925, 2. **La Rose Noire:** *S*, June 26, 1924, 3; July 19, 1925, 3; **Le Moscovite:** *S*, April 30, May 7, 1925, 3.

226–228 **tourism increases:** *S*, March 2, 5, 10, 1925, 2; July 3, 1926, 2; Hoover, Fisher, March 20, 1925. **the most audacious plan:** *S*, Aug. 25, Nov. 27, 1925, 2; *S*, July 2, 1926, 2. **Serra's financial deal:** *S*, April 29, 1927, 2; *Yildiz*; DPT 539. **Hagia Sophia:** Interview, June 16, 2009. **American companies write to consulate general:** CPI 398. **"American Association of Jazz Bands":** "Would Jazz in St. Sophia," *NYT*, Jan. 12, 1927, 6; "Sophia Mosque for Dances," *NYT*, Dec. 16, 1926, 10. **Maxim's entertainments:** *S*, July 2; Aug. 5, 25, 31; Nov. 7, 11, 13; Dec. 24, 1925, 3; Jan. 28, 1926, 3; Feb. 11, March 10, 1926, 2; *La République*, Nov. 26, 1925, 3.

228–229 **caliph leaves:** Shaw, IV, 1965; *S*, March 10, 1924, 2. **fez abandoned, Soviet Union takes over embassy:** Hoover, Fisher, Sept. 26, 1925; Lewis, 253, 283–84. **new laws:** *S*, March 12, May 25, 1924; May 25, 1925; Feb. 28, March 6, 11, 1926, 2; Hoover, Fisher, Feb. 1, 1924; *Vp*, Feb. 2, 1925, 3. **restrictions on foreign workers:** Hoover, Anna V. S. Mitchell Papers, Stokes to Bouimistrow, Feb. 18, 1926, box 1. **Turkish language mandatory:** *S*, Jan. 18, 1926, 2. **Nansen:** Nansen, 36.

230–231 **"Villa Tom":** *S*, May 6; June 24; July 14, 21, 27, 1926, 2; June 10, July 1, 1926, 4; Aug. 19, 1926, 3. **Olga:** CPI 393. **waiter at Maxim, flower merchant:** CPI 403.

232–234 **Yildiz Municipal Casino:** DPT 539; Greer, 318–20. **Frederick tries to continue:** *S*, Dec. 18, 1926; Jan. 2, 10, 11, 1927; Feb. 17, 1927, 2.

Englishman: "Finds Trade Dull in Constantinople," *NYT,* July 31, 1927, E2. **new restrictions:** *S,* Jan. 2, 11, 19, 1927, 2. **Greer:** Greer, 319–20.

234–236   **Frederick flees to Angora, city character and population, "Villa Djan":** *S,* May 5, 1927, 2; Ahmad, 91. **competition:** Argus; "Angora Made into a City of Jazz Bands," *CDM,* Oct. 6, 1926, 14; "Life Is Less Hectic in Constantinople," *NYT,* July 8, 1928, 50. **French consul general:** French Consul to American Consul, June 18, 1927, DPT 660. **creditors seize Maxim:** *S,* May 18, 19, 21; Dec. 19, 1927, 2; June 17, 1927, 3. **"ex-Villa Tom":** *S,* June 17, 1927, 3. **job in Angora:** "Mr. Thomas de Maxim invite ses créanciers à Angora," *P'st,* April 26, 1928, 3; the note is dated April 1 and mentions that the report of Frederick's sighting in Angora was "delayed"; other evidence also suggests that the encounter was during the last half of 1927.

236–237   **in Angora prison:** "Dancing Negro in Angora Jail for Old Debts," *Milwaukee Journal* (The Green Sheet), Monday, Jan. 16, 1928, n. p.; Allen to USSS, Nov. 1, 1928, CPI 409; Elvira to Allen, March 8, 1933, CPI 443; Argus. **demise of Yildiz Casino:** Crosby to USSS, Sept. 28, 1927, DPT 539; Grew to USSS, Oct. 24, 1927, DPT 539.

237–238   **Constantinople prison:** "Sultan of Jazz Dies in Poverty," *Boston Post,* July 9, 1928, 10. **prison conditions:** *Constantinople To-Day,* 336–43; *S,* Nov. 20, Dec. 22, 1927, 2; "Prison Life Is Easy in Constantinople," *NYT,* Feb. 2, 1930, 53. **illness:** Allen to West, July 20, 1928, CPI 409. **death and funeral:** *S,* June 13, 1928, 3; Sperco, 144; SE; FC. **"Sultan of Jazz":** W. G. Tinckom-Fernandez, "Life Is Less Hectic in Constantinople," *NYT,* July 8, 1928, 50.

Epilogue

239–240   **Elvira in Czechoslovakia, restrictions on employment, legal problems, journey to Germany, return to Constantinople:** Elvira to Allen, March 8, 1933, CPI 443.

240–241   **brothers' difficulties, Fred's passport applications, U. S. government changes mind:** DPT 423, 430, 629.

241–242   **Elvira's appeal:** DPT 629; USSS to Consul General, Sept. 17, 1935,

Central Decimal File, box 577, 367.1115, Thomas, Bruce, and Frederick/2, RG 59. **SS Excello:** Bruce Thomas, Application for Passport Renewal, June 20, 1938, box 16, General Records, U.S. Consulate General, Istanbul, RG 84. **Fred's work in Manhattan:** Frederick Thomas Jr.'s application for Social Security Number, Sept. 1, 1938. **Bruce tries to enlist:** Central Name Index, 1940–1944, box 1219, RG 59. **African-American newspapers:** *New York Amsterdam News*, February 7, 1948, 2; a garbled variant appeared in *CDe*, February 14, 1948, 7. **Fred asks for State Department's help:** Central Name Index, 1945–1949, box 456; 1950–1954, box 463, RG 59.

242–244 **Bruce travels to United States:** Central Name Index, 1950–1954, box 463, RG 59. **meeting with Mikhail:** Interview, Nov. 8, 2006. **Bruce's death:** Bruce Thomas Certificate of Death, State of California, County of Los Angeles, Registrar-Recorder/County Clerk. **Fred's death:** Death Notice, February 12, 1970, *Democrat and Chronicle* (Rochester, NY), 7B; e-mail from Younglove-Smith & Ryan Funeral Home, Rochester, NY, October 30, 2008. **Olga's traces:** Interview, Nov. 8, 2006. **Irma's fate:** CPI 383; interviews, Nov. 8, 2006; June 16 and 18, 2009. **Mikhail's life, Chantal Thomass:** Interview, Nov. 8, 2006; http://www.chantalthomass.fr.

INDEX